Sport, Children's Rights and Violence Prevention:

A Sourcebook on Global Issues and Local Programmes

Celia Brackenridge, Tess Kay and
Daniel Rhind (Editors)
2008, 2012 and 2015

Sport, Children's Rights and Violence Prevention:

A Sourcebook on Global Issues and Local Programmes

Celia Brackenridge, Tess Kay and Daniel Rhind (Editors)

2008, 2012 and 2015

Brunel University London

Acknowledgement

The editors wish to thank Susan Bissell of UNICEF for giving permission for this e-book to be published and for kindly contributing the Foreword.

Year of original collation: 2008

Year of final publication: 2015

Publishers: Total Health Publications and Brunel University Press

Author contact: Dr Daniel Rhind daniel.rhind@brunel.ac.uk

CONTENTS   Page

Tables

Figures

FOREWORD

In line with the Convention on the Rights of the Child (CRC), UNICEF has been a strong advocate of children's right to leisure and play. It recognizes the intrinsic value sports have in promoting the child's health and well-being, education and development, and social inclusion, including by fostering the culture of tolerance and peace. Every child has the right to play safely, in an enabling and protective environment. However, although under-researched, evidence shows that children have been subjected to various forms of violence, abuse and exploitation ranging from undue pressure to achieve high performance, beatings and physical punishment, sexual harassment and assaults, to child labour and trafficking. The violence that children experience can lead to lifelong consequences for their health and development. It can also have devastating consequences.

Article 19 of the CRC asserts that all children have the right to be protected from violence, calling on State Parties to take all appropriate measures for the protection of children, including while in the care others. Measures include strengthening child protection systems; increasing awareness and strengthening the protective role of parents, teachers, coaches and others caregivers as well as the media; developing and implementing standards for the protection and well-being of children in sports; implementing sport for development and other international programmes and initiatives; and improving data collection and research to develop an evidence-base of "what works". Above all, the protection of young athletes starts by ensuring that those around children regard them in a way that is appropriate to their needs and that is respectful of their rights - as children first and athletes second.

This book provides an expanded set of evidence and resources to back up the 2010 report from the UNICEF Innocenti Research Centre in Florence, Italy - *Protecting Children from Violence in Sport: A review with a focus on industrialized countries.* I am delighted to provide a Foreword as it complements the ongoing work being done by UNICEF in development and humanitarian environments to make sport a safer place for children.

Susan Bissell
Head of Child Protection Policy Division
UNICEF
New York

November 2012

AUTHOR DETAILS

The editors - Celia Brackenridge, Tess Kay and Daniel Rhind - all work at Brunel University London, UK in the Brunel Centre for Sport, Health and Well-being (BC.SHAW). In 2010 they established the Brunel International Research Network for Athlete Welfare (BIRNAW), an international resource for exchange of information on research, policy and practice aimed at enhancing the welfare and well-being of athletes of all ages. Readers interested in joining BIRNAW should contact Dr Rhind at Daniel.rhind@brunel.ac.uk

In 2008, when these contributions were first collated, the authors were based as follows:

Filip Boen – Lecturer, Department of Human Kinesiology, K. U. Leuven, Belgium

Steve Boocock - NSPCC Child Protection in Sport Unit, UK

John Brady - Director of Media and Communications, National Rugby League, Australia

Joy D. Bringer - Senior Sport Scientist (Sport Psychology), Sports Council for Wales

Tristan Collins - Consultant and Director, Performance Impact Associates Ltd., UK

John Cooper - Co-ordinator of Athletics, Community Services Department, City of Kitchener, Canada

Paulo David - Regional Representative of the Office of the United Nations High Commissioner for Human Rights in the Pacific

Bert De Cuyper – Department of Human Kinesiology, K. U. Leuven, Belgium

Brooke de Lench - CEO, MomsTEAM.com, USA

Kristine De Martelaer - Faculty of Physical Education and Physiotherapy, Vrije Universiteit Brussel, Belgium

Mary Duncan - Coordinator, Play by the Rules, Australian Sports Commission, Australia

Jocelyn East - University of Ottawa, Canada

Kari Fasting – Professor of sport sociology, Norwegian College of Sport Sciences, Oslo, Norway

Misia Gervis - Principal Lecturer, School of Sport and Education, Brunel University London, UK

Michael Hartill – Lecturer, Edge Hill University, Ormskirk, UK

Lynne Johnston – Clinical doctorate student, University of Newcastle upon Tyne, UK

Gretchen Kerr - Associate Professor and Associate Dean, Faculty of Physical Education and Health, University of Toronto, Canada

Sandra Kirby - Associate Vice President, University of Winnipeg, Canada

Nadia Knorre – National Olympic Committee, Czech Republic

Trisha Leahy - Chief Executive Officer, Hong Kong Institute of Sport, China

Ian Male - Consultant Community Paediatrician, Southdowns NHS Trust, Brighton/Mid Sussex, UK

Kristine De Martelaer - Faculty of Physical Education and Physiotherapy, Vrije Universiteit Brussel, Belgium

Marc Mazzucco - Doctoral student of law, University of Toronto, Canada

Petra Moget - National Olympic Committee*National Sports Confederation, The Netherlands

Leon Van Niekerk - Department of Psychology, University of Johannesburg, South Africa

Joke Opdenacker - Department of Human Kinesiology, K. U. Leuven, Belgium

Phil Prescott – Edge Hill University, Ormskirk, UK

Elaine Raakman – Originator and coordinator, We Just Play, Canada

Debbie Simms - Manager, Sport Ethics Unit, Australian Sports Commission, Australia

Ashley Stirling - Doctoral student, Faculty of Physical Education and Health, University of Toronto, Canada

Hamish Telfer - Senior lecturer, Cumbria University, UK

Anne Tivaas - NSPCC Child Protection in Sport Unit, UK

Jan Toftegaard Stoeckel - Assistant Professor at the Research Centre for Sport, Health and Civic Society, Institute of Sport, University of Southern Denmark, Odense, Denmark

Trine Thoreson – masters student, Norwegian College of Sport Sciences, Oslo, Norway

Yves Vanden Auweele - Department of Human Kinesiology, K. U. Leuven, Belgium

Leon Van Niekerk - Department of Psychology, University of Johannesburg, South Africa

Nicolette van Veldhoven - National Olympic Committee*National Sports Confederation, The Netherlands

Tine Vertommen – student, Faculty of Arts and Philosophy, Vrije Universiteit Brussel, Belgium

John Waser - Manager of National Coach and Athlete Career and Education, Australia

Maarten Weber – police officer and research collaborator with Marianne Cense, The Netherlands

Michelle Zubrack – Kinesiology student, University of Winnipeg, Canada

PREFACE

Celia Brackenridge, Tess Kay and Daniel Rhind

Editorial note at 2012

UNICEF is the world's largest child protection agency. The work of UNICEF is delivered through diverse agencies and national settings. Frequently, sport is used by the agency as a mechanism for repairing broken communities after human conflicts or natural disasters. However, sport itself is by no means neutral when it comes to the safety and welfare of the child. In 2007 this issue was recognised as a gap in the provisions of UNICEF. To their credit, and thanks largely to the persuasive powers of Susan Bissell, then working at the UNICEF International Research Centre in Florence, Italy, the staff at UNICEF convened a roundtable of experts in research and policy on welfare in sport. Over the next few years, the group drew together a report on the state of evidence about violence to children in sport and a summary of available prevention policies. This report, authored by Celia Brackenridge (UK), Kari Fasting (Norway), Sandra Kirby (Canada) and Trisha Leahy (Hong Kong) was published as a United Nations Innocenti Research Centre Review in 2010 and entitled *Protecting Children from Violence in Sport: A review with a focus on industrialized countries.*

It was not possible within that relatively short document to provide many details of the research and policy issues that it addressed. Hence it was agreed that a second, companion volume would be compiled to give interested readers further information and practical examples of both global and local projects to prevent violence to children in sport. For several reasons, that companion volume sat on the presses for some years. We have decided to publish it here in the state that it was left in 2008, to stand as a record of the issues at that time and to fill a gap in the ever-widening trail of literature about child rights and safety in sport. Inevitably, both science and practice have moved on in the intervening years. Several significant initiatives for child athlete welfare have started and the growth of scientific studies in this field has been exponential. As one example, the editors launched BIRNAW in 2010, a network of some 45 interested researchers, policy makers, sport organisations and other stakeholders who wish to advance the field, whose first publication is available as a free download (Brackenridge and Rhind, 2010, see Note 1 below). There are also now new websites, research projects and coalitions of advocates and scientists across the world that were not active before 2008. We make no apology for omitting these here: others are working on texts that will take the story forward from 2008. For our part, this book represents simply one step in recording the journey towards child safety in and through sport.

Future developments in this field are likely to explore how the different research and policy interests in sport and international development might coalesce. One exciting initiative in this regard is the launch of a set of *International Standards for Safeguarding and Protecting Children in Sport* that were first publicised by UNICEF's Child Protection through Sport Working Group at the 2012 Beyond Sport Summit in London. We look forward to seeing how these standards impact on the many sport for development projects.

2008

The welfare and protection of the child athlete has assumed growing significance in the past decade, as the scale of international sport has expanded. Child rights have, at last, begun to impinge on sport in ways that were previously unthinkable. Rights advocates, for example, have now found a voice in some of the world's most important sporting organisations, from the International Olympic Committee down. This has happened both as a result of research work *within* sport and pressure from *outside* sport. Sport has been traditionally resistant to incursions from equity and rights advocates and has had a tense relationship with groups pressing for a better deal for women, black and minority, LGBTQ and disabled athletes. In some parts of the world is it still dangerous for anyone who challenges the status quo in sport. At the same time, we need to recognise that significant advances have been made and that models of good practice are available in some countries that can perhaps stimulate positive social change elsewhere.

One of the reasons for producing this book is to help sport organisations around the world to compare their own environments with those elsewhere and to learn from others who have already introduced measures to prevent violence, exploitation and abuse against child athletes. The book serves as a companion volume to the UNICEF report on violence against children in sport. [3] Readers of this unique volume should be able to use it as a reference resource that draws together all the key issues and literature sources in one volume. This sourcebook provides a comprehensive overview of the global state of child protection and welfare research and policy in sport as it was in 2008. Its purpose is to draw together in one, easy-to-access volume a range of disparate material that has not previously been readily available.

Researchers, students, policy makers and sport administrators have been hampered in the past by lack of knowledge about the range, type and scale of abuses to child athletes and to the protective interventions that have been implemented to address these problems. Indeed, research into child abuse and protection in sport is in its infancy when compared with issues such as race or gender equity, doping or performance enhancement. The studies that do exist are published in specialist academic sources. Digests of extant research projects are therefore provided here to focus attention on the evidence base that underpins child protection and welfare policy in sport.

One of the practical outcomes of child advocacy work in sport has been the proliferation of international, national and local charters, codes, training programmes and related initiatives. This volume also provides a summary of these key initiatives, both as reference material and also to show how positive benefits have emerged from what is sometimes a very negative subject.

The book sets out the global context of child abuse and protection in sport from the perspective of policy, sport science, management and practice. It also presents a range of protective interventions by way of a series of case studies. Helpfully, UNICEF has already published a framework for policy development: below, this framework is introduced and discussed in relation to children's sport. [4]

Eight elements of a protective sport environment

1. Attitudes, traditions, customs, behaviour and practices

Cultural traditions are deep seated in most countries, rooted in centuries of history. In its modern institutionalised form, however, sport is only about two hundred years old. Sport historians and sociologists differ on whether sport is *constitutive* of culture (i.e. emerges from it) or *generative* of culture (i.e. develops it). [5, 6] Either way, we know that, the older sport formations are, the more closely they reflect the customs and values of their country of origin.

Complicating this picture is the effect of two major socio-economic forces – one is nineteenth century colonialism and the other is twentieth and twenty first century globalisation. Colonialism helped to spread sport disciplines from Western Europe to many parts of the globe, chiefly from Great Britain to the countries of the British Commonwealth. Globalisation resulted from the rise of capitalism and the consequent spread of trade and competitive markets to virtually all parts of the world, including the former communist states. In many ways, sport is a microcosm of globalisation, both reflecting its values and processes and also helping to accelerate global flows.

What are the implications of this for children in sport? Some would argue that as sport has become ever more shaped by the forces of capitalism so its participants – whether they be children or adults – have become subjected to the pressures of the marketplace. By this explanation, extreme training regimes, high workloads, restricted nutrition and unquestioning submission to technical authority are perhaps inevitable – the price of success. [7]

The doomesday scenario is that the ethic of 'winner takes all' associated with commercialised sport will eventually bring about the downfall of marketised sport and force a return to the values of street play and casual recreation. For some, this would not be unwelcome! Whatever the long term impacts of globalisation on sport, there is an opportunity for all of us to use the process positively to spread messages about children's rights and safety both *within* and *through* sport.

No sporting environment will protect children from violence if its attitudes or traditions condone harmful practices against children. The difficulty is that definitions of harm vary culturally: this is why is it so important that we have the UN CRC as a *universal* statement against which to benchmark our local (country/sport) situation.

2. Governmental commitment to fulfilling protection rights

Sport organisations have different relationships to governments in different countries. At one extreme, they are entirely government-funded and controlled as a mechanism of the state apparatus: at the other, there is virtually no government intervention in sport at all. Without government backing, it is very difficult for federal sport bodies or individual sport organisations to argue that child protection is necessary or, indeed, to procure financial or political support for the development of protective mechanisms, whether this be coach education or criminal record checks for volunteers. In the best case scenario, government displays a strong commitment to international legal standards and, rather than merely supporting sport organisations in their child protection work, actually *requires* them to do such work. There are several examples in this book of countries whose governments have linked revenue grant aid for sport to the development of child protection measures.

3. Open discussion and engagement with child protection issues

It is clear from the geographic skew in this volume that some countries are more active in pursuing child protection in sport than others. Where severe political conflicts, natural disasters or long term deprivations are evident, then a country is less likely to have a developed system for sport, recreation and play, and much less likely to have considered how child protection can or should be embedded within such a system. However, it may be argued that such countries are often targetted by international aid programmes using sport as a tool for reconstruction and reconciliation. The child protection expertise and measures adopted outside sport can readily be transferred into the sport setting just as long as sport developers recognise the need for this.

4. Protective legislation and enforcement

Virtually all countries have committed to the UN's children's rights agenda, exemplified in the UN CRC, and most have local legal frameworks through which such commitments can be enforced. Nonetheless, because of its Cinderella status, sport all too often lies beyond the 'mental map' of legislators. Assumptions about the goodness of sport need to be challenged if the sport domain is ever to be held to account for the same levels of security and safety as, say, schools or child care institutions.

5. The capacity to protect among those around children

The sport workforce is often under-skilled for leadership, teaching and coaching, let alone for broader sport-related medical, scientific or welfare roles. Even the apparent international leaders in child protection in sport have not all engaged in capacity building among their sport personnel. This lapse is perhaps understandable for countries whose resources for delivering sport are limited. But, paraphrasing Archbishop Desmond Tutu's comments at the time of the apartheid regime in South Africa, on the impossibility of achieving non-racial sport in a racist society, it is also the case that "there can be no safe sport in an unsafe society". The message is thus that *anyone* involved in delivering sport to children and young people – whether as coach, manager, volunteer, bus driver or medic – should be given training in essential welfare-related skills and equipped with the necessary knowledge to refer concerns or disclosures to those with professional child protection expertise.

6. Children's life skills, knowledge and participation

The benefits of engagement in sport and a physically active lifestyle are widely affirmed through research and through UNICEF's own review of sport. [8] Further, the contribution of sport to wider life and social skills has also been recognised within formal education and local communities. Denial of sporting opportunities, provision of sport programmes tainted by abuse or bullying, or failure to embed child protection within sport, all diminish the potential to achieve such benefits.

7. Monitoring and reporting

We cannot say with confidence that what is offered in this book is necessarily *best* practice since monitoring and evaluation of child protection in sport is only in its infancy, but we hope that the examples given in Part 5 are at least *good* practice. It is to be hoped that this volume will encourage more researchers and advocates to become involved in this field of endeavour and to develop better tools for monitoring and reporting improvements in violence prevention.

8. Services for recovery and reintegration

Sport is often seen as an ideal vehicle for recovery among child victims of abuse and violence. Sport certainly has a role to play in the recovery and reintegration of *some* children following trauma. But its potential as such is curtailed unless sport itself is a child-safe environment.

The structure of this book

This book is organised in five parts. Part 1 sets out the context for violence prevention work in children's sport. First, Jocelyn East explores issues of cause and culpability. Trisha Leahy then sets out a powerful argument for an integrated approach to sport in her explication of sport as a biopsychosocial system. Australia is one of the leading countries for child protection work in sport: Australian John Waser next describes how management systems have been developed and implemented in his country. Along with parents, the coach is arguably one of the most important figures in the life of the child athlete: from his extensive experience as a youth coach and child protection advocate, Hamish Telfer (UK) gives an account of safe coaching practices. This is followed by Ian Male's analysis of the paediatrician's role in both diagnosis and prevention of violence and abuse-related trauma in youth sport. Ashley Stirling and Gretchen Kerr (Canada) have both been involved in the practice and academic analysis of youth sport and in advocating for better child protection. They set out a rationale for child-centred sport which is echoed many times in other chapters. Finally in this section, Celia Brackenridge (UK) rehearses some of the challenges of researching violence in the context of sport-for-development programmes.

The main focus of Part 2 is on policy-related issues, summarising the scope, implementation and impact of various policies for child welfare in sport around the world. Marc Mazzucco begins with a discussion of the way in which Canada has used the UN CRC as a tool for the promotion of child welfare in sport. This is followed by an explanation of how the UK established the world's first dedicated Child Protection in Sport Unit: Steve Boocock was the

Unit's first Director and tells of the early milestones and impacts of its work. Next, Debbie Simms describes the development of the Australian Member Protection Policy which was an attempt to be inclusive in considerations of welfare in sport. Two chapters follow that focus on the impact of child protection policies in sport, both from the UK: first, Phil Prescott and Michael Hartill report on their research for the Rugby Football League in England and then Celia Brackenridge summarises her research on child protection impacts in twelve national governing bodies of sport in Scotland. Tristan Collins concludes this section with an overview his research on the impact of child protection on the coaching of high performance gymnastics in the UK.

Part 3 consists entirely of summaries of extant research data on harassment and abuse in sport, from Canada, Norway, Australia, The Netherlands, Denmark, the Czech Republic, Belgium and England. Part 4 brings together a range of important national and international policy statements and charters relating to sport ethics, children, and violence prevention. Finally, in Part 5, a number of practical examples are offered of national and local programmes designed to enhance child safety in sport.

The contents of this book reflect the authors' own opinions which are not necessarily endorsed by UNICEF. Corrections are welcome: kindly inform the editors to help facilitate accurate revisions by writing to daniel.rhind@brunel.ac.uk

Notes

1. Brackenridge C.H. and Rhind, D. (eds.) (2010) *Elite Child Athlete Welfare: International perspectives*. London: Brunel University Press. ISBN: 978-1-902316-83-3. Free download available at
http://www.brunel.ac.uk/about/acad/sse/sseres/sseresearchcentres/youthsport/birnaw
2. Brackenridge, C.H. Fasting, K., Kirby, S. and Leahy, T. (2010) *Protecting Children from Violence in Sport: A review with a focus on industrialized countries*. Florence: United Nations Innocenti Research Centre Review.
http://www.unicef-irc.org/publications/pdf/violence_in_sport.pdf
3. Brackenridge, C.H. Fasting, K., Kirby, S. and Leahy, T., ibid. 2010
4. Based on Landgren, K., 'The protective environment: Development support for child protection', *Human Rights Quarterly*, 27, 214-248, 2005.
5. Gruneau, R. *Class, Sports and Social Development*. Windsor, ON, Human Kinetics, 1999.
6. Dunning, E., *Sport Matters: sociological studies of sport, violence and civilization*. London, Routledge, 1999.
7. Brackenridge, C.H., Pitchford, A., Nutt, G. and Russell, K., *Child Welfare in Football: An exploration of child welfare in the modern game*. London, Routledge, 2007.
8. Brackenridge, C.H. Fasting, K., Kirby, S. and Leahy, T., op cit. 2010

Part 1
CONTEXT

CHAPTER 1. THE CAUSES OF VIOLENCE IN SPORT: WHO IS TO BLAME?

Jocelyn East

Children are exposed to violence in many aspects of their lives. Violence is common in children's movies and cartoons, in their books and games, and on television programmes. Children hear and live violence at home, on the street, at school, from strangers and from their peers. At a young age they do not understand what violence is and why humans are hurting each other physically or psychologically. They progressively understand or feel the difference between bad and good behaviours by the way people react to violence. As they get older, they start to see that violence is sometimes used as a tool to fulfil personal desires and to earn respect. Those contradictory messages and values put children in a clash of values.

As a microcosm of society, the world of sport does not escape the presence or impact of violence. Thus it also sends out contradictory messages. Sport can be a tool to help youth develop, as it acts on several dimensions of the body and the mind. However, the presence of violence certainly harms the potential of sport to contribute to positive development of individuals and communities. The goal of sport is to determine a winner, so it is fertile ground for the expression of frustration and associated violence. Sport can easily generate disappointment and lead to violent behaviour. Moreover, in several professional sports, violence is tolerated as a strategic means to intimidate opponents. Thus, sport icons adopt violent behaviour, and children who admire them tend to reproduce the same behaviour on their playgrounds, far from the spotlight or the media.

Anyone who believes in the potential of sport wants children to have positive experiences they will remember for the rest of their lives and that will help them to adopt and preserve healthy life habits. That is why children need to be taught how to behave ethically and avoid committing bad behaviour in sport. However, before ethics can be built through sport education programme or policies, it is important to understand what sparks violent behaviour and its root causes. This chapter thus aims to highlight the origins of violence in sport and to propose some strategies for reducing children's exposure to it.

Definition of Violence in Sport

Violence is hard to define, especially in the context of sport, which has a continuum from willing to win to dangerous violent acts.[1, 2] In any sport involving physical contact between players, the line between fair play and unnecessary violence is sure to be equivocal.[3] The difficulty in defining violence makes it hard for societies to even be aware of the presence of violence in their sport community. It seems that sport writers, commentators and academics fail to understand the true nature of aggression and violence in sport, and this ambiguity leaves the door open for numerous justifications by people who commit violent acts.[4]

As this text aims to expose the impact of violence in sport for children, an appropriate definition is:

Behaviour that transgresses the rules of sport, leading to pain, either physical or emotional, and an abnormal risk of injury, harm, mutilation or death.[5]

Causes, Typologies and Theories of the Origins of Violence

Different explanatory theories, typologies and models try to explain violence in sport. Most authors agree that it should not be viewed as an isolated phenomenon requiring its own explanations, but rather should be studied in a wider social context. One of the most common explanations for violence in sport is linked to tolerance of it by participants, coaches, parents, spectators, officials and sport administrators. In fact, people tolerate violence because they misperceive it or do not see it as 'true' violence.[7] Often violence is seen as part of the game, especially in certain contact sports (such as rugby, ice hockey, boxing, wrestling, American football), where it is seen as a means to intimidate and to win and as a tool to develop masculinity and 'character'. This perception could come from the military model, which accepts violence and toughness as part of military training, making it normal to take risks and get injured. It is important to look like a man in order to be able to protect the country.[8] Some sports, such as ice hockey, have convinced the public that intimidation, violence and cheating are 'natural'.[9] The tolerance of violence by professional sport sends a message to youth and children that violence is necessary to reach the highest levels of success.

These perceptions can explain why public opinion is often silent about violence in sport, except when tragedies occur. This silence seems tacitly to condone athletes' aggressive behaviours, and those same athletes sometimes become popular sport heroes.[10] It is therefore important to ask whether violence in sport really outrages spectators or rather appeals to them.

This public perception of violence is reinforced by ambivalence towards violence among management, athletes and fans, who fail to take personal responsibility for it. This dynamic can be explained as follows:

- Coaches and managers tend to blame fans, saying that violence attracts them to the game.
- Athletes frequently say they oppose violence but that the coaches expect it of them.
- Fans justify violence by attributing aggressiveness to individual athletes and to situational aspects of certain games, such as hockey and football. Indeed, in the recent past, brutality in sport was accepted without comment.[11]

Several psychological theorists agree that sport violence seems to be the result of a long evolutionary process that is either innate or acquired through cultural and social adaptation, or by a mix of the two. Freud's 'Innate theory' suggests that humans have a basically untrustworthy inner nature and are universally and instinctively aggressive.[12] Similarly, 'drive theory' suggests that drives are the internal impellers of action. Accordingly, any frustration of goal achievement induces an aggressive response, designed to injure the person or object causing the frustration.[13] Feshbach has argued that the ultimate goal of an individual's drive to aggress is not the infliction of injury on others but the restoration of the aggressor's self-esteem and sense of power.[14]

Arguably the most important theory on violence is social learning theory, which proposes that watching violent sport behaviour increases tendencies for future athletic aggression, as participants learn to be violent by watching others.[15] According to this theory, aggression and violence are acquired through a long, exceedingly complex process of cultural adaptation.[16] Part of this process involves internalizing acceptance of violence in sport as a form of catharsis or safety valve, an opportunity to reduce aggressive tendencies by releasing energy in a socially desirable way.[17] However, recent studies have concluded that this is not the case.[18]

Causes of Violence – External factors

Participants are put in a special context when they play sport. They are part of a pre-determined environment set by rules, opponents, spectators and sometimes even by weather. The sport environment brings together several external factors that influence participant behaviours. Heat, noise, crowd density, proximity to spectators and spectator use of alcohol can all heighten irritability, which in turn can exacerbate rule-breaking and diminish respect among athletes, coaches, spectators and others involved in sport.[19] The development of the score during the game, the importance of the game for the participants and its effect on league standings are external factors that can also influence the eruption of violence.

Professional sport has important influences on children's sport, both positive and negative. In several professional sports, violence is a best-seller formula because it attracts both the fans and the media. Professional sport operates virtually as a self-regulated industry, deciding its own rules and whether or not to comply with amateur or international sport rules.[20] It has also been argued that tolerance towards violence, failure to apply rules and inconsistent application of sanctions teaches unrelenting aggression as well as the value of breaking rules, being aggressive, being tough and showing courage in playing while injured.[21]

Even George Orwell suggested that in several professional sports you have to hate your opponent to give your best and to beat them:

> "Serious sport has nothing to do with fair play. It is bound with hatred, jealousy, boastfulness, disregard of rules, and sadistic pleasure in witnessing violence: in other words, it is war without the shooting."[22]

The media also have an impact on violence in sport. The proliferation of television channels has resulted in people seeing more sports and more specific violent behaviours. Shocking or violent behaviour is seen over and over again. Experts disagree about whether this shapes social behaviour, especially for youth. In recent studies children's perceptions of violence were extremely diverse, and they were able to distinguish between realistic and unrealistic violence, between real and fictional violence. Children were more affected by mild depiction of real violence in news bulletins than watching sport violence, as they saw the sport violence as unreal. Repetitive televised violence appears to desensitize people, to the point that sport violence is perceived as not real and not serious in its consequences.[23, 24]

Finally, peer approval is also a strong external factor affecting violence in sport. The socialization of participants in many sports includes learning violent tactics. Especially among youth and teenagers, violence is often seen as a sign of strength that brings respect to the individual from the peer group. Athletic aggression is sometimes valued because it reflects qualities such as strength and toughness, especially among male youth. This can lead the young athlete to want to learn other violent tactics from his teammates or senior players because he may then feel even more a part of the group.

Significant individuals in sport can also become external factors influencing violence among participants through their behaviour. In some situations, for example, athletes temporarily abdicate their own moral responsibility to their coaches. This is especially the case when coaches transfer their moral values and attitudes to the young participants.[25] Even if they do not always realize it, coaches are ethical and moral educators as they teach children how to behave in sport. In fact, several studies point to coaches as one, or even the major, influence on their young athletes with regard to the use of violence in sport. The importance of the coach as a role model should never be underestimated.[26]

Referees' game decisions may influence individual emotions, leading to violent behaviour. Frustrations often arise from a feeling of unfairness following a referee's decision or from an accumulation of decisions that seem to favour the opponent. Unpopular official decisions also constitute the most frequent precipitants of crowd violence. Referees must therefore accept that they have a role to play in determining the boundaries of violence both within and beyond the field of play.

Though it may be hard to accept, humans seem to like watching violence. Fans are not bound by the same rules as players. In fact, there are usually no rules for spectators but rather socially expected norms that permit them to express their emotions. Sport spectators should realize that they have a dual role towards violence in sport. If they show their emotions in the wrong way, they become violence actors. They can also legitimize athletes' violent behaviour by cheering and encouraging fights or violent conduct.

All these external factors can lead to social tolerance of violence in sport, qualifying sport as a place where social norms are temporally suspended, where people can 'wear a mask' and where normally unacceptable behaviours are accepted. As Michael D. Smith suggests, the tolerance of violence is often worse than the violence itself: Tolerance tends to amplify violence because nothing is done to stop it.[27]

Causes of Violence – Internal Factors

External factors interact with factors that are internal to participants. Indeed, sport players are bombarded by influences from other people's behaviour, values and decisions, including constant changes in the sport environment. The psychological state and health of the participant are all tested at different levels. Indeed, Kerr argues that some individuals are predisposed to violence because of their psychological profile.[28] He suggests there are four types of violence from a participant perspective:

- Thrill violence: satisfaction in breaking the rules;
- Power violence: desire to dominate the opponent, or using violence as a strategic tool;
- Anger violence: searching for revenge or reacting to unfairness;
- Play violence: satisfaction from using minor aggression with minor consequences, such as a penalty.

It seems that violence is used in sport as a way to enhance self-esteem depending on the culture of the sport and the response to the person committing the violent act. Violence creates an aggressor-attacked relationship in which the aggressor can use violence and domination to restore his or her sense of self-esteem and power over the 'other' and over his or her reality. In many ways, sport offers a space and time for the athlete to wear a mask and act in ways that would not be acceptable outside the sport context.

Sports participants often justify their violent behaviour as a response to unfairness that frustrated them. Perhaps a goal was not achieved or the players feel that they or their teammate were not treated with respect, which then lowers their self-esteem. Violence seems to be more frequent in situations where the individual perceived that he or she received treatment outside of the established sport rules. Personal judgements about what is unfair play a major role in creating or preventing violence in sport, highlighting the importance of sound knowledge and good ethics. Internal factors also include an individual's skills in controlling violence. It is hard to determine precisely how or why a given individual reacts violently in a given sport context, but self-esteem seems to play a major role, as it influences emotional stability and ability to tolerate frustrations. Overall, explanations of violence in sport are multi-factoral; the core element is undoubtedly the interaction between the internal and external factors.

Preventing Violence in Sport

To avoid violence in sport, particularly in children's sport, it is imperative to work on the climate. In some sports, more violence takes place in the stands than on the playing field, underlining the importance of including spectators, parents, friends and fans in violence-prevention initiatives.[29] As a first step, those individuals must recognize that they have a role to play in preserving a safe and welcoming sport environment for the players they watch, especially in children's sport. Coaches and referees who are more directly involved in the competition must be aware of the issue and must recognize their important role in eliminating violence from sport. Once this is achieved, different tools (such as codes of conduct, specific rules, explanations of the consequence of violence, etc.) can be elaborated to reduce tolerance for violence.

Steps should also be taken within the existing sport infrastructure (changes in rules, stricter enforcement) and, on a wider scale, by providing ethical education for children in sport as early as possible.[30] This should be as important a teaching component as the technical and tactical aspects of sport education usually given to children. The ethics-in-sport component should also be promoted through public policies and educational curricula, such as physical education and health classes. The goal is to change the attitudes, values and perceptions of participants, managers and fans and to reduce tolerance for violence. As a last step, we should heed Leizman's proposal to reprogramme our tolerance towards violence in professional sport.[31] This mind shift might be possible if we can start to dispel the myth that using violence helps to achieve excellence in sport.

Notes

1. See an extended discussion of definitions in *Protecting Children from Violence in Sport: A review with a focus on industrialized countries.* Florence: United Nations Innocenti Research Centre, 2010.
2. *Rapport final du Comité d'étude sur la violence au hockey amateur au Québec (Final report of the committee studying violence in amateur hockey in Quebec),* Québec, Haut-Commissariat à la jeunesse, aux loisirs et aux sports, 1977, p. 47.
3. Goldstein, J.H., *Sports Violence,* New York: Springer-Verlag, 1983, p. 3.
4. J.H. Kerr, *Rethinking Aggression and Violence in Sport,* Routledge, 2005. Kerr (pp. 6-7) cites Bandura (1973), who argues that the definition of aggression is a semantic jungle because of the difficulty of determining the true intent behind a behaviour. Kerr (pp. 6-7) also cites Renfrew (1997) in concluding that no clear definition of aggression exists that is commonly accepted by professionals.
5. *Dictionnaire de la pensée politique hommes et idées (Dictionary of Political Thought, Men and Ideas).* Paris, Hatier (Coll. J. Brémond), 1989, p. 828.
6. Goldstein, op. cit., p. 3.
7. Smith, M.D., 'What is sports violence? A sociolegal perspective of sports violence' in: *Sports Violence,* New York: Springer-Verlag, 1983, p. 17.
8. Bridges, J.C., *Making Violence Part of the Game: A socio-legal history of violence in American sport,* Commack, Kroshka Books, 1999.
9. *Manifeste sur le hockey : Pour un sport au service de l'humain (Manifesto for Hockey: For a Sport in the Service of Humanity),* Fédération québécoise de hockey sur glace, 1988, p.15.
10. Ibid, p. 56.
11. Goldstein, op. cit., pp. 68, 77, 101.
12. Leizman, J., *Let's kill'em: Understanding and controlling violence in sports,* M.D. Lanham, University Press of America, 1999, p. 50.
13. LeUnes, A.D. and J.R. Nation, *Sport Psychology: An introduction,* Chicago, Nelson-Hall, 1989, p. 200.
14. Feshbach, S., 'The dynamics and morality of violence and aggression', *American Psychologist,* vol. 26, 1971, pp. 281-292.
15. Goldstein, op. cit., p. 51.
16. Leizman, op cit., p. 53.

17. Goldstein, op. cit., p. 55.
18. Kerr (ibid. [pp. 197-198]) reports on Wann (2001), saying that there is virtually no empirical evidence validating the existence of catharsis in sport. However, Kerr (p. 128) also cites Conroy 2001 and Smith 1979, who have shown that young athletes are very aware of the nature of aggression and violence in sport and perceive them as expected and legitimate under certain circumstances but that there is no evidence that young athletes carry these perceptions about the legitimacy of violence into everyday life.
19. LeUnes and Nation, op. cit., p. 202.
20. Bridges, op. cit., p. 227.
21. Vaz, E., 'The institutionalized rule violation in professional hockey: Perspectives and control system', *Canadian Association for Health, Physical Education and Recreation Journal*, 1977:43, pp. 6-34.
22. George Orwell, 1948, 'The Sporting Spirit', *Collected essays, journalism and letters of George Orwell*, vol., 4, London, Secker and Warburg, cited in J.H. Kerr, *Rethinking Aggression and Violence in Sport*, London, Routledge, 2005, Introduction page.
23. Buckingham 1993, 1996, 2000 and Hargrave 2003, cited in J.H. Kerr, *Rethinking Aggression and Violence in Sport*, London, Routledge, 2005, p. 126.
24. Goldstein, op. cit, pp. 1-2.
25. Shields, D. and B. Bredemeier, 1989, cited in J.H. Kerr, *Rethinking Aggression and Violence in Sport*, London, Routledge, 2005, p. 83.
26. Kerr, op. cit.
27. Smith, op. cit., p. 62.
28. Kerr, op. cit., pp. 39-42.
29. Commission de l'aménagement du Territoire., *La Problématique de la Violence dans le Hockey Mineur (Problematic Violence in Minor Hockey)*, Assemblée Nationale du Québec, 2002, p.15.
30. Goldstein, op cit., pp. 68, 77, 101.
31. Leizman, op.cit., p. 54.

CHAPTER 2. BIOPSYCHOSOCIAL SPORTS SYSTEMS AND THE ROLE OF SCIENTIFIC SUPPORT IN ATHLETE WELFARE

Trisha Leahy

In many countries organized competitive sport forms a social institution that specifically addresses two key articles of the Convention on the Rights of the Child: article 31, the right to play, and article 29, the right to develop talents and mental and physical abilities to their fullest potential. High-performance sport systems, often funded by governments, have become more prevalent in recent years as countries compete to develop athletic giftedness and perform successfully on the world stage of elite sport. It is now recognized that individual success at the elite level is a function of a complex interplay of multiple factors. Apart from individual talent and expert coaching to facilitate that talent, developing athletic giftedness to its fullest potential requires a comprehensive support infrastructure to minimize risk and maximize results. It is made up of a 'scientific support team' – the physicians, sports physiologists, trainers and others who form part of the elite athlete's entourage.

This chapter proposes that the foundation of an elite athlete's support infrastructure is a biopsychosocial paradigm, which integrates the biological, psychological and social factors that lead to an individual's development. The chapter will highlight the role of scientific support personnel from within this framework, particularly with reference to facilitating the development of athletic giftedness within a safe, ethical delivery system.

The Biopsychosocial Model

The biopsychosocial paradigm underpins many international elite sports support systems, targeting all aspects of each athlete's medical, physiological, psychological, social support and welfare needs. This paradigm includes five characteristics, as described below.

1) Multidisciplinary approach

The biopsychosocial paradigm assumes that athletes rarely if ever exhibit unidimensional problems. Therefore solutions invariably result from a multidisciplinary, integrated intervention that provides the necessary breadth and depth of services, facilitating coordinated service delivery. The obvious advantage of a multidisciplinary approach is that each member of the team has different expertise and clinical skills. Nevertheless, the approach faces many challenges. Communication and coordination of services require a greater outlay of time. Case management, shared decision making and confidentiality require collaborative negotiation and monitoring. Both psychological and sport injury research confirm that one of the key elements in successful intervention programmes, whether rehabilitation or psychotherapeutic, is the quality of the relationship between the practitioner and the athlete.[1-2] This requires careful and informed relationship management, both within the scientific support team and between the team and the athletes.

2) Scientist-practitioner model of service provision

In the high-performance arena, research and practice have to be linked, each informing the other. In this regard, service providers are more than technicians; they are scientists, applying evidence-based interventions. The service provided needs to be based on state-of-the-art science, specific to the particular athlete population. Within the biopsychosocial framework, effective science-based interventions must be based on multidisciplinary, collaborative research.

3) On-field service provision

Office-based services are the exception in elite sport. Scientific support staff members need to be highly mobile, travelling to local and overseas training and competition venues. This is an important principle of specificity of service. On-field scientific observations and testing data provide valuable, immediate input to inform coaching decisions at key points in performance programming and evaluation.

4) Sport-specific expertise

Each sport has different characteristics and requirements, which may call for different levels and types of scientific support from different disciplines. Generalist, ad hoc interventions have minimal, if any, usefulness and are not cost effective. Scientific support staff thus need to be completely familiar with the characteristics of specific sports to provide the level of integrated service necessary to support high-performance athletes on the world stage.

5) Individualized service provision

There is no universal 'elite athlete' profile identifying the appropriate interaction between biological, psychological and social factors. By definition, elite athletes have unique characteristics that enable them to perform at the highest levels of physical endeavour. Effective servicing must therefore cater to highly individual needs and training requirements.

Issues of Gatekeeping

Within the biopsychosocial model, scientific support personnel are key front-line members of the athletes' entourage, responsible for providing a scientific methodology to support coaching, training and performance. In recent years, with research yielding more and more science-based evidence, the elite sport sector has produced increasingly sophisticated interventions to enhance coaching methods and training systems, thereby improving individual athletic performance. However, these developments have taken place largely along the biological-psychological spectrum of the model; little attention has been given to socio-cultural factors in athletes' development and their possible impact. These issues now require attention if the biopsychosocial framework is to be used as the operating model of high-performance service delivery.

Sport as an institution has social responsibility and requires thoughtful stewardship. However the sport industry, like other industries, is a complex social system in which structural and relational characteristics are inherently value laden. A successful professional coach must produce winning teams; a successful professional sport must attract fans, both to entertain and to earn income for sponsors. To attract and retain young gifted athletes, sport at all levels needs to provide developmentally appropriate and safe training environments. In a climate of competing interests, how can socially responsible and ethical methods be ensured and the rights of young athletes protected?

A safe environment is psychologically and physically healthy. A psychologically unsafe environment is marked by abusive, threatening or humiliating coaching styles, uncontested peer bullying and harassment.[3-4] Psychological abuse not only causes immediate stress on athletes but has also been linked to long-term psychological harm.[5-6] A physically unsafe environment is marked by the use of extreme physical activities as punishment for errors or failure to perform, age-inappropriate training regimens and acceptance and implicit tolerance of hazing rituals.[7] Sexual abuse of young athletes has been documented in many countries, and some research has found victims suffering from long-term post-traumatic stress (see Part 3).[8-11]

Documentation of these various forms of harm to athletes has led to a more critical analysis of the sporting environment itself as a socio-cultural system, as well as assessment of its impact on young people. Both human rights frameworks and the scientific biopsychosocial paradigm are being brought to bear in developing policy and practice aimed at preventing harm. At the highest level of elite sport, the International Olympic Committee (IOC) has recently issued a Consensus Statement regarding sexual harassment and abuse in sport (see chapter 29). The IOC has stated that its aim is to improve the health and protection of all athletes through promotion of effective policies and to increase awareness of these among the athlete's entourage. The IOC specifically recognizes all the rights of athletes, including the right to a safe and supportive sport environment, where athletes are most likely to flourish and optimize their performance.[12] UNICEF has now taken up the issue under its mandate, defined by the Convention on the Rights of the Child, of working to prevent violence against children, which it defines as those under the age of 18.

These issues raise questions about the role and preparedness of scientific support staff to ensure safety for athletes. The team members are in a key position to monitor the sporting environment and therefore have an important 'gatekeeping' responsibility in terms of protecting young athletes' rights and maintaining a psychologically, physically and sexually safe sporting environment. Because of their close involvement with the team, these staff are often the first point of contact for athletes in distress. They therefore need to be aware, first, of the potential for these forms of harm, and second, of the relevant policies and procedures for reporting and referral. Members of the scientific support team can use their positions to help prevent harm, advocate for appropriate protection policies and develop "a culture of dignity, respect and safety in sport", as called for by the IOC Medical Commission.[13]

Ethical Guidelines

To effectively contribute to protecting the rights of young people in sport, scientific support team members need to be educated, and they need clear ethical guidelines and codes of conduct. Indeed, a code of ethical conduct and a professional body to regulate the code are key components of the professionalism of the sports industry.[14] However, it has become clear in recent years that rule-driven approaches to compliance will have, at best, only a limited effect on professionals' functioning.[15] But when compliance becomes articulated as a shared responsibility that protects *all* parties (scientific support staff as well as athletes), rather than an imposition, it is much more likely to be accepted and applied in practice.

The values and norms of any institutional culture must be looked at routinely from the perspective of ethics.[16] This needs to be applied more effectively in sport, and particularly to preventing violence against children in sport.[17] Ethical commitment must be built formally and informally into the sport system through the vision, mission goals and objectives of sport organizations.

Ethical Competency Training

The competitive sport sector is beginning to develop a framework of ethics. Sport bodies in the leading countries in this field, such as Australia and Canada, have produced clearly defined ethics policies including goals and related codes of behaviour for coaches, athletes and scientific support staff. Such policies generally include ethical principles and beliefs along with mandatory and aspirational behavioural guidelines. However, these constitute only one aspect of preventing violence against children in sport. Frequently lacking are systematic education and training in ethical competencies and decision-making needed to deal with the often complex and intense relationships in the world of sport.

Presuming a theoretical set of ethical competencies does a disservice to sports professionals who, with little or no training, are presented with prescriptive and proscriptive ethical guidelines that the profession apparently sees as self-evident. For example, it is common for scientific support staff to be given a code of professional conduct that may simply state, 'avoid sexual intimacy with athletes'. Given the complex, emotionally intimate relationships that evolve in the high-pressure field of elite athletics, support staff need more guidance and training than provided by these simple declarative statements. Ethics education needs to address the definition of an ethical relationship, how relationships become exploitive, the meaning of harm in relationship terms and how relational errors of judgement can occur.

Conclusion

Only by maximizing the resources of the scientific support team and empowering each individual through appropriate ethical guidelines and training will the scientific, medical and welfare support system be able to provide an environment that promotes the health, welfare and performance of athletes across the entire spectrum of the biopsychosocial model.

Notes

1. Ray, R., and D.M. Weiss-Bjornstal (eds), *Counseling in Sports Medicine*, Champaign Il: Human Kinetics, 1999.
2. Waddington, L., 'The therapy relationship in cognitive therapy: A review', *Behavioural and Cognitive Psychotherapy*, 2002:30, 2, pp. 179-192.
3. Kirby, S. and G. Wintrup, 'Running the gauntlet: An examination of initiation/hazing and sexual abuse in sport', *Journal of Sexual Aggression*, 2002:8, 2, pp. 49-68.
4. Stephens, D. E., 'Predictors of likelihood to aggress in youth soccer: An examination of co-ed and all-girls teams', *Journal of Sport Behavior*, 23:3, pp. 311-325.
5. Leahy, T., 'Preventing the sexual abuse of young people in Australian sport', *The Sport Educator*, 2001:13, pp. 28-31.
6. Leahy, T., G. Pretty and G. Tenenbaum, 'A contextualised investigation of traumatic correlates of childhood sexual abuse in Australian athletes', *International Journal of Sport and Exercise Psychology*, 16:4, pp. 366-384.
7. Holman, M. and J. Johnson, 'Hazing and peer harassment', IOC Consensus Statement, Conference on Sexual Harassment and Abuse in Sport, Lausanne, Switzerland, 3-5 October 2006.
8. Fasting, K., C. Brackenridge and J. Sundgot-Borgen, *Sexual Harassment In and Outside Sport*, Oslo, Norwegian Olympic Committee, 2000.
9. Kirby, S., L. Greaves and O. Hankivsky, *The Dome of Silence: Sexual harassment and abuse in sport*, Halifax, N.S., Fernwood Publishing, 2000.
10. Leahy, T., G. Pretty and G. Tenenbaum, 'Prevalence of sexual abuse in organised competitive sport in Australia', *Journal of Sexual Aggression*, 2002:8, pp. 16-35.
11. Leahy, T., G. Pretty and G. Tenenbaum, 'Childhood sexual abuse narratives in clinically and non-clinically distressed adult survivors', *Professional Psychology: Research and Practice*, 2003:34, pp. 657-665.
12. IOC Medical Commission, *Consensus Statement on Sexual Harassment and Abuse in Sport.* Available at http://multimedia.olympic.org/pdf/en_report_1125.pdf , retrieved 17 August 2008.
13. IOC Medical Commission, ibid.
14. Lyle, J., *Sports Coaching Concepts: A framework for coaches' behaviour*, London, Routledge, 2002.
15. Newman, J. L. and D.R. Fuqua, 'What does it profit an organization if it gains the whole world and loses its own soul', *Consulting Psychology Journal: Practice and Research*, 2006:58, pp. 13-22.
16. Newman and Fuqua, ibid.
17. See *Protecting Children from Violence in Sport: A review with a focus on industrialized countries.* Florence: United Nations Innocenti Research Centre, 2010.

CHAPTER 3. PROTECTIVE MANAGEMENT: AUSTRALIA'S NATIONAL ATHLETE CAREER AND EDUCATION PROGRAMME

John Waser

During the 1990s there were growing concerns that Australia's elite athletes were foregoing development of essential life skills in their pursuit of sporting excellence. This led to frequently traumatic transitions out of sport. These concerns increased with the advent of the Olympic Athlete Programme in 1995, which placed extra pressures on Australian athletes to satisfy gold medal expectations at the Sydney 2000 Summer Olympic Games. This led to an international evaluation of research into athletes' lives and how they balance sport with work and life. Also assessed were centres offering athlete life skills programmes.

In response to the findings, the Australian Institute of Sport (AIS, the government's elite national training centre for athletes), established the National Athlete Career and Education Programme in 1995. It provides assistance in educational, vocational and personal development to national sporting organizations and AIS athletes through the AIS and the State Institutes of Sport/State Academies of Sport (SIS/SAS) network.

In 2006, the programme was extended to include coaches and was renamed the National Coach and Athlete Career and Education (NCACE) programme.[1] Responsibility for its management was transferred to the National Sports Programmes Division of the Australian Sports Commission (ASC), the government agency for sport.

Programme Framework

The NCACE programme has been one of the catalysts in forging cooperative links among elite sport networks in Australia. Delivered through the SIS/SAS network, it has received federal and state funding. To be eligible for assistance, athletes must be involved in the national senior squad or on scholarship with the AIS or SIS/SAS. Approximately 3,000 eligible athletes have accessed the programme each year, with a further 300 professional athletes making use of it on a fee-for-service arrangement. The programme is coordinated nationally consistent with reporting and accountability guidelines.

The NCACE programme aims to provide services to assist elite athletes in exploiting educational, vocational and personal development opportunities while pursuing and achieving excellence in sport. Seven strategies support this objective:

- A structured process to assess individual athletes' educational, vocational, financial and personal development needs;
- Competency-based personal development training courses;
- Nationally consistent career and education planning to enable elite athletes to manage their individual vocational requirements;

- Fostering of opportunities for elite athletes from the business and education sectors and local communities;
- A career and education transition programme;
- Professional development for NCACE personnel through research into, and implementation of, cutting-edge practices in athlete career development and education;
- Integration of NCACE personnel and services into programmes offered by the Australian Institute of Sport and SIS/SAS.

NCACE Programme Evaluation/Research

The University of Queensland undertook a national evaluation of the NAACE programme with 867 athletes in 1998.[2] The findings were used to further develop the framework and service delivery protocols. The evaluation found that:

- The programme was beneficial due to establishment of systematic procedures for its national implementation and administration;
- A high proportion (86.7 per cent) of eligible athletes saw the need for the programme (95 per cent in Queensland, Victoria, the Australian Capital Territory and Western Australia);
- A high proportion (88.8 per cent) of athletes reported satisfaction with the programme.

The major recommendations were to:

- Develop a national database to enable access to information when athletes relocate;
- Develop flexible delivery methods for athlete training courses;
- Modify athlete assessment procedures so they can be undertaken by telephone or in groups.

State surveys conducted with athletes and coaches on the quality and types of services offered also provided valuable data for programme modification. Athlete and coach satisfaction ratings with NCACE are consistently over 80 per cent, and quantitative data from these surveys have shown that a high number of athletes see the need for this programme.

Since 2003, NCACE personnel have been trained to ensure that all those involved in elite athlete development are aware of and support the integration of the programme into athlete service models. Implementation of NCACE has been as flexible as possible to meet the needs of sport and of athletes. Adaptation of the model has been extremely successful in some cases. Coach awareness and support of the programme has increased significantly through formal and informal learning opportunities, but given the chase for gold, it is often last on the list in tight funding climates. The availability of extra funding for NCACE through the Olympic Athlete Programme, however, has raised acceptance of the benefits of life skills development from the perspective of both athletes and coaches. The challenge in Australia is to maintain the momentum.

A longitudinal research study of the programme, jointly conducted by NCACE and the University of Southern Queensland, was completed in 2007. The results were the culmination of tracking athletes over five years. In the final data collection phase 423 athletes returned surveys, which revealed these findings:

- 94 per cent indicated they knew of the NCACE programme;
- 80 per cent were aware of all services offered by NCACE;
- 78 per cent of athletes who had accessed NCACE felt it contributed to improvement in their athletic performance.

Transition Programme

Exclusive commitment to sport may preclude participation in other activities and subsequently hinder achievement in other areas of life. With appropriate education, support and planning, it is possible for athletes to balance their various commitments and deal with challenges.

An athletic career has phases and transitions, which require athletes to cope with change. A transition, defined as an event or non-event that results in a change in one's behaviour and relationships,[3] can be positive and beneficial if dealt with correctly. Indeed, the greatest learning and development opportunities for athletes often come from the transitions they experience.

The NCACE programme is responsible for assisting athletes in managing transitions through appropriate career, education and personal development planning at all stages of their sporting career. It also refers them to other professionals to address issues that arise outside of the NCACE programme mandate. The programme also works with significant people in the athlete's life, such as parents, siblings and partners, to assist him or her in managing transitions. The transitions that affect elite athletes include:

- Career phases
  - Retirement;
  - Change in employment status, such as between unemployment, part-time employment and full-time employment;
  - Change in employment position through promotion, demotion, new job/duties;
  - Movement between study and work, both full time and part time;
  - Movement through school, from primary to tertiary levels, both full-time and part-time;
  - Failure, such as being asked to leave a job or a school.

- Relocation – intrastate, interstate or overseas

- Sport developments
  - De-selection (due to performance, age, injury, discipline, restricted numbers);
  - Change in seniority or role in squad;
  - Transition between squads, such as from the developmental squad to the senior squad;

- o Change in participation model, such as from part-time to full-time participation due to moving from state to national squads;
- o Move from squad to individual status and vice versa;
- o Gain or loss of benefits such as scholarships and contracts.

- Recognition
  - o Changes brought about by success or failure;
  - o Increased public attention, through either positive or negative media portrayal.

- Personal
  - o Experience of a major loss, such as the death or illness of a family member, or a major gain, such as a new partner or child;
  - o Change in relationship with a partner, family, friends, sport personnel, work colleagues, etc.;
  - o Legal concerns;
  - o Sexuality;
  - o Discrimination.

Where possible, athletes moving off scholarship within the AIS/SIS/SAS network should have access to an NCACE exit interview to ensure their action plan fits with their transition environment.

Evolution of the Programme

The NCACE programme has evolved in its products, services and reach. It now:

- Offers athletes access to multiple methods of information delivery, including face to face, hard copy and online (ACEonline);
- Uses the Elite Athlete Friendly University collaborative agreement to support athletes in the community (thirty four Australian universities are working to ensure that athletes can combine tertiary studies with high-performance sports);
- Uses new technology to map and monitor delivery of services, including a secure Internet gateway so all staff can access and update materials.

In an effort to broaden its reach, NCACE entered into a contract to provide services to dancers, coaches and professional footballers.

SCOPE (Securing Career Opportunities and Professional Employment)

Recognizing that elite athletes face similar career transition issues as dance artists, Ausdance approached NCACE with the idea for a similar programme to help its transitioning artists. SCOPE developed through a partnership between the Australia Council for the Arts and the ASC, it uses the expertise of NCACE to deliver professional development and career and education services to elite dance artists and choreographers. SCOPE aims to help dance artists develop their professional capacities within and beyond their career in performance and/or choreography. It recognizes that transition from active performance is inevitable and therefore must be a key consideration in a dancer's professional life. In Canada, the Netherlands, Switzerland, the United Kingdom and the United States, dancer transition centres have been established to help dance artists transition to non-performing careers.

Coach Career Management Programme

The Coach Career Management Programme, the more recent initiative of NCACE, is delivered nationally by Coach Career Management Consultants. The programme was designed to support coaches in managing their careers, education and personal development. Consultants work with coaches to develop individual action plans. Coaches can access a range of services and educational opportunities to help them develop their skills and plan their career transitions.

Professional sports

In addition to the amateur athletes that have benefitted from these services, professional sporting organizations have also contracted NCACE to provide career building services for their teams and federations, such as the Football Federation of Australia, which has been serviced by NCACE since 2005.

Notes

1. For more information on the NCACE programme see
   <www.ausport.gov.au/participating/athletes/career_and_education>.
2. Gorely, B., D. Bruce and B. Teale, *Research Report: Athlete career and education program 1997 evaluation*, University of Queensland, 1998.
3. Schlossberg, N.K., 'A model for analysing human adaption to transition', *The Counselling Psychologist*, 1981:9, 2, p. 5.

CHAPTER 4. PROTECTIVE PRACTICE: COACHING CHILDREN AND YOUNG PEOPLE

Hamish Telfer

The coach is a pivotal figure in the lives of children and young people involved in sport. Coaches set standards and expectations that go beyond sport experiences. Sport serves a number of functions as children grow, often providing and facilitating the conditions and social situations for their most enjoyable and significant achievements. Jones et al. highlight the varying roles that coaches are required to embrace, emphasizing the importance of skilled, personalized coaching with this age group.[1] In particular, it is essential for coaches working with children and young people to understand the performer's world. Coach education courses alone seldom equip coaches with the range of interpersonal skills required to fulfil all the requirements of working with young performers.[2] This chapter outlines the need for sports practitioners to embed athlete welfare within their practice and to be aware of the cultural context in which they operate.

The skills that underpin coaching the child athlete, and indeed all performers, are often gained through informal learning. As such, they are considered of relatively low impact compared with formal education and training. Such courses often centre on technical skills (what to coach), which are usually considered more important than pedagogical skills (how to coach). Thus, coaches seldom place enough emphasis on examining their experiential learning and how this contributes to their practice. As a result, interpersonal skills and informal learning are often given less credence, and the narrow definition of coaching results in practitioners overlooking this essential skill set.

Nor are coaches generally equipped to understand how their power position affects those they coach. Consequently, they often fail to recognize the impact of their role, words and actions. Consideration of athlete welfare is therefore sometimes low on the list of demands that coaches perceive to be important.

Coaching and Child Protection

The relationship between coaching practice and children's rights to protection and prevention of harm is only now beginning to influence the experience of children in sport. Awareness is growing, though, and coaches are reorienting their approaches to reflect both emerging good practice and recent changes in international and national law that govern work with children and young people.

One of the key dilemmas of this reorientation is how coaches can achieve a balance between focusing on outcome (success/results) and focusing on process (developing the performer). Indeed, much of sport engagement at all levels is centred on striving to bridge the gap between sport as recreation and the development of sporting excellence through systems designed to identify and nurture talent.

Until recently, sport has singularly failed to identify the key skills needed to deliver quality coaching to children and young people that take account of this outcome/process balance. Sports systems theorists such as Côté, who place the child at the centre of the coaching process, are helping redefine the nature of the coaching skills and systems required to ensure that the child's development and welfare are at the heart of coaching.[3] These changes are influencing how people think about the long-term development of young athletes and are redefining attitudes about the role of sport in the lives of young people. Such issues are affecting structural shifts in coaching frameworks in Australia, Canada and the United Kingdom.[4]

However, sport governing bodies still generally fail to distinguish between coaching the recreational performer and coaching those who are loosely grouped under 'performance and excellence'. This often leads coaches to focus on performance rather than individual development. The performance and excellence approach is usually underpinned by the requirement of national systems to identify and nurture talent, which rewards those who achieve externally driven outcomes (winning medals) rather than those who achieve relative to their own abilities. The sports coach is therefore often in personal conflict over value systems that represent competing goals.[5] Indeed, the performer often becomes a form of 'coaching capital' for the coach, since coaches are assessed and recognized through the outcomes of performers.

Embedding consideration of long-term athlete welfare within coaching practice is essential to meet the responsibilities of coaching children and youth. Situating the welfare of the young performer within coaching practice ensures that children have positive sport experiences. Coaches must therefore understand their responsibilities and be able to identify and evaluate the key elements of welfare within coaching practice. This will, in turn, enhance the coached experience of children and young people. The central tenet of this approach is to keep the focus on the young athlete as an individual rather than simply as a producer; in short, valuing the performer rather than the performance. This will ensure achievement of a balance that serves the child's best interests.

Coaching Practice

An understanding of the key principles of child and athlete welfare is essential for coaching practice to reflect contemporary thinking and the requirements of international and national law. The Convention on the Rights of the Child has influenced countries' social policies and is now filtering into national sport policies. In the United Kingdom, for example, the government's Every Child Matters agenda has influenced coaching practice through safeguarding workshops aimed at integrating coaching practice with national policy for child welfare.[6]

Coaches working with child athletes now have a clear and unambiguous set of child welfare principles, and they are required to evaluate their practice based on these principles.[7] They need to understand the uneven power relationships inherent in sport coaching environments. To avoid 'inappropriate' practice in working with young performers, the coach needs to take account of the physical and emotional context of coaching and ensure respect for boundaries of sexual propriety.

Coaches must also address the varying levels of capacity among young performers,[8] balancing the demands of 'competitive readiness' against the age and maturity of athletes. This often requires different approaches for different age groups; given young performers' variation in capacities, coaches need to consider how to work with young people based on their relative ability and physical maturation, rather than their age. This should result in less stress for young performers who may be less mature or 'ready' than others in their age group.

Coaches must also be able to determine the appropriate training intensity relative to a child's growth and development, both within a specific training session and cumulatively.

Having a range of coaching methods is vital when coaching young performers. Coaches are often directive, since 'telling' is a simple mechanism for imparting information. This approach emphasizes the coach's power and ignores the development of the athletes' decision making skills and opinions. Coach-centred training can give the coach a sense of security, which can be threatened by athlete-centred coaching. Shifting practice from coach-centred to performer-centred is a significant challenge, especially given that coaches who work with children are often the least qualified and experienced.

The real challenge for coaches is to understand the impact of their own behaviours on young performers. These behaviours are often rooted in coaches' practice orientation, and they serve to reproduce the traditional, hierarchical sport culture, which works against athlete welfare. A key question is 'what is the essential purpose of competition for children?' Selecting the best team inevitably leads to repeated exclusion of some players and inclusion of others. But if competition is seen as a development opportunity for all, selection becomes more inclusive. This sends a positive message, demonstrating that the young performer is valued as a person rather than as a performer. This is particularly illustrated when performers come through as 'late maturers'. Coaches therefore need to ensure that the competition experience is balanced.

In athletics as in all other fields, children should be valued and need to be protected through compliance with the principles of good practice. Child protection and athlete welfare should become embedded within practice as a deliberate set of actions based on a clear set of principles about the purpose and function of coaching with this age group.

Communication methods are also part of protective practices. Coaches need expertise in communication, especially in the key task of giving feedback, which needs to be balanced and timed appropriately. Messages should encompass both the technical and general and should always be supportive. This does not necessarily rule out observations of what went wrong, but corrective messages should always centre on the action rather than the individual. How coaches speak is key to perceptions of equitable behaviour; they need to be aware of their tone and pitch. Shouting intimidates or frightens; it does not encourage; and physical punishment is unacceptable coaching practice. Young performers should not be asked to show wrong

techniques in front of their peers; instead the correct techniques should always be emphasized. Coaches also need to consider how they use humour, which can be interpreted as hostile or humiliating.

Coaches need to understand what is not said but inferred. Silences, ignoring performers or inappropriate non-verbal behaviours all emphasize 'coach control', often causing the young performer to feel disempowered and apprehensive about expressing an opinion. This controlling environment is the antithesis of an open and mutually respectful coach-performer relationship.

Understanding the nature of protective practice is perhaps most important in relation to physical contact. While it is not necessarily wrong to touch children and young people in demonstrating techniques, coaches must consider the appropriateness of physical contact. They should always make sure the young performer is comfortable with and consents to physical contact in advance, which communicates sensitivity to the performer.

Codes of Conduct and Athlete Welfare

A key response to the emphasis on athlete welfare is the proliferation of codes of conduct or practice for coaches. But codes alone provide little guarantee of ethical conduct. They often exist in a vacuum, failing to take account of coaches' experiences and the coaching environment. Codes of ethics that address coaching practice need further development to avoid the air of 'moral certainty' and turn them into guidelines based on key ethical principles.[9]

Sports coaching is starting to embrace self evaluation, which is leading to more self-critical examination.[10] 'Reflective practice', a developing area in coach education programmes, encourages coaches to view their practice as a craft rather than the delivery of a set of technical skills. It encourages coaches to take more account of their experiential learning and to integrate these experiences into their teaching. Reflection provides a framework for validating their practice and making sure their techniques are based on evidence.

This approach is aimed at ensuring that athlete welfare is at the heart of coaching practice. The relevant skills are increasingly being adopted in programmes that work with children and young people. They help in ensuring that coaches consider the relational aspects of their work, such as setting boundaries related to social relationships, delivery style and reward and goal management.[11] Reflective practice encourages them to address both their actions (what did I do and was it correct) and the impacts of those actions (why did I do that and what were the consequences).

The interpersonal skills required in coaching young performers need to reflect what Loland identifies as the interface of competing values[12] in terms of the nature of childhood, participation in sport and the emphasis on outcomes. Coaches of children and young people need to focus sharply on the welfare of their athletes. Sensitivity to the ages of child athletes and the stages of their participation in sport makes coaching practice more robust in helping the young performer move from play *within* sport to practice *of* sport. By embedding athlete welfare principles in their coaching, coaches can reflect an ethos of 'doing the right thing' rather than one concerned merely with impression management.

Notes

1. Jones, R., K. Armour and P. Potrac (eds.), *Sports Coaching Cultures*, Routledge, London, 2004.
2. See Strean, W., 'Possibilities for qualitative research in sports psychology', *The Sport Psychologist*, 1998:12, pp. 333-345.
3. Fraser-Thomas, J.L., J. Côté and J. Deakin, 'Youth sport programs: An overview to foster positive youth development', *Physical Education and Sport Pedagogy*, 2005:10, 1, pp. 19-40.
4. Sports coach UK, *The United Kingdom Coaching Framework*, sports coach UK, Leeds, 2008.
5. Lee, M. (ed.), *Coaching Children in Sport*, Routledge, London, 1993.
6. UK Child Protection in Sport Unit, *Strategy for Safeguarding Children in Sport*, Leicester, National Society for Prevention of Cruelty to Children, 2006.
7. Sports coach UK, *Safeguarding and Protecting Children*, sports coach UK, Leeds, 2006.
8. Lyle, J., *Sports Coaching Concepts. A framework for coaches' behaviour*, Routledge, London, 2002.
9. McNamee, M., 'Celebrating trust: Virtues and rules in the ethical conduct of sports coaches', in: M. McNamee and J. Parry (eds.), *Ethics and Sport*, E&FN Spon, London, 1999, pp. 148-168.
10. Knowles, Z., A. Borrie and H. Telfer, 'Towards the reflective sports coach: Issues of context, education and application', *Ergonomics*, 2005:28, 11-14, pp. 1711-1720.
11. Lyle, op. cit.
12. Loland, S., *Fair Play in Sport – A moral norm system*, Routledge, London, 2002.

CHAPTER 5. SAFEGUARDING CHILDREN IN SPORT: A PAEDIATRICIAN'S PERSPECTIVE

Ian Male

In recent years, the United Kingdom has moved from the concept of child protection to the broader approach of safeguarding. This approach encompasses "protecting children from maltreatment; preventing the impairment of children's health and development; ensuring children are growing up in circumstances consistent with the provision of safe and effective care; and taking all reasonable measures to ensure that risks of harm to children are minimised".[1] For statutory agencies such as the government's Department of Health, this has opened the question of whether the responsibilities remain solely around protecting children from abuse largely within the family setting, or in advocating for the safety of children in wider society. This could include a role in the field of sport.

Sports Medicine and Child Protection

To understand the following perspective, it is helpful to comprehend the role of the paediatrician, and more specifically the community paediatrician working within the British National Health Service. All are trained initially as doctors and then specialize in working with children. This brings a detailed understanding of anatomy and physiology both in health and ill health, as well as how health changes over a child's development. Doctors are also trained in the science of pharmacology, bringing an understanding of the potential risks and benefits of drug use, whether prescribed or otherwise. Community paediatricians specialize clinically in neurodisability, mental health and special needs. They often play a key role in child public health, including accident prevention and health promotion, as well as in child protection. This latter includes both a clinical role, in identifying or assessing possible abuse, and a strategic role, working with Local Safeguarding Boards. (These are Local multi-agency groups representing health, education and other relevant sectors that together oversee child protection, which is now called 'safeguarding' in England.)

While sports medicine at the adult level has recently been granted professional (Royal College) status, it has not yet even reached sub-specialty status within paediatrics. As a result, there is no national response for tackling child protection issues within sport. Much of what follows comes from marrying paediatric responsibilities with a personal interest in safeguarding children in sport, which stems from my role both as a girls' football coach at local level and as a parent of three children who participate in a number of sports, from school to county level.

From the perspective of public health alone, there are significant advantages to encouraging children to have a lifelong involvement in sport. With current concerns about childhood obesity, the reduction in sedentary lifestyle and associated weight reduction are high on the list.[2] However, there are also potential benefits to mental health and self-esteem, a reduction in anti-social behaviour and the possibility of future careers, whether as a competitor or in support services. Calum Giles, a former England hockey player who had suffered from attention-deficit hyperactivity disorder, explains this well:

"I had very little self-esteem at school, and was in trouble on a daily basis. Hockey was the only thing that kept me happy; when I was at hockey I was made to feel talented, the people there made me feel like I was worth something."[3]

At a lower level, a recent study[4] has shown a similar positive effect from sports in boys with developmental coordination disorder. This disorder is associated with poor motor coordination, which results in a tendency to be the last one chosen for any team. Boys with the disorder recorded higher loneliness scores that were statistically significantly (38/80 compared with 22/80) and significantly lower participation rates in all group physical activities (participation in team sports of one session per week compared with four sessions per week), when compared with boys without it. Involvement in non-physical activities whether in a group (e.g. choir) or individually was similar in both groups. For the boys with developmental coordination disorder, however, involvement in team sport, but not other activities, significantly reduced feelings of loneliness.

Despite these undoubted benefits, many children and adolescents either do not participate in sport or drop out. The reasons for this are manifold but include availability of somewhere to play; cost (for example, it now costs £20 for a family of five to swim at our local swimming pool, which is beyond the budget of many families); attitudes about clothing; and, for the less able, the difficulties of getting onto a team, which is often very competitive even at local level. Recent research suggests that coaching or parenting methods may also have an impact, at times overstepping a line into what could be considered emotional abuse.[5-7] One retrospective study of 12 former elite child athletes who had dropped out of their sport revealed that they had experienced frequent abusive behaviour by their coaches, including belittling and shouting (12/12), frequent threatening behaviour (9/12), frequent humiliation (9/12), scapegoating, rejection and isolation.[8] Comments included:

"I gave up because … she constantly told me I was crap and worthless."

"I think being humiliated is so horrible, and the pain of that I'll always remember."

"I was upset and depressed most of the time I was training."

Losing these athletes from their sport is bad enough; however, such coaching methods also resulted in significant psychological harm, both at the time and in the longer term. Prior to the study, the athletes had had little opportunity to share their experiences or to seek help, yet many suffered long-term mental health difficulties such as low self-esteem and depression.

Evidence is growing that other forms of abuse, in particular sexual abuse, are also commonplace in sport.[9] The impact on the victim can be severe and lifelong. Sheldon Kennedy has written at length about his experiences of repeated sexual abuse by his ice hockey coach and the impact this had, leading to a self-destructive lifestyle and failure to fulfil his sporting potential.[10] Adding to his vulnerability was the fact that he was good enough to represent his country (Canada) at youth level, and therefore spent long periods of time away from home, often staying with his coach. In his book, *Why I Didn't Say Anything*, he describes his feelings when he finally was able to go to the police:

> "Suddenly, the last twelve years of my life made perfect sense to everybody who loved me. All the drinking and drugs and self abuse and silence. All the acting out, and anger, how I couldn't look anybody in the eyes … but I was still a mess, full of irrational fears and anxiety."

The Impact of Abuse in Child Sports

Little research has been undertaken specifically on the impact of sexual or other child abuse in the context of sport. But several studies outside of sport have confirmed that such abuse frequently results in the long-term mental health problems described so vividly by Sheldon Kennedy, such as post-traumatic stress disorder, depression, drug and alcohol abuse, and relationship difficulties. Given the potential mental health benefits from involvement in sport and the significant burden mental health difficulties place on the economy, it is tragic that some coaches are actually adding to the problem. Sadly, as Sheldon Kennedy describes, our assumptions and stereotypes of how a paedophile should appear have left child athletes particularly vulnerable to those who would take advantage of them:

> "Sometimes his defenders brought these things up because they were having trouble believing … We've all been taught to think that sexual offenders are the losers of society – dirty old men in trench coats … (but) sexual abusers are often trusted members of the community who are in positions of authority over children. They are the priests at the local church, the coach of the softball team … and they have all learned to hide their behaviour … What better way to find new victims than to be put in charge of dozens of vulnerable, impressionable children who are eager to please the authority figures in their lives."[11]

A recent campaign in the United States by the National Athletic Trainers Association and American Academy of Orthopedic Surgeons asked the question: 'What will they have longer, their trophies or their injuries?' While the nature of most sports carries a risk of injury, we do need to ensure these risks are kept to a minimum. This may involve considering whether some sports carry an unacceptable risk to children's safety and modifying the rules and equipment to reduce risk (for example, cricket now demands that all youth players wear a helmet when batting or wicket keeping). But it may also involve monitoring coaching practice to prevent children from exposure to risk. Bringing this into a child protection framework, it may be helpful to consider whether exposing children to such risk amounts to 'physical abuse' or 'neglect'.

'Physical abuse' implies that a child has received a physical injury as a result of an act by the parent or guardian (with a coach effectively taking parental responsibility while in charge of the child) or through failure to take reasonable steps to prevent physical harm.[12] This could include administration of a harmful substance or tampering with a child's normal physiology. 'Neglect' implies failure to meet the needs of the child whether deliberately or not, for example in failing to protect from danger or carry out important aspects of care. These clearly have implications in a sporting context. For example, while an adult may choose to accept the physical (and legal) risks of taking performance-enhancing drugs or of using rapid dehydration to reach a competition weight limit, children should be protected from such practices. In prescribing any medicine, doctors constantly weigh the potential benefits with the risk of side effects. Some people may justify taking such risks for the potential to improve performance or to win that elusive gold medal. However, the need to safeguard the child from harm should override any possible gain, which in many cases may primarily be for the benefit of the adult, whether coach or parent. For one example, the side effects of anabolic steroids include:

- Liver damage;
- High blood pressure and heart disease;
- Stroke;
- Sleep problems;
- Early cessation of growth;
- Drug dependence;
- Aggressive behaviour;
- Paranoia;
- Depression and thoughts of suicide.

Equally, acute dehydration developing over several hours – as seen medically in severe gastroenteritis, for example – may present as a medical emergency and may lead to electrolyte imbalance, acute renal failure, hypovolaemic shock, potential seizures and even death. To deliberately expose a child to rapid dehydration therefore carries a high risk. The American Academy of Pediatrics has also emphasized the increased potential for heat-induced illness, including dehydration, resulting from differences in physiology and morphology between children and adults. These include a high ratio of surface area to body mass, increased metabolic heat production during exercise and decreased sweating capacity.[13] Aside from the risks of deliberate dehydration, the danger may bring into question the wisdom of running all-day tournaments at the height of summer, as is common practice in children's soccer in the United Kingdom.

Protecting Children from Harm

While deliberate infliction of physical harm is clearly unacceptable, failure to prevent harm, such as by demanding that children train or play through known injuries, should also be considered. Joan Ryan's book, *Little Girls in Pretty Boxes*,[14] describes how such an approach among American gymnasts, fuelled by the nation's desire for gold at the Olympics in the 1990s, had devastating consequences, including paralysis and the subsequent death of one girl.

Similarly, we need to challenge the pressure exerted in certain sports, where size is important, to maintain an inappropriately low body weight. For a girl (or, for that matter, a boy) whose weight is already worryingly low to be told by a coach – or worse still, international judges – that she is 'too fat' to win a medal is dangerously irresponsible.[15] Not surprisingly, the female athlete triad of anorexia (and other eating disorders), amenorrhoea and osteoporosis is now well recognized; the American Academy of Pediatrics reports that 32 to 62 per cent of female collegiate athletes engage in unhealthy weight control behaviours.[16] Eating disorders in general remain notoriously difficult to treat and on occasion end in death. As with so much in medicine, therefore, prevention is far easier than cure. Given that the perfectionist and obsessive personality often seen in those hoping to reach the top in sport predisposes them to eating disorders, it is important that we develop an approach to coaching and parenting that protects children and adolescents from such problems, rather than encouraging their development.

The public health community has discussed whether to use the term 'accident' when describing an event leading to injury, given that with foresight many such incidents, and the resulting harm, are avoidable. For example, wearing cycling helmets significantly reduces the risk of brain injury for a cyclist involved in a traffic accident. Within the neglect framework, it is therefore important to consider the management of children in sport – whether at school, club or governing body level – to ensure that each sport is run in a way that minimizes the risk of 'accidental' (or deliberate) injury occurring.

A recent systematic review found a lack of research examining injury prevention programmes for children in sport beyond that suggesting the effectiveness of strategies focussing on pre-season conditioning, functional training and education.[17] Research, however, suggests that the nature of certain sports, particularly those emphasizing early specialization, may predispose to long-term injury. Examples of this include the impact on spinal growth and injury seen in children focussing on a single asymmetric sport such as tennis where the child uses one side of their body more than the other, or the observation of a local orthopaedic surgeon of an increase in knee operations in field hockey players with the move from grass to artificial surfaces. A recent study that used magnetic resonance imaging to compare adolescent cricketing fast bowlers with swimmers (swimming is a symmetrical sport) showed that the cricket players were prone to developing an imbalance in their spinal muscles, resulting in symptomatic lumbar spinal injury.[18]

Equally, the American Academy of Pediatrics has reviewed the incidence of spinal injuries, including those resulting in paralysis, in ice hockey.[19] Many of these injuries result from body checking (bumping the opponent with one's body), with one study showing a twelvefold increase in injuries in a league allowing body checking compared to one that did not.[20] Interestingly, these injuries became more common after helmets and face masks were introduced to *reduce* facial injury. It has been suggested the increase occurred due to players with protection playing more aggressively because they felt less vulnerable to injury. The report recommends not allowing body checking in children aged 15 years or younger. The Academy also recommended rewarding fair play, following one study that showed injury rates were quartered in the qualifying rounds of a tournament using fair play rules, compared with the rest of the tournament using normal rules.

So what would make a difference? Children involved in sport, regardless of level or ability, have the right to be treated as children, and in a safe environment. This means examining our motives in pushing young children into long hours in a single sport: 10,000 hours of training from age 7 to 17 may have turned Maria Sharapova into a Wimbledon champion, but how many other children were discarded along the way? Allowing children to be children also means having acceptable standards of interaction and relationship between coach and child athlete. In addition it is important to consider how coaches operate at senior elite level, because methods that achieve success will be copied at lower levels of sport, regardless of their appropriateness. Until now, sport has been largely left to self-regulate, although increasingly there is input and support from bodies such as the Child Protection in Sport Unit (in the United Kingdom).

As the statutory agencies involved in safeguarding children become more involved in areas such as sport, it will be important to work in partnership to achieve an approach that keeps children safe while avoiding losing coaches from sport through fear that their actions may be misinterpreted. For example, many coaches now worry about how to respond to an injured child, for fear that handling the child in assessing and responding to the injury may risk an accusation of inappropriate handling. We also need to achieve a balance that can fulfil each nation's desire for success in the sporting field while making sport an enjoyable experience for children of any age or ability. The story by E.J. Nolan about a learning-disabled boy carries this lesson in a way accessible to everyone:

Shay and his father had walked past a park where some boys Shay knew were playing baseball. Shay asked, "Do you think they'll let me play?" Shay's father knew that most of the boys would not want someone like Shay on their team, but the father also understood that if his son were allowed to play, it would give him a much-needed sense of belonging and some confidence to be accepted by others in spite of his handicaps. Shay's father approached one of the boys on the field and asked (not expecting much) if Shay could play. The boy looked around for guidance and said, 'We're losing by six runs and the game is in the eighth inning. I guess he can be on our team and we'll try to put him in to bat in the ninth inning.'

Shay struggled over to the team's bench and, with a broad smile, put on a team shirt … Now, the potential winning run was on base and Shay was scheduled to be next at bat. At this juncture, do they let Shay bat and give away their chance to win the game? Surprisingly, Shay was given the bat. Everyone knew that a hit was all but impossible because Shay didn't even know how to hold the bat properly, much less connect with the ball.

However, as Shay stepped up to the plate, the pitcher, recognizing that the other team was putting winning aside for this moment in Shay's life, moved in a few steps to lob the ball in softly so Shay could at least make contact. The first pitch came and Shay swung clumsily and missed. The pitcher again took a few steps forward to toss the ball softly towards Shay. As the pitch came in, Shay swung at the ball and hit a slow ground ball right back to the pitcher. The game would now be over. The pitcher picked up the soft grounder and could have easily thrown the ball to the first baseman … Instead, the pitcher threw the ball right over the first baseman's head, out of reach of all team mates. Everyone from the stands and both teams started yelling, 'Shay, run to first! Run to first!' Never in his life had Shay ever run that far, but he made it to first base. He scampered down the baseline, wide-eyed and startled. Everyone yelled, 'Run to second, run to second!' … Shay reached third base because the opposing shortstop ran to help him by turning him in the direction of third base, and shouted, 'Run to third'… Shay ran to home, stepped on the plate, and was cheered as the hero who hit the grand slam and won the game for his team. 'That day', said the father softly with tears now rolling down his face, 'the boys from both teams helped bring a piece of true love and humanity into this world'. Shay didn't make it to another summer. He died that winter, having never forgotten being the hero and making his father so happy…"[21]

What would you have done?

Notes

1. Child Protection in Sport Unit, *Play Sport Stay Safe: Strategy for safeguarding children and young people in sport 2006-2012*. London, National Society for Prevention of Cruelty to Children, 2006.
2. Christodoulos, A., A. Flouris and S. Tokmakidis, 'Obesity and physical fitness of pre-adolescent children during the academic year and the summer period: Effects of organized physical activity', *Journal of Child Health Care*, 2006:10, pp. 199-212.
3. Giles C., *My Story*, <www.stickwise.com>, 2007.
4. Poulsen, A., J. Ziviani, M. Cuskelly and R. Smith, 'Boys with developmental coordination disorder: Loneliness and team sports participation', *American Journal of Occupational Therapy*, 2007:61, pp. 451-462.
5. Gervis, M. and N. Dunn, 'The emotional abuse of child athletes by their coaches', *Child Abuse Review*, 2004:13, pp. 215-223.
6. Sagar, S., D. Lavallee and C. Spray, 'Why young elite athletes fear failure: Consequences of failure', *Journal of Sports Science*, 2007:25, pp. 1171-1184.
7. Myers, J. and B. Barrett, *In at the Deep End*, NSPCC/Amateur Swimming Association, Leicester, 2002.
8. Gervis, M. and N. Dunn, op cit.
9. Kennedy, S. and J. Grainger, *Why I Didn't Say Anything: The Sheldon Kennedy story*, Insomniac Press, Toronto, 2006.
10. Kennedy, S. and J. Grainger, ibid.
11. Kennedy, S. and J. Grainger, op cit.
12. Hobbs, C., H. Hanks and J. Wynne, 'Physical abuse' in: *Child Abuse and Neglect*, Churchill Livingstone, Edinburgh, 1993, pp. 47-75.
13. American Academy of Pediatrics Committee on Sports Medicine and Fitness, 'Climatic heat stress and the exercising child and adolescent', *Pediatrics*, 2000:106, pp. 158-159.
14. Ryan, J., 'If it isn't bleeding, don't worry about it: Injuries', in: *Little Girls in Pretty Boxes*, London, The Women's Press, 1996, pp. 15-49.

15. Ryan, J., 'They stole her soul and they still have it: Eating disorders', in: *Little Girls in Pretty Boxes*, London, The Women's Press, 1996, pp. 50-84.

16. American Academy of Pediatrics Committee on Sports Medicine and Fitness, 'Promotion of healthy weight-control practices in young athletes', *Pediatrics*, 2005:116, pp. 1557-1564.

17. Abernethy, L. and C. Bleakley, 'Strategies to prevent injury in adolescent sport: A systematic review', *British Journal of Sports Medicine*, 2007:41, pp. 627-638.

18. Engstrom, C., D. Walker, V. Kippers and A. Mehnert, 'Quadratus lumborum asymmetry and L4 pars injury in fast bowlers: A prospective MR study', *Medicine and Science in Sport and Exercise*, 2007:39, pp. 910-917.

19. American Academy of Pediatrics, 'Safety in youth ice hockey: The effects of body checking', *Pediatrics*, 2000:105, pp. 657-658.

20. Regnier, G., R. Bioleau, G. Marcotte, et al., 'Effects of body checking in the Pee-Wee (12 and 13 years old) division in the province of Quebec', in: C. Castaldi and E. Hoerner (eds.), *Safety in Ice Hockey*, Philadelphia, PA, American Society for Testing and Materials, 1989, pp. 84-103.

21. Nolan, E., *The Day Shay Got to Play.* © 2001 E. J. Nolan (all rights reserved).

CHAPTER 6. PROTECTING CHILDREN IN SPORT THROUGH AN ATHLETE-CENTRED SPORT SYSTEM

Ashley Stirling and Gretchen Kerr

Concern has been growing over child maltreatment, also defined as volitional acts that result in or have the potential to result in physical injuries and/or psychological harm.[1] Despite the secrecy surrounding childhood experiences of abuse, emerging incidence and prevalence data indicate that child abuse and neglect is a substantial problem affecting a significant proportion of children and youth both in society generally[2] and in sport specifically.[3,4-8] As sport is a highly child-populated domain, the establishment of child protection measures to reduce the potential for child maltreatment in sport is critical. We propose that a multifaceted, athlete-centred approach is required to protect young athletes from experiences of maltreatment in sport. This chapter reviews the philosophy of athlete-centred sport and offers recommendations for the implementation of child protection policy, education, research and advocacy in sport.

The Philosophy of Athlete-centred Sport

Athlete-centred sport espouses a value-based approach emphasizing developmentally appropriate child-focused participation. It is both a philosophy and an approach to delivering sport programmes that recognizes athletes as active agents in the sport experience. The basic tenet is that sport should contribute to the overall development of the person: physically, psychologically, socially and spiritually.[9] The health and well-being of the athlete takes precedence over performance outcomes and is the primary focus in the development of policies, programmes and procedures.[10-11] In this way, sport is a vehicle for achieving personal development, teaching life skills and pursuing ethical conduct and citizenship.

Advocates of this approach maintain that only through full development of the person can he or she achieve optimal athletic performance. The most significant misconception about athlete-centred sport, held by many sport leaders, is that holistic athlete development comes at a cost to performance. Rather, performance excellence is possible only through personal excellence. As performance excellence still remains the end product of the athlete-centred development approach, according to this philosophy, an athlete-centred sport model can exist within a high-performance sport environment.

The philosophy of athlete-centred sport is unique from previous promotions of positive youth development in and through sport in that it recognizes athletes as active participants.[12] As author Lynn Kidman states, "The key to the athlete-centred approach is a leadership style that caters to athletes' needs and understandings where athletes are enabled to learn and have control of their participation in sport."[13]

In an athlete-centred approach, the adults – coaches, parents, administrators and support staff – have responsibilities to protect and enhance the well-being of athletes above and beyond all other goals and objectives. Furthermore, adults have 'extended responsibility',[14] or the responsibility to prioritize the health and well-being of the young person beyond the athletic career. As such, adults are guided by questions such as: How will the decisions we're making today affect this young person as an athlete, and as a person, long after the competitive career is over? Will these decisions contribute to the development of a well-rounded individual upon retirement from sport?

Coaches, given the amount of time they spend with athletes and their influence on young people, play a particularly important role in actualizing an athlete-centred sport system. Proponents of this approach advocate a coach-athlete relationship that functions as a partnership, where planning, decision making and evaluations are shared responsibilities, within the parameters of the developmental status of the athlete (see table 1).[15] Within the framework of an athlete-centred approach, "empowered athletes have the authority and are enabled to engage actively and fully in shaping and defining their own direction," according to Kidman,[16] who includes these components in an athlete-centred sport model:

- The use of teaching games for understanding;
- Developing thinking and decision making in athletes through questioning;
- Pursuing a culture in which athletes gain responsibility for establishing and maintaining goals for themselves or the team;
- The use of role rotation on teams to enhance empathy, understanding, trust and decision making skills.

Table 1: Key principles of the athlete-centred philosophy

✓	Sport is a vehicle through which personal development occurs, life skills are taught, and ethical conduct and citizenship are pursued.
✓	Optimal athletic performance is achieved only though holistic athlete development.
✓	Sport should contribute to the overall development of the person: physically, psychologically, socially, and spiritually.
✓	Dynamic needs of the child (developmental and temporal) drive the nature, content and delivery of the sport programme.
✓	The health and well-being of the athlete take precedence over all other goals and objectives in sport, particularly performance.
✓	Adults in leadership positions in sport have an extended responsibility to consider the long-term effects of the child's experiences in sport.
✓	Athletes should be active participants in the sport experience.
✓	Relationships with athletes should function as a partnership in which planning, decision-making and evaluation are shared in a developmentally-appropriate manner.

Additionally, David outlined the 10 following principles as fundamental to a child-centred sport system: [17]

1) Equity, non-discrimination, fairness;
2) Best interests of the child: children first;
3) Evolving capacities of the child;
4) Subject of rights, exercise of rights;
5) Consultation, the child's opinion, informed participation;
6) Appropriate direction and guidance;
7) Mutual respect, support and responsibility;
8) Highest attainable standard of health;
9) Transparency, accountability, monitoring;
10) Excellence.

Implementing an Athlete-centred Sport System

To protect young athletes from maltreatment in sport, an athlete-centred, multifaceted approach requires four interrelated pillars (see figure 1):

1) Policy;
2) Education;
3) Research;
4) Advocacy.

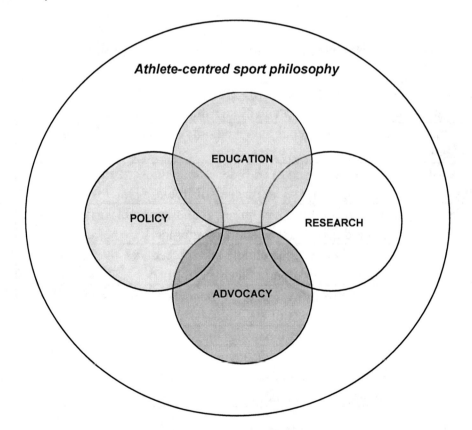

Figure 1. Athlete-centred approach to child protection

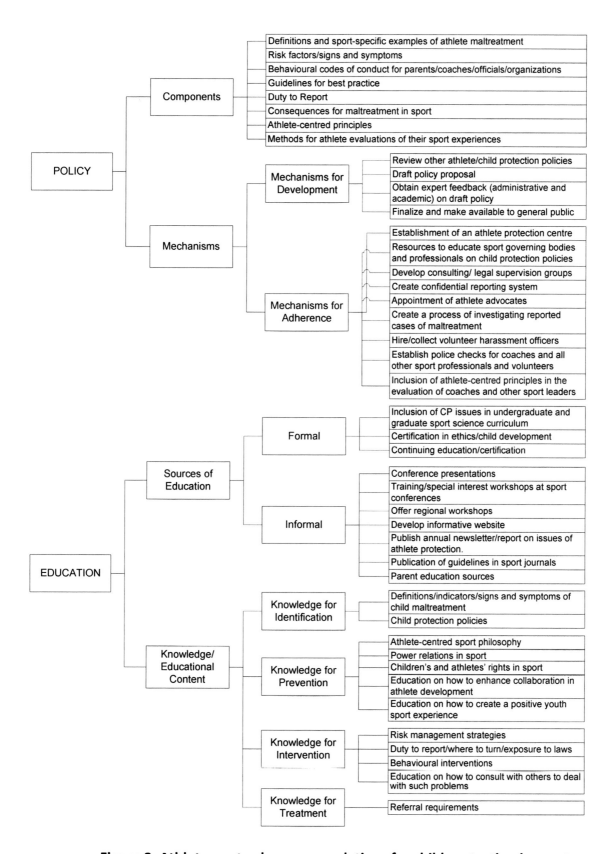

Figure 2. Athlete-centred recommendations for child protection in sport

The athlete-centred philosophy puts the child's holistic development and well-being at the forefront of sporting initiatives. Implementation of the model would assure prevention of child maltreatment.

Each of the four pillars, along with specific athlete-centred recommendations for child protection in sport, is illustrated in figure 2. While these suggestions do not represent all possibilities, they should stimulate further discussion and development. The scope of influence of sport leaders and professionals will vary across cultures, sport systems and levels of sport.

Conclusion

An athlete-centred approach to sport is proposed as a valuable method to promote child protection. More specifically, prioritizing athletes' safety, developmental needs and health may be the most effective way to protect children from maltreatment in sport. Not only would an athlete-centred model help protect children, but athletes would also benefit personally from the holistic development associated with such an approach to sport.

Notes

1. Crooks, C.V. and D.A. Wolfe, 'Child abuse and neglect', in: E.J. Mash and R.A. Barkley (eds.), *Assessment of Childhood Disorders* (4th ed.), New York, Guilford Press, 2007, p.3.
2. Ibid.
3. Kirby, S. and L. Greaves, 'Foul play: Sexual harassment in sport', paper presented at the Pre-Olympic Scientific Congress, Dallas, Texas, United States, 11-15 July 1996.
4. Brackenridge, C.H., '"He owned me basically …" Women's experience of sexual abuse in sport', *International Review for the Sociology of Sport*, 1997, 32:2, pp. 115-130.
5. Kirby and Greaves, op. cit.
6. Fasting, K. and C.H. Brackenridge, 'The grooming process in sport: Case studies of sexual harassment and abuse', *Auto/Biography*, 2005, 13:1, pp. 33-52.
7. Stirling, A.E. and G.A. Kerr, 'Elite female swimmers' experiences of emotional abuse across time', *Journal of Emotional Abuse*, 2007, 7:4, pp. 89-113.
8. Stirling, A.E. and G.A. Kerr, 'Defining and categorizing emotional abuse in sport', *European Journal of Sport Science*, 2008, 8:4, pp. 173-181.
9. Clarke, H., D. Smith and G. Thibault, *Athlete-centered Sport. A discussion paper.* <www.athletescan.com/Images/Publications/AthleteCentredDiscussion.doc>1994, September, retrieved 11 November 2006.
10. Canadian Heritage, *The Canadian Sport Policy.* <www.pch.gc.ca>, 2002, May, retrieved 1 March 2007.
11. Clarke, Smith and Thibault, op. cit.
12. Miller, P.S. and G.A. Kerr, 'Conceptualizing excellence: Past, present, and future', *Journal of Applied Sport Psychology*, 2002:14, pp. 140-153.
13. Kidman, L., *Athlete-centred Coaching: Developing inspired and inspiring people*, Innovative Print Communications, 2005, p. 16.

14. Clarke, Smith and Thibault, op. cit.
15. Clarke, Smith and Thibault, op. cit.
16. Kidman, op. cit., p. 16.
17. David, P., *Human Rights in Youth Sport: A critical review of children's rights in competitive sports.* New York, Routledge, 2005.

CHAPTER 7. MANAGING RESEARCH ON VIOLENCE TO CHILDREN IN SPORT[1]

Celia Brackenridge

For the past two decades my research has focused mainly on athlete welfare, notably addressing abuse and social inclusion. Here I will explore some of the difficulties of managing such research and trying to compile an evidence base about violence to children in sport in the sometimes challenging environment of sport-for-development programmes. This chapter offers some definitions of violence to children, drawing on work done for UNICEF.[2] It also outlines general limitations to generic and sport-based violence research and examines management issues that affect violence research, which are often hidden from view in the reporting of such research. Finally, it offers a way of interpreting the tension in the researcher-manager relationship as a creative tension that may aid sport-for-development work.

Defining Violence to Children in Sport

Violence is the term adopted by UNICEF to encompass physical, sexual and psychological/mental forms of maltreatment, including abuse and assault. This has a much wider compass than, for example, the term 'child abuse' by which the National Society for the Prevention of Cruelty to Children describes four main types of abuse: sexual, physical and emotional abuse and neglect.[3] An important definition of violence comes from article 19 of the Convention on the Rights of the Child:[4]

> "...all forms of physical or mental violence, injury or abuse, neglect or negligent treatment, maltreatment or exploitation, including sexual abuse..."

The World Health Organization, in the *World Report on Violence and Health*, defines violence as:[5]

> "...the intentional use of physical force or power, threatened or actual, against a child, by an individual or group, that either results in or has a high likelihood of resulting in actual or potential harm to the child's health, survival, development or dignity."

A related term is torture, defined by the Convention against Torture and Other Cruel, Inhuman or Degrading Treatment or Punishment:

> "...any act by which severe pain or suffering, whether physical or mental, is intentionally inflicted on a person for such purposes as obtaining from him or a third person information or a confession, punishing him for an act he or a third person has committed or is suspected of having committed, or intimidating or coercing him or a third person, or for any reason based on discrimination of any kind, when such pain is inflicted by or at the instigation of or with the consent of or acquiescence of a public official or other person acting in an official capacity.[6]

In the context of sport, violence to child athletes by their peer athletes or authority figures may be expressed through:

- Discrimination and harassment on the basis of sex, race or sexual orientation;
- Sexual violence, including:
  - Groomed or forced sex/rape;
  - Use of pornography;
  - Sexual degradation;
  - Sexualized initiations, bullying and hazing;
- Physical maltreatment, including:
  - Overtraining;
  - Playing while injured;
  - Peer aggression;
  - Parental maltreatment;
  - Doping/drug abuse;
  - Alcohol abuse;
- Emotional and psychological abuse;
- Neglect;
- Child labour and trafficking.[7]

Violence has multiple meanings for those who experience and perpetrate it. Parkes' account of violence among primary school children in South Africa, for example, shows how children perceive, make sense of and cope with violence in one community that has a post-apartheid legacy of violence by males, exacerbated by economic deprivation. Despite being in what she describes as a "constraining and disempowering context … characterized by high levels of interpersonal conflict, violent crime and gangsterism,"[8], the children strive to express agency in their social positions – at once both rejecting and yet incorporating violence into their own beliefs and social practices and using violence as a form of capital. Some forms of violence, such as beatings or physical punishment, were not defined by these children as violence at all but as part of their normal expectations of everyday retribution in school, home or community. Indeed, there was a normalcy to their descriptions of violence that might challenge the experiences and assumptions of many researchers from so-called developed nations.

Limitations in Researching Violence to Children in Sport

Prevalence of violence and violence-related behaviour is notoriously difficult to measure, for a host of reasons. First, violence is a sensitive subject, which many victims and most perpetrators are reluctant to discuss or report. Second, with little legal, policy or academic agreement about what constitutes violence to children, definitions and age boundaries vary from study to study and country to country. Third, athletes are often hesitant to report such problems because of their marginal status, or they are silenced by virtue of them. Those who do speak out may face safety and other negative consequences. Fourth, it is difficult to compare studies across cultures because of differences in definition, sampling, ethics, consent, underreporting and non-response. Finally, ethical research practice stipulates that children cannot consent but merely assent to be research participants; even when they assent, there is a real question over their freedom to refuse.

Establishing validity and reliability is as difficult with violence as with any other type of social research.[9] Some studies adopt proxy measures to assess prevalence, such as number of violence-related hospital visits by children or number of court convictions related to violence against children. But such measures are crude and often underestimate the true scale of violence. Longitudinal studies are the most accurate if trends are required but are also expensive and thus rare. Finding accurate measures for child violence is thus a huge challenge to the research and policy communities.

Research on violence in sport suffers from the same limitations as do mainstream violence studies. For example, many of the published studies do not distinguish between grades of violent behaviour (harassment, physical injury or sexual abuse, for example); some do not differentiate athletes under 18 years old from adult athletes in their research samples; some use legal definitions while others adopt everyday norms as threshold measures;[10, 11] and some do not differentiate on the basis of gender, rendering invisible the gendered nature of violence.

Sport psychologists and sport sociologists approach the study of child violence from different perspectives and thus adopt different methods and tolerances for what counts as violence. For example, some psychology research measures violence as a one-off *event* or perhaps a series of events (number of fouls in a game, number of red or yellow cards issued by a referee). But this can also mask prevalence: sociologists might argue that violence arises from a (social) *process* whereby unequal power relations are exercised by those with authority over those without it. This might assist with relational explanations of violence but overlook the fine details of violent behaviour that need to be identified if we are to design successful violence prevention interventions. As yet, there are no standardized scales for measuring violence to children in sport.

Street play and adult-free recreation may be the only instances in which children have real autonomy over their sport – though even in such cases they are often under adult surveillance. In contrast, children in organized, competitive sport usually lack authority; they are generally excluded from decision-making and may even have their voices silenced by coaches, assertive parents or carers, or senior athletes.[12] Participation in sport is therefore defined as a *physical* but not a *political* right. As a consequence, children are rarely allowed to shape their own competitive sporting experiences and may be subjected to violence if they fail to comply with the wishes of sport authority figures.

This exclusion from the right to participation as defined by the Convention on the Rights of the Child renders children vulnerable to a range of violence types, from bullying to sexual abuse to commercial trafficking.[13] As yet, we have virtually no idea of the prevalence, scale or depth of violence to children in sport, or of the consequences for their well-being. Such is the concern about this issue that the Committee on the Rights of the Child, which is charged with monitoring governments' adherence to the Convention on the Rights of the Child, has established a Working Party on Children and Sport and is to collaborate with UNICEF to improve knowledge on this subject.

Management Issues Influencing Violence Research in Children's Sport

Davies Banda, from Zambia, has worked and coached in Zambia and Botswana and has performed research on HIV/AIDS and sport development projects. He argues:

> "There is need for research in issues of abuse in this [sport for development] sector due to the vulnerability of the participants that attend sports sessions organized by sport-for-development NGOs. This vulnerability is mainly to do with power relations – abuse is always about the misuse of power by those who have more power within the organization ... The vulnerable mostly are the orphans who depend entirely on financial support from such NGOs to fund their school expenses. Abuse or violence does happen to such young people ... [There is a] lack of systematic policies and procedures for NGOs to vet those that apply as volunteers with the organizations. On the part of the NGO, there is also fear of losing the 'faithful' volunteers if such suspect that they are being investigated for a child abuse allegation.[14]

Problem definition and ownership

Research management begins with problem identification and ownership. Who defines the problem? How is the research question shaped and understood? Who stands to gain or lose from the research enquiry? Who is included or excluded by the way a project is framed? How might access difficulties mediate the course of the research and thus influence the nature of the findings?

Managing political expectations and avoiding cultural imperialism

Questions about the politics of research apply to most social science projects, but they become sharply relevant in the field of sport for development. Almost by definition, the moral direction of sport for development is one of 'doing good'. Widespread use is made of sport as a social and economic panacea – not unlike nineteenth century 'rational recreation' and 'muscular Christianity'[15] – and sport-for-development programmes are stuffed full of assumptions about their benefits. The expectations of sponsors and gatekeepers thus bear heavily on the research manager. Which government agency wants to hear that its international development funds have had no positive effect or, worse, may have damaged local conditions? Which international peace organization wants to learn that sport cannot deliver social inclusion, reduce community crime or integrate rival youth groups? Lidchi argues for avoiding the 'transplant' programme "that fails to adjust to engage with the surrounding social reality and culture".[16] Similarly, it is important to avoid the assumption that western rational research models can necessarily be transplanted effectively into other social realities.

Managing subjectivity

Conventional scientific approaches to social research offer no space for reflecting about how researchers influence their own work, no scope for situating the personal or locating one's own subjectivity. Yet in sport-for-development research one is often challenged by the unfamiliar, or even culturally alienated. The suppression of subjectivity thus has an effect on the research process and the reported findings that might lead at best to distortion (we only see what we want to see) and at worst to deceit (we only report what we are allowed to report).

Managing insider-outsider relations

Linked to the issue of subjectivity is that of managing insider-outsider relations. However much effort we might put into social acclimitization, cultural sensitization, habituation to the setting or recruiting trusted local gatekeepers, few of us can claim insider status in the sport-for-development projects that we observe.

Managing the gender politics of fieldwork

Just as sport is a deeply gendered social practice, so too is research.[17] The gender politics of researching violence in sport-for-development programmes thus present particular challenges to female researchers that can compound their pre-existing status as alien (for example, by virtue of their age, economic advantage or non-indigenous background). Of course many sport-for-development schemes are targeted at girls, at health and at physical activity, and some are led by women. But there is still distributive (more) and relational (more power) male dominance in sport that questions the place of female as athlete or as researcher. Warren suggests that merely being female "can result in a lack of credibility in the presentation of research …"[18] Equally, there is danger in the false labelling of women ethnographers, as 'sociability specialists', able to communicate well and get respondents to open up.[19]

Managing our own conceptual frameworks

Taken-for-granted definitions and norms in one culture may not translate easily into sport-for-development settings. Examples of how such issues might challenge researchers include:

- (Re)constructing a concept of childhood in communities where people as young as 10 years old might be orphaned and responsible for looking after their siblings or elders;

- Drawing on the human resources of a community that has no formal child care, social services or medical support infrastructure;

- Defining violence in a culture in which sexual bargaining may be linked to social or financial survival and domestic violence may be normative;

- (Re)defining sport for development as social work by another name;

- Defining sport as the problem rather than the solution; that is, locating violence within sport and not assuming that it only occurs within families and communities.

These kinds of issues are well illustrated in Gary Armstrong's potent account of the Don Bosco football project in Liberia, 'Lords of Misrule'.[20] He wrote:

"One internationally well-known enterprise declared in 2001 that it was going to locate community football teams and work with them to save children. This brought exasperation from Father Joe [founder of the project] who predicted: "They'll swamp the area. Give out footballs will-nilly and have photos taken of kids with balls for their brochures. After six months it'll all end, the balls will burst, or get lost, and there won't be any replacements. The kids meanwhile get the idea what they want some Western agencies will get for them – free. NGOs are without shame, they start an idea, spend a fortune in the short term and don't follow it through. But then their duty is to their policy makers …"

Davies Banda reinforces this from his own observations:

"Child abusers from other parts of the world find it easy to operate in some of the African countries in sports for development projects due to lack of systematic policies and procedures; anecdotal data from female participants narrate how abuse by leaders (foreign) is prevalent in some organizations."[21]

Effective Researcher-Managers in Children's Sport for Development

How can we become effective research(er)-managers within the sport-for-development context? One way is to adopt reflexive sociology, through which we move back and forth between the subjective and the objective. Techniques such as bracketing, research diaries, writing in the first person or in the present tense can all assist us to cope with the emotional content of our work and to ground us in our subjective realities rather than assuming that there is only one objective reality to be defined or explained. As Evelyn Fox Keller notes, "the persistent scientific call to objectivity, distance, and caution is quintessentially male."[22] Suspending assumptions of validity and adopting trustworthiness criteria instead are not new ideas: Andrew Sparkes has done much to humanize sport psychology research by promoting such techniques.[23]

Focussing on process evaluation and studying organizational capacity building rather than outcomes[24, 25] can also bring us closer to the projects and the people we study. By joining up with advocates and practice organizations – getting our hands dirty –

we are very deliberately politicizing the research process, but not necessarily in ways that render our research 'biassed'. The very terms 'findings' and 'results' imply an end point to research that, in the sport-for-development context, is simply unrealistic. Life and daily struggles continue, with or without researchers around and with or without sport-for-development projects and facilitators.

Finally, our work in both sport for development and the management of research on sport for development will be enhanced if sport NGOs become more closely tied to child rights NGOs.[26-28] We can learn much from the way that UNICEF conducted its recent global study on violence against children, actively involving children as participants in the research process across all the regions of the world.[29] This work exemplified what is so often missing in 'traditional' sport research, as it made outsider-insider relations work for children and helped their voices to be heard.

Notes

1. This chapter is based on a presentation to the conference The Management of Sports Development held at Brunel University, West London, United Kingdom, 25-26 April 2008.
2. UNICEF, *Exercising Rights: Preventing and eliminating violence against children in sport*, Florence, UNICEF Innocenti Research Centre (in press).
3. National Society for Prevention of Cruelty to Children/Sport England Child Protection in Sport Unit, <www.thecpsu.org.uk>, retrieved 3 March 2008.
4. United Nations, *Convention on the Rights of the Child*, New York, United Nations, 1990.
5. Krug, E.G., L.L. Dahlberg, J.A. Mercy, A.B. Zwi and R. Lozano (eds.), *World Report on Violence and Health*, Geneva, World Health Organization, 2002, p.5.
6. Adapted from United Nations, *Convention against Torture and Other Cruel, Inhuman or Degrading Treatment or Punishment*, article 1, Geneva: United Nations, 1984.
7. UNICEF, op cit.
8. Parkes, J., 'The multiple meanings of violence: Children's talk about life in a South African neighbourhood', *Childhood*, 2007:14, pp. 401-414.
9. **Dahlberg, L.L., S.B. Toal, M. Swahn and C.B. Behrens, *Measuring Violence-Related Attitudes, Behaviors, and Influences Among Youths: A compendium of assessment tools.* 2nd edition, Atlanta, GA, Centers for Disease Control and Prevention, National Center for Injury Prevention and Control, 2005.**
10. Fasting, K., C.H. Brackenridge and J. Sundgot-Borgen, *Females, Elite Sports and Sexual Harassment. The Norwegian women project*. Oslo, Norwegian Olympic Committee, 2000.
11. Leahy, T., G. Pretty and G. Tenenbaum, 'Prevalence of sexual abuse in organized competitive sport in Australia', *Journal of Sexual Aggression*, 2002:8, 2, pp. 16-36.
12. Kirby, S. and G. Wintrup, 'Running the gauntlet: An examination of initiation/hazing and sexual abuse in sport', *Journal of Sexual Aggression*, 2002:8, 2, pp. 49-68.

13. David, P., *Human Rights in Youth Sport: A critical review of children's rights in competitive sports*, London, Routledge, 2005.
14. Banda, D., personal communication, October 2007.
15. The descriptions were applied to nineteenth century missionaries who used sport to spread their Christian messages.
16. Lidchi, V.G., 'Reflections on training in child abuse and neglect prevention: Experiences in Brazil', *Child Abuse Review*, 2007:16, pp. 353-366.
17. Warren, C.A.B., *Gender Issues in Field Research*, Qualitative Research Methods Series 9, Newbury Park, CA: Sage, 1988.
18. Warren, ibid, p. 353.
19. Warren, op cit.
20. Armstrong, G., 'The Lords of Misrule: Football and the rights of the child in Liberia', *Sport in Society*, 2004:7, 3, pp. 473-502.
21. Banda, D., Personal communication, October 2007.
22. Fox-Keller, E., 1985, cited in Warren, op cit, p. 60.
23. Sparkes, A., 'Writing people: Reflections on the dual crises of representation and legitimation in qualitative inquiry', *Quest*, 1995:47, pp. 158-195.
24. Coalter, F., *Sport-in-Development: A monitoring and evaluation manual*, Stirling University and UK Sport, London, 2006.
25. Coalter, F., *A Wider Role for Sport: Who's keeping the score?* London, Routledge, 2007.
26. Bilson, A., Editorial: International issues in children's participation and protection', *Child Abuse Review*, 2007:16, 6, pp. 349-352.
27. Harwin, J. and T. Barron, 'The role of service delivery non-governmental organisations in policy reform', *Child Abuse Review*, 2007:16, 6, pp. 367-382.
28. Parkes, op.cit.
29. Pinheiro, P.S., *World Report on Violence Against Children*, 2006. Details at <www.violencestudy.org/r54>, retrieved 3 March 2008.

Part 2
GLOBAL ISSUES: CHILD RIGHTS AND CHILD PROTECTION POLICY

CHAPTER 8. USING THE CONVENTION ON THE RIGHTS OF THE CHILD TO PROTECT CHILDREN IN CANADIAN SPORT

Marc Mazzucco

In Canada, sport organizations have historically been characterized as private bodies. They obtain their legal authority from their own constitutions, which are contractual in nature and confer upon them a self-regulating and autonomous status. As a result, the Canadian government has refrained from, and in some cases has been discouraged from, intervening in the operations of sport organizations. This makes the protection of child athletes more difficult.[1] In response, academic commentators have suggested integrating domestic and international child rights standards into Canadian sport.[2]

The Convention on the Rights of the Child (1989), as one source for external enforcement of children's rights in Canadian sport, has both advantages and limitations. First, Canada has not adopted specific legislation to introduce the Convention into its domestic law.[3] As a result, the Convention and the obligations it imposes have only moral force in Canada; sport authorities are not legally obligated to implement and enforce its provisions. Nor can it be used as a direct basis for any claim in a Canadian court or tribunal; judicial decisions have previously forced sport organizations to amend policies and practices due to human rights violations.[4] Second, provincial monitoring bodies, which oversee the implementation of children's rights, are limited by their enabling statutes to investigate and remedy rights violations involving provincial government departments and agencies, rather than provincial sport ministries and organizations.[5] Even in provincial monitoring bodies, the Convention cannot be used as a direct basis for any claim in a Canadian court or administrative tribunal, whereas judicial decisions have previously forced sport organizations to amend policies and practices due to human rights violations.[6]

Despite these limitations, the Convention is still a valuable tool for the enforcement of children's rights by sport governing bodies, and it could exert considerable moral influence on the hierarchy of sport governance in Canada. National and provincial sport organizations are overseen by Sport Canada with funding from the Department of Canadian Heritage; due to this public funding, Sport Canada is in a position to hold them accountable for implementing all policies, administrative measures and educational requirements aimed at protection of children's rights. A review of existing sport policies and measures in relation to the Convention is essential to appreciate the remedies required to protect the rights of child athletes nationally.

Athlete-centred Policies

In Canada, sport policies aimed at athlete welfare focus on the notion of 'athlete centredness'. This approach to sport looks beyond performance objectives to the physical, psychological, social and spiritual development of the athlete.[7] Consistent with article 5 of the Convention, the athlete-centred philosophy reinforces the responsibilities of sport providers to create an athletic environment in accordance with the 'evolving capacities' of the child athlete.

Athlete centredness is expressed in various national sport policies[8] and has been included as a policy directive for publicly funded national sport organizations.[9] Unfortunately, a disconnect exists between the concept and the implementation of athlete centredness. This limitation arises from the divergent interpretations of the concept among sport providers and a general lack of accountability for sport organizations to implement policies and practices promoting it.

Under the sport funding and accountability framework (SFAF), publicly funded national sport organizations are required to establish a formal policy on athlete centredness and to demonstrate the direct involvement of high-performance athletes in decision making.[10] However, many national sport organizations have included only policies that require the representation of athletes on decision-making committees, while forgoing formal policies on athlete centredness. The absence of broader athlete-centred policies within national sport organizations not only reflects a narrow interpretation of athlete centredness but also a lack of accountability for such policy directives.

Harassment and Abuse Policies and Procedures

Under the SFAF, a publicly funded national sport organization (NSO) is also required to implement a formal policy on harassment and abuse and to appoint a harassment officer for investigation of complaints arising from abuse and harassment.[11] NSOs are responsible for ensuring that these policy guidelines, which are consistent with articles 19 and 34 of the Convention, permeate down to regional athletic clubs in the form of codes of conduct.

Canada has become a leader with respect to such policies. In developing them, several NSOs have sought the assistance of professionals in child welfare and abuse prevention, such as the Canadian Red Cross and its RespectED programme, which promotes education to prevent abuse and exploitation. The Centre for Sport and Law, a sports governance firm, also provides online resources to help sport organizations develop risk management policies.[12] The Canadian Red Cross and Hockey Canada, the NSO for ice hockey, have jointly developed and implemented the programme 'Speak Out! It's More Than Just a Game' (see chapter 39) and several national policies on abuse, harassment and bullying prevention.[13] The Canadian Red Cross has similarly influenced sport organizations in the provinces of Manitoba and Saskatchewan.

Despite these successes, several limitations remain with respect to harassment and abuse policies. First, such policies are more likely to be effective in preventing sexual abuse and more overt forms of physical abuse such as corporal punishment or peer violence. Less likely to be reported are emotional abuse and certain types of physical abuse, such as excessive intensive training and imposed dietary restraints.[14]

Second, harassment and abuse policies vary in quality, and there is lack of standardization in the appointment and training of harassment officers in sport organizations. While most sport organizations have appointed harassment officers, many have not ensured that they are appropriately trained to respond to complaints.[15]

Third, there is a significant lack of accountability among publicly funded sport organizations to implement harassment and abuse policy directives under the SFAF. It requires them to submit annual strategic and operating reports to Sport Canada, which reviews implementation of harassment and abuse policy directives in relation to national standards.[16] Based on this assessment, Sport Canada provides recommendations and allocates funding to NSOs.[17] This funds allocation procedure has been criticized by sport policy researchers for placing performance indicators, such as high-performance excellence and sport participation, ahead of 'non-performance' directives, including harassment and abuse prevention.[18] Furthermore, a lack of transparency in this funding procedure has led to criticism that Sport Canada does not adequately review annual reports to ensure sufficient implementation of certain policy directives.[19]

Best Practices and Coach Education

Several initiatives exist to educate coaches on best practices for safe and ethical sport. One measure is the Coaching Code of Ethics Principles and Ethical Standards, developed by the Coaches of Canada, a national organization representing Canada's professional coaches.[20] The Code describes four principles that govern ethically appropriate behaviours for coaches: respect for all participants, responsible coaching, integrity in relationships and honouring sport. The ethical principles reflect many of the key principles and specific rights expressed in the Convention.

The Coaches of Canada has the authority to order disciplinary sanctions for its members who fail to meet these standards of ethical conduct.[21] However, membership in Coaches of Canada is not mandatory, and most coaches are not professionals, thus limiting the enforceability of the Code.[22]

A second initiative is the Long-Term Athlete Development model, which addresses issues such as early sport specialization, over-training and the use of adult training programmes in youth sport. Widely adopted by sport organizations,[23] the model is consistent with articles 3, 5, 6, 31 and 32 of the Convention. For instance, it avoids basing sport training and competition procedures solely on the child athlete's chronological age by recognizing the wide variation in the evolving physical, cognitive and emotional capacities of the child athlete.[24] However, the model lacks a reference to the child athlete's moral and psychosocial development and political autonomy, which has the effect of reinforcing the power imbalance in the coach-athlete relationship.[25] Nor does it include a formal mechanism to monitor its use by coaches. As a result, there is reason to be sceptical of the model's actual influence on coaching practices, particularly in elite sport, which has traditionally condoned early, intensive and specialized training to produce short-term results.

A final initiative concerns three coach education programmes: the National Coaching Certification Programme, RespectED and Respect in Sport. The certification programme prepares coaches with several core competencies, such as problem-solving and critical thinking, to help them engage in ethical decision-making.[26] Each NSO is required to determine the appropriate content of the programme to make it relevant to their sport. The programme helps coaches understand their moral and legal obligations to respect the interests of athletes. It also attempts to address problems of previous coach education programmes, which overvalued technical expertise relative to other coaching abilities such as interpersonal skills.[27]

Despite such positive aspects, the certification programme does not address the Convention or children's rights per se or educate coaches on children's rights, as mandated by article 42 of the Convention. It also lacks minimum certification requirements and fails to adequately address harassment and abuse prevention or an athlete-centred coaching philosophy.[28] Sport Canada has yet to implement policy directives requiring NSOs to enforce coach certification.

The RespectED and Respect in Sport programmes educate coaches on prevention of harassment, neglect and abuse of young athletes, and are pursuant to articles 4, 19, 32 and 34 of the Convention. The RespectED programme also enables coaches and administrators to conduct risk assessments of their sport associations in accordance with article 25 of the Convention. RespectED has recently partnered with Respect in Sport, an NGO that trains sport organizations in promoting respect, to provide the content for an online programme of coach education. The advantages of online delivery are its flexibility, potential for broad dissemination and privacy.

Despite these positive steps, the efficacy of these initiatives has not been assessed.

Recommendations

Many provisions of the Convention on the Rights of the Child are reflected in Canadian sport policies and practices. However, several limitations impede the protection of children's rights, including fragmentation of policies and initiatives; lack of a widespread and comprehensive education programme for coaches and other sport providers; absence of research on the effectiveness of policies, initiatives and educational programmes; and lack of accountability. The following suggestions are aimed at addressing these shortcomings.

Government intervention

- Canadian non-governmental organizations, such as the Canadian Coalition for Children's Rights, can submit 'alternative' reports to the Committee on the Rights of the Child regarding the status of measures to protect children's rights in Canadian sport. The Committee, through its subsequent Concluding Observations, could recommend that the Canadian government pursue more effective remedies.

- Sport researchers may be able to pressure the federal government through research documenting children's rights violations in sport.[29]

Education and training

- Current coach education programmes should be evaluated to determine their efficacy.

- A comprehensive approach to coach education could then be developed that addresses ethical issues, including prevention of harassment and abuse with reference to children's rights.[30] Sport Canada could direct all NSOs to ensure their coaches obtain this minimum certification (consistent with article 3.3 of the Convention).

- Education modules could also be developed for sporting officials, parents and athletes (article 42).[31] An athlete-specific module would empower athletes by informing them of their rights (articles 17 and 29).

- The Long-Term Athlete Development model could be expanded to incorporate the child athlete's moral and psychosocial development and political autonomy, enabling coaches to share decision making with the child athlete (articles 12 and 13).

Policy development and implementation

- The federal government could commission a task force to investigate implementation of children's rights in Canadian sport (article 4). The task force could develop an action plan to advance children's rights.[32]

- A federal policy covering children in sport could be developed based on the action plan and the Convention. Formulation of the policy would require the varied expertise of organizations within and outside sport.[33] The policy would include national standards prescribing the components of an athlete-centred sports system and the responsibilities of all stakeholders.[34]

- National and provincial sport organizations would be able to use the standards as a benchmark in developing their own policies and by-laws (see chapter 25 on standards for protecting children in sport in the United Kingdom). Implementation of the children-in-sport policy would be included as a directive under the SFAF to ensure compliance by national sport organizations.

- The SFAF would be amended to improve accountability. This would include:

  o Making NSO funding contingent on addressing broader social objectives, such as the human rights of athletes; those that fail to meet national standards expressed in the children-in-sport policy would be penalized, such as by reducing funding;

- o Offering underperforming sport organizations help (through a clearing house, described below) to improve their policies and practices;
- o Designating a formal SFAF review committee, composed of officials from Sport Canada, to perform a more comprehensive assessment of NSOs' operating plans and provide them with recommendations in the form of concluding observations. The operating plans and concluding observations would be made available to the Department of Canadian Heritage and the public to ensure transparency and accountability. The review committee would also control funding for NSOs;
- o Annual reporting by the SFAF review committee to the Department of Canadian Heritage, summarizing the use of funds provided to each NSO and clearly outlining the influence of wider social objectives in the allocation of this funding.

- A clearing house could be designated to provide information and support and create partnerships, similar to the functions of the United Kingdom's Child Protection in Sport Unit[35] (see chapter 9). All national, provincial and regional sport organizations would be informed about the tools offered by the clearing house.

- Federal and provincial ombudspersons could be created as a mechanism to help coaches, parents and athletes in filing children's rights complaints, such as through the Sport Dispute Resolution Centre of Canada, harassment officers within each sport, the Coaches of Canada or provincial children's rights agencies (articles 4 and 12). The ombudspersons would also be responsible for periodic monitoring of all sport programmes, centres and institutions, especially those engaging in intensive training (article 25).[36] The national ombudsperson office would also keep a database of complaints and the monitoring assessments of all sport associations. The information from this database would be communicated to the SFAF review committee.

Conclusion

The Convention on the Rights of the Child provides a unique tool for protecting children's rights in Canadian sport. The strength of the Convention lies in the moral obligations it creates for sport governance organizations to protect the rights of child athletes. Moreover, the Convention contains provisions that provide the procedural means to inform policy development and best practices, guide the expansion of educational programmes and direct research initiatives.

Notes

1. See C.L. Dubin (Commissioner), Ministry of Supply & Services, *Commission of Inquiry into the Use of Drugs and Banned Substances Intended to Increase Athletic Performance*, Ottawa, 1990. Justice Dubin warned against the Canadian

government's intrusion into the operations of sport organizations. Ironically, it was believed that less government involvement in sport administration would alleviate some of the problems encountered in elite sport in Canada, namely, the use of performance-enhancing substances.

2. David, P., *Human Rights in Youth Sport: A critical review of children's rights in competitive sports*, New York, 2005. Provincial child labour laws: H. Cantelon, 'High performance sport and the child athlete: Learning to labor', in: A. Ingham and E. Broom (eds.), *Career Patterns and Career Contingencies in Sport*, Vancouver, University of British Columbia, 1981; P. Donnelly, 'Child labour, sport labour – Applying child labour laws to sport', *International Review for the Sociology of Sport*, 1994:32, vol. 4, pp. 389-406.

3. Standing Senate Committee on Human Rights 'Children: The silenced citizens – effective implementation of Canada's international obligations with respect to the rights of children', <www.senate-senats.ca/rights-droits.asp>, 2007, retrieved 11 May 2007.

4. Barnes, J., *Sports and the Law in Canada*, Butterworths, Toronto, 1996.

5. Standing Senate Committee on Human Rights, op. cit.

6. Canadian Heritage, 'The Canadian sport policy', <www.pch.gc.ca/progs/sc/pol/pcs-csp/2003/polsport_e.pdf>, retrieved 7 January 2007.

7. Clarke, H., D. Smith and G. Thibault, 'Athlete-centred sport. A discussion paper', <www.athletescan.com/Images/Publications/AthleteCentredDiscussion.doc>, 2006, retrieved 10 October 2006.

8. Canadian Heritage, op. cit. and 'Canadian strategy for ethical conduct in sport – Policy framework', <www.pch.gc.ca/progs/sc/pol/eth2002/StEthic.pdf>, retrieved 7 January 2007.

9. Canadian Heritage, 'Sport funding and accountability framework', <www.canadianheritage.gc.ca/progs/sc/prog/cfrs-sfaf/index_e.cfm#1>, retrieved 7 February 2007.

10. Ibid.

11. Ibid.

12. <www.sportlaw.ca/writings.php>.

13. Hockey Canada, 'Workshop guideline – Speak Out! It's more than just a game' (3rd ed.), Ottawa, Hockey Canada Safety and Insurance, 2005.

14. This is despite recent research in Canada documenting such forms of abuse among Canadian athletes: A. Stirling and G. Kerr, 'Elite female swimmers' experiences of emotional abuse across time', *Journal of Emotional Abuse*, 2007:7, p. 4; G. Kerr, E. Berman and M.J. De Souza, 'Disordered eating in women's gymnastics: Perspectives of athletes, coaches, parents, and judges', *Journal of Applied Sport Psychology*, 2006:18, pp. 28-43.

15. Kerr, G. and A. Stirling, 'Child protection in sport: Implications of an athlete-centred philosophy', *Quest*, 2008, 60:2, pp. 307-324.

16. Canadian Heritage, op cit.

17. Ibid.

18. Green, M., 'Power, policy, and political priorities: Elite sport development in Canada and the United Kingdom', *Sociology of Sport Journal*, 2004:21, pp. 376-396.

19. B. Kidd, personal communication, 12 February 2007.

20. Coaches of Canada, 'Coaching Code of Ethics – Principles and ethical standards', <www.coachesofcanada.com/files/PDF/06-04-01-CodeofEthics.pdf>, retrieved 17 November 2006.

21. Coaches of Canada, 'Code of Conduct', <www.coachesofcanada.com/Professionals/Conduct.asp>, retrieved 17 November 2007.

22. Donnelly, P. and R. Sparkes, 'Child sexual abuse in sport', *Policy Options*, 1996:18, 3, pp. 3-6.

23. Robertson, S. and A. Hamilton (eds.), 'Long-term athlete development – Canadian sport for life', <cms.nortia.org/Org/Org180/Groups/Downloads/English/LTAD_Resource_Paper.pdf>, retrieved 21 February 2007.

24. Balyi, I. and A. Hamilton, 'Long-term athlete development: Trainability in childhood and adolescence. Windows of opportunity. Optimal trainability', Victoria, National Coaching Institute British Columbia and Advanced Training and Performance Ltd., 2004, p. 7.

25. Brackenridge, C.H., 'Women and children first? Child abuse and child protection in sport', *Sport in Society*, 2004:7, 3, pp. 322-337.

26. Demers, G., 'The new national coaching certification program and its implications for women coaches', *Canadian Journal for Women in Coaching*, 2003:3, p. 5.

27. Mercier, R., 'Changing the androcentric world of sport', *Canadian Journal for Women in Coaching*, 2001:1, p. 6.

28. Kerr, G. and A. Stirling, op. cit.

29. This approach was recommended in Canada's national action plan for the implementation of children's rights. The plan specifically calls upon researchers and academics "to enrich the government's knowledge of child development, to help them understand the complex interaction of children in *all aspects of society*, and to inform best practices" (para. 180). Canada, 'A Canada fit for children – Canada's plan of action in response to the May 2002 United Nations special session on children',<www.hrsdc.gc.ca/en/cs/sp/sdc/socpol/publications/2002 002483/canadafite.pdf>, retrieved 15 January 2007.

30. Hockey Canada has initiated a pilot project that integrates its Speak Out! programme on harassment and abuse prevention with the National Coaching Certification Program on ethical decision making.

31. Together RespectED and Respect in Sport have already launched an educational module on harassment and abuse prevention for parents and are preparing one for officials.

32. Sam, M.P., 'The makers of sport policy: A (task) force to be reckoned with', *Sociology of Sport Journal*, 2005:21, pp. 28-99.

33. Amis, J. and T.L. Burton, 'Beyond reason: Formulating sport policy in Canada', *Avante*, 1996:2, 2, pp. 17-36.

34. Clarke et al. (op. cit.) has conceptualized an athlete-centred sport system around 10 fundamental principles, all of which reflect key principles and specific rights found in the Convention. They include accountability, mutual respect,

empowerment, equity and fairness, excellence, extended responsibility, health, informed participation, mutual support and athletes' rights.

35. Brackenridge, op. cit.
36. David, op. cit.

CHAPTER 9. THE UNITED KINGDOM'S CHILD PROTECTION IN SPORT UNIT

Steve Boocock

Sport, like society at large, has been slow to accept the idea that it needs to address the issue of child abuse. This unwillingness, particularly in terms of sexual abuse, has been based on beliefs commonly seen by any professional working with child abuse. As a practitioner in this field for many years, I have heard strikingly familiar views expressed within sport at all levels of participation, from recreational to elite. They include denial ("it doesn't happen in this sport"), blaming or externalizing the issue ("it's someone else's fault") and minimization ("it's not a big issue").

The reality is that child abuse *does* happen in sport, as in any other sector of society, and failing to address it leaves victims, clubs and sports isolated, vulnerable and, in the long term, damaged. Achieving acceptance of this reality has been a slow and difficult process, but the establishment of the Child Protection in Sport Unit (CPSU) in the United Kingdom marks a significant change in attitude. The CPSU is an effective model for changing attitudes and practice and reducing the risks of abuse.

Responding to Concerns on Child Abuse in Sport

Despite a number of high-profile criminal cases, sporting organizations (other than those directly involved in allegations) were at first reluctant to respond to child abuse issues. A 2001 study in the United Kingdom showed that less than half of grant-aided bodies had a child protection policy or responsible child welfare officer in place.[1]

In response to community, club and parental concerns, individual sporting bodies approached the National Society for the Prevention of Cruelty to Children (NSPCC) and SportsCoach UK[1] to develop child protection policies, training and other resources. After initial reluctance to formally address the issue, in 1999 Sport England[2] became instrumental in establishing the child protection in sport task force, with a view to developing a blueprint to address this issue. This group represented key stakeholders from sport and child protection, and its work led to production of an action plan and a framework for a coordinated response. The action plan identified specific areas in which sports were vulnerable and strategies to address these. It was based on a number of principles:

- Children have the right to have fun and be safe in sport;
- Child protection in sport is about best practice;
- Given the largely unregulated nature of sport and the many volunteers involved, sport provides easy access to someone who wants to harm children;

---

[1] The lead organization for training coaches.

[2] The government agency responsible for sport.

- Due to the close proximity of coaches and the intense and competitive atmosphere of sport, children and adults are frequently placed in vulnerable situations;
- Sport is uniquely placed to contribute to the positive development of children.

The action plan set out proposals to:

- Establish benchmarks and minimum standards of competence for sports organizations in child protection;
- Establish mechanisms to support child protection officers in sport organizations;
- Develop knowledge and understanding with respect to the incidence and nature of child abuse in sport and set targets for reduction;
- Develop a sports-wide child protection training strategy for working with children and young people;
- Enable a system for reporting suspicious or abusive behaviour towards children;
- Establish systems for dealing effectively and efficiently with allegations of child abuse;
- Ensure that those involved in sport have access to case-specific advice and support on all child protection issues;
- Minimize opportunities for inappropriate individuals to enter or operate in sport;
- Raise awareness at all levels on the issue of child protection in sport.

Sport England's formal acceptance of this plan was strengthened by two crucial decisions – its willingness to fund the establishment of an independent child protection unit and to link future financial support for sports directly to their development and implementation of child protection policies. These decisions ensured that sport organizations would address the issue of child protection. To their credit, the sport national governing bodies responded positively.

The Child Protection in Sport Unit

Acceptance of the plan led to creation of the CPSU in 2001. The goals shaping the unit's work are to:

- Minimize incidents of abuse within sport;
- Fully integrate children's and young people's safety and welfare into all areas of sporting organizations and sport activities;
- Establish an open sport culture in which children's interests are paramount;
- Ensure that sport makes a full and positive contribution to inter-agency child protection systems;
- Increase public confidence in sport's commitment and ability to safeguard the interests of children.

The CPSU aims to provide strategic leadership and specialist advice to sport governing bodies and clubs to prevent abuse and, where appropriate, to campaign for action on the part of others, such as sport clubs, officials and parents. While sport bodies recognize that statutory agencies are responsible for investigating allegations of abuse, the national governing bodies and their clubs have an important role in responding to reported incidents of abuse. The CPSU helps by providing advice to sport organizations on child protection issues and likewise giving information and assistance to the statutory agencies on sports issues.

Few national governing bodies have permanent child protection staff. Many sports have located responsibility for dealing with child protection in coach development programmes; others rely on individuals in the national governing bodies. To ensure that all sports can respond appropriately to child protection matters, the CPSU established mechanisms to support child protection officers in national governing bodies. This involves providing training and learning opportunities, giving access to support and information, and producing regular briefing papers (on such issues as use of photography and adult:child ratios) for these officers.

Policies, procedures and training

An organization's ability to protect children depends partly on the quality of its policies and procedures. Indeed, to receive government funding, national governing bodies must have a child protection policy. A key task for the CPSU has been establishing benchmarks and minimum standards of child protection competence for sport organizations. Accordingly, it has developed and implemented national standards of child protection practice, a consultancy service to help organizations achieve the standards and a mechanism to facilitate evaluation of evidence of implementation.

Training and education for all those involved in sport is central to the success of the child protection strategy. In the future and in partnership with other bodies, the CPSU will develop a sports-wide child protection training strategy for people working with children and young people in sport.

Systems of response

As awareness of child protection issues in sport develops, it is safe to assume that more abuse incidents will be reported. To maintain the confidence of victims and others, it is essential for sport to establish systems for dealing effectively and efficiently with such allegations. Telephone helplines play a significant role in contributing to an effective child protection network, as the NSPCC and Childline have already demonstrated.[2] Already some sports, including swimming and football, operate child protection helplines, with some success.

A limited number of sports have experience in responding to and investigating abuse-related concerns. Some sports have found their processes inappropriate or ineffective. In some cases frustrated parents have involved politicians, the media or sponsors, placing additional pressures on national governing bodies. The CPSU therefore plans to develop practice guidance on internal investigations of reported child protection concerns. It is also important to provide support to children and young people, parents and the accused. The CPSU will therefore develop and support a network of individuals able to provide services to those involved in allegations of abuse.

Safe recruitment of volunteers

Central to developing a safe and protective sport environment is minimizing opportunities for inappropriate individuals to enter or operate in the field. Within the United Kingdom, sport depends almost entirely on large numbers of adult volunteers, whose participation gives them access to children and young people. The Criminal Records Bureau[3] enables sport to perform background checks on these individuals. Given the number of adults involved in sporting organizations, it will be a huge task to obtain, process and store information about them. While the information provided by the Criminal Records Bureau is important in recruitment and selection, it is only part of a much wider effort needed to create and sustain a safe environment for children. National governing bodies also need guidance, tools and training in best practice in recruitment and risk assessment of individuals, and the CPSU will work to facilitate this.

Advice and guidance

The establishment of the CPSU and the high expectations now placed on national governing bodies has changed the attitude towards child protection in many sporting organizations. These bodies have sought to respond more positively and constructively and are now more open in acknowledging incidents. However, changing culture and practice will take time and resources. Very few sports have the resources to deliver training and education on the scale required, so links to local resources will be essential.

As it seeks to change its approach, sport will, justifiably, expect to be involved at all levels of child protection practice and procedures, and it will demand high-quality advice and support. Sport policies make it clear that when a concern is identified, the local procedures must be followed and the relevant agencies involved. This will inevitably raise issues relating to the exact criteria for decision-making, definitions and appropriate responses. Sport is beginning to develop a clearer definition of abusive practice, and it is important that mainstream child protection organizations participate in developing definitions of abuse within sport. Equally, child protection agencies need to incorporate the knowledge and experience of sports and develop responses appropriate to their needs.

---

[3] A centralized computer database that records information about court convictions. All paid employees and volunteers whose work brings them into contact with children must undergo a clearance check through it as a condition of hire. Details available at <www.crb.gov.uk>.

Conclusion

Sport has begun to address the issue of child abuse, though belatedly in the view of some. The response of some sports has led the way for other organizations, including some outside sport, to develop policy and practice that contribute significantly to improving children's experiences and opportunities. The development of work in this field has also opened (or re-opened) a major debate about ethical practice in all levels of sport. It is now widely accepted that children have the right to be safe – so why not other vulnerable groups involved in sport, such as disabled people? And, if it is right for these, then is it not right for all athletes to be protected from abuse and harassment?

Notes

1. Safeguarding the Welfare of Children in Sport, *Towards a Standard for Sport in England*, NSPCC, London, 2001.
2. The NSPCC/ChildLine telephone helpline is a generic child abuse helpline that serves approximately 2,500 enquiries each day. Details available at <www.childline.org.uk>, retrieved 25 March 2008

CHAPTER 10. THE AUSTRALIAN APPROACH TO CHILD PROTECTION IN SPORT

Debbie Simms

Over the past decade child protection has emerged as a key ethical issue for the sport industry in Australia. Factors driving this have included the introduction of new child protection legislation in several states as well as regular media coverage of court cases involving abuse of children in sport. As a result, awareness of child protection has grown throughout society, as have expectations for those working with children. Government authorities have responded by introducing funding criteria that require sporting organizations to meet specific child protection obligations.

In the mid- to late 1990s, the Australian Sports Commission[4] developed a comprehensive approach, the Harassment-free Sport Strategy, for tackling harassment and discrimination in sport. Initially the strategy comprised education workshops and training courses, research, provision of resources and an anti-discrimination policy template for sports. In 2001 the Commission expanded the strategy to include child protection with a view to:

- Increasing the sport industry's awareness and understanding of child abuse and the industry's related legal and moral obligations;
- Obtaining the commitment of sport organizations to work proactively to minimize the risk of a child being abused;
- Ensuring organizations can respond appropriately to allegations or incidents of child abuse.

The strategy is constantly evolving as a result of feedback from the sport industry, new findings (both domestic and international) and the introduction of new legislation. The strategy has three phases.

Phase 1: Research, Legislation and Policy Development

The Commission first reviewed domestic and international research on child abuse in sport as well as in the broader community.[1] Further information was sought through consultation with the sport industry and the education sector as well as various commissions for children and young people, police units targeting child sexual assault, child protection advocacy groups, youth-based organizations (such as Scouts) and other relevant bodies.

Relevant legislation was also closely examined to determine the requirements for sporting organizations. As a federation, Australia has a proliferation of child

---

[4] The government body that supports and invests in sport at all levels, working closely with national sporting organizations, national and state governments, schools and community bodies to ensure that sport is well run, accessible and safe. Through the Australian Institute of Sport, it assists talented, motivated athletes to reach their potential.

protection legislation on federal, state and territorial levels, making this task an enormous and ongoing challenge. A comprehensive review of policies and procedures addressing child protection inside and outside sport was also undertaken to establish best practice models and guidelines.

This research exposed the reality that sporting organizations knew little about child abuse, had no child protection policies or procedures in place, and were unaware of their legal obligations under previous and new legislation. As part of the process to redress this situation, the Commission developed a member protection policy template.[5] It is a generic framework designed to help organizations write their own policies and procedures. It includes:

- Position statements on child protection, discrimination, harassment and intimate relationships;
- Organizational and individual responsibilities;
- Codes of behaviour;
- Child protection legislative requirements;
- Processes such as complaint handling, tribunals and investigations;
- Reporting documents.

The template, regularly reviewed and updated, is easily accessed via the Commission's website.[2]

Phase 2: Commitment and Education

The next step involved obtaining a commitment from sport organizations at all levels to address member protection issues and then commencing an education process. The Commission recognizes and provides funding to over 80 national sporting organizations. To ensure they address member protection issues, the Commission introduced funding criteria for the national-level bodies requiring development, implementation, review and regular updating of member protection policies.

It is more difficult, however, for the Commission to obtain a commitment to member protection and child protection issues from state-level sport associations and local clubs that are not directly funded by the Commission. Instead, it aims to influence these bodies indirectly by working with the national sporting organizations and state and territory departments of sport and recreation. Funding agreements are in place between the Commission and these local government departments to deliver a range of outcomes at the state level, several of which relate to implementation of the strategy. As a result, most departments have introduced funding criteria that require implementation of member protection policies by state sporting organizations and clubs.

---

[5] 'Member protection' is a term used in Australia to describe the policies and practices required to protect individuals and organizations from harassment, discrimination, child abuse and other forms of inappropriate behaviour in sport.

The Commission also works closely with departments to ensure provision of consistent messages and information relating to member protection and child protection at the state level.

As with any initiative involving social issues, education is a vital component. During the second phase, the Commission reviewed educational material and courses from a range of sectors including child protection, education, religious groups and child care, and organizations such as Scouts. It found that child protection information needed to be further developed specifically for the sport context.

Using various experts, the Commission developed resources and training materials on member protection and child protection. Education was largely targeted at coaches, who were considered high priority for a number of reasons:

- Coaches typically have more power in the coach/child relationship. It is crucial that coaches do not exploit this power and that they understand and establish clear professional boundaries with children.
- Coaches may be in a position to notice abuse that occurs both within and outside the sporting environment. It is important that they understand, recognize and report such abuse and know how to handle these disclosures.
- Many coaches are confused about whether, how or when it is appropriate to touch athletes.
- Coaches are concerned about the possibility of false allegations by 'disgruntled' athletes or parents.

Information was developed to assist coaches to feel confident about meeting their legal and ethical responsibilities as well as to help them establish positive, respectful and safe relationships with children. This information is now incorporated into coaching materials and online training for all beginner courses under the Commission's National Coaching Accreditation Scheme. Child protection information is also regularly included in coaching and officiating conferences, seminars and publications and on the Commission's website.

Another group receiving training is member protection information officers, who are the first point of contact in a sport for people with concerns regarding harassment, abuse and other inappropriate behaviour. Two-day training, refresher workshops and regular network meetings help these officers understand protection policies, learn active listening skills and acquire the tools to provide guidance to complainants.

Administrators and decision-makers were the final target audience for education.

State departments of sport and recreation coordinate training, workshops and meetings using either private or government trainers who specialize in anti-discrimination or a combination of presenters from various fields. One of the most difficult aspects of the education strategy is ensuring sufficient numbers and quality of workshops and courses held at suitable times, given the challenge of working with volunteers' schedules. To overcome these problems, much of the training material is being revised and converted to an online format. This will significantly increase accessibility of the programmes as well as offering flexibility and 'blended learning opportunities' (which incorporate different learning styles with physical and virtual resources) and reducing the cost and time commitment for individuals.

Phase 3: Partnerships and Resources

Establishing and maintaining links and partnerships with government agencies involved expanding educational opportunities and developing additional materials. The Commission determined that the sport industry needed expert advice to assist it in embracing the issue of child protection. Given the seriousness and complexity of the issues and the differences in legislation from state to state, the Commission decided it needed to establish links with relevant specialist agencies in every state and territory. These agencies included anti-discrimination commissions and commissions for children and young people, as well as police units in some states.

In conjunction with state departments of sport and recreation, the Commission works closely with these agencies to help them understand the sport industry while also helping the sport industry understand child protection. To maintain the relationship, the Commission conducts an annual workshop with representatives from each agency, distributes a quarterly newsletter and maintains regular liaison.

The Commission has also contributed content for the Play by the Rules website, which aims at preventing and managing inappropriate behaviour in sporting clubs.[3] Play by the Rules (see also chapter 32) is a major component of Australia's harassment-free sport strategy and has helped strengthen partnerships with protection agencies. The Commission provides financial and administrative support and works closely with this programme.

Information on specific topics continues to be developed in response to sport industry concerns and requests, such as the risks posed to children through the use of photographs on sport web sites and in publications. Evidence in Australia indicated that information published on the Internet site or in a print publication could be used to target, locate and then 'groom' or prepare children for abuse or exploitation by gaining their trust. It is also known that offenders visit sporting events to photograph or videotape young people for inappropriate use. In response, the Commission produced an information sheet on acquiring and displaying images of children.

The Commission continues to look at ways of incorporating child protection issues and information into its other programmes, including coaching and officiating, junior sport, disability sport and indigenous sport.

Conclusion

It is very difficult to measure the impact of the Commission's approach to child protection on the sport industry. The response to date in Australia is similar to that experienced in the United Kingdom and Canada: On the one hand, some national sporting organizations have embraced policies, procedures and practices positively and proactively, acknowledging that child protection is an important issue and committing time, effort and resources to address it. On the other hand are organizations that implement policies and procedures only because it is required, not because they view child protection as an important issue.

Awareness of child abuse in the sport industry has definitely gone up, which has led to an increase in the number of queries about and/or complaints alleging child abuse in sport received by the Commission, state departments of sport and child protection authorities. The Commission does not yet know to what extent this increase is a result of its strategy and awareness raising or whether its efforts have made sport safer for children.

The Commission continues to review and develop its approach to ensure it remains relevant, practical, effective and current. It recognizes that it has only begun the journey to ensure that all sports in Australia provide child-safe environments.

Notes

1. Key sources: C.H. Brackenridge, '"He owned me basically": Women's experience of sexual abuse in sport', *International Review for the Sociology of Sport*, 1997, 32:2, pp. 115-130; C.H. Brackenridge, *Spoilsports: Understanding and preventing sexual exploitation in sport*, Routledge, London, 2001; C.H. Brackenridge, 'So what? Attitudes of the voluntary sector towards child protection in sports clubs', *Managing Leisure – An International Journal*, 2002:7, 2, pp. 103-124; Child Wise, *Choose with Care: Building child safe organizations*. Child Wise: Melbourne, 2004, www.childwise.net; A. Garrison, 'Child sexual abuse accommodation syndrome: Issues of admissibility in criminal trials', *Institute for Psychological Therapies Forensics Journal*, 1998:10, <www.ipt-forensics.com/journal/volume10/j10 2.htm>; M. Hartill, 'Sport and the sexually abused male child', *Sport, Education and Society*, 2005:10, 3, pp. 287-304; K. Kovacs and N. Richardson, *'Child Abuse Statistics' Resource Sheet 1*, National Child Protection Clearinghouse, Australian Institute of Family Studies, 2004, <www.aifs.gov.au/nch/sheets/rs1.html>; T. Leahy, *Preventing the Sexual Abuse of Young People in Australian Sport*, Australian Institute of Sport, Canberra, 2001; A. Morrone, *The Right to Play Safely: A report on violence against women in sport and recreation*, Centre Against Sexual Assault & the Royal Women's Hospital, Melbourne, 2003; J. Myers and B. Barrett, *In at the Deep End: A new insight for all sports from an analysis of child abuse within swimming*, NSPCC/Amateur Swimming Association, London, <www.britishswimming.org>; National Association for the Prevention of Child Abuse and Neglect (NAPCAN) www.napcan.org.au; NSW Sport and Recreation, NSW Department of Tourism,

Sport and Recreation, <www.dsr.nsw.gov.au/children/index.asp>; NSW Commission for Children and Young People, <www.kids.nsw.gov.au>; Queensland Commission for Children and Young People and Child Guardian, <www.ccypcg.qld.gov.au>; S. Smallbone and R. Wortley, 'Child sexual abuse: Offender characteristics and modus operandi', *Trends and Issues in Crime and Criminal Justice*, 193, Australian Institute of Criminology, Canberra, 2001; A. Tomison, 'Update on child sexual abuse', *Issues in Child Abuse Prevention*, 5, Australian Institute of Family Studies, Melbourne, 1995, <www.aifs.gov.au/nch/issues5.html>.

2. Member Protection Policy Template, <www.ausport.gov.au/supporting/ethics/member_protection>.

3. www.playbytherules.net.au.

CHAPTER 11. THE IMPACT OF CHILD PROTECTION ON SCOTTISH SPORT GOVERNING BODIES[1]

Celia Brackenridge

Although child protection is a comparative newcomer to the sport policy agenda in the United Kingdom, it has rapidly taken its place alongside race, gender and disability as one of the key ethical issues facing governing bodies of sport.[2] Scottish involvement in child protection in sport dates back to the mid-1990s in the post-Dunblane period[6] when public concern about the safety of voluntary sector recreation was highlighted. By 2002, a three-year action plan for child protection in Scottish sport had been collated by sportscotland, the government agency for sport.[3]

Scotland's Child Protection in Sport Programme, delivered in collaboration with the national charity Children 1st, embraced an estimated 800,000 children who took part regularly in organized sport as well as the adults who worked with them.[4] The establishment of the programme reflected a view that, while it is possible to deliver child protection generically, it is most effective when delivered in an applied way through agencies that understand the legal and social work implications of child protection and also have empathy for the cultural traditions and working practices of sport. The overall objective of the Child Protection in Sport Programme was to assist and support governing bodies of sport in Scotland to establish policies, procedures and programmes that promote the protection of children through good practice.

This chapter describes a study of the impact of the programme on a selected number of Scottish national sport governing bodies (SGBs) between 2002 and 2004.

Research Design

Methodologies for measuring implementation of social inclusion and ethics in sport frequently draw on social marketing techniques or stage models of health behaviour change. But at the time of this study these techniques had not been applied to child protection. For most voluntary sport organizations, introducing child protection involves a process of cultural change in which the individual stakeholders – such as officers, coaches, members and parents – exhibit a variety of 'activation states' towards child protection:[5]

- Inactive = no knowledge or commitment;
- Reactive = reluctant commitment and engagement;
- Active = satisfactory awareness and involvement;
- Proactive = full commitment and advocacy;
- Opposed = either overtly critical of, or covertly against, the initiative.

These states are evidenced by analysing the following:

---

[6]In 1996 a self-styled recreation leader shot dead 16 people in the Dunblane Primary School gymnasium.

83

- Voices/discourses: What people **say** about child protection in sport;
- Knowledge and experience: What people **know** about child protection through experience – their awareness, interest or understanding;
- Feelings: What people **feel** – their attitudes and emotions regarding child protection;
- Action: What people **do**/have done about child protection – their achievements and behaviour.

Experience in England has shown that governing bodies respond in a variety of ways to child protection, ranging from those who are willing to embrace policies and procedures to those who are unwilling and resist them. Similarly, the state's approach to child protection in sport can range from permissive (such as giving advice and guidance only) to prescriptive (such as requiring compliance with standards as a condition of funding). The combination of possible state approaches and governing body responses is illustrated in the conceptual model in figure 3.

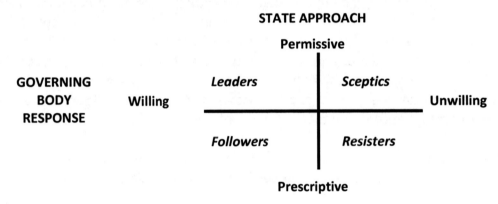

Figure 3. Conceptual model of state approaches and governing body responses to child protection in sport

Leaders. These governing bodies are willing to cooperate and are proactive in developing child protection initiatives on their own, often because they or others in their sport have faced a challenging case involving adverse publicity. They may have drawn from social work, teaching, probation or police skills within their own ranks and have used child protection materials from outside sport to develop their policy infrastructure. They offer models of practice (not necessarily evaluated yet as best practice) to other governing bodies.

Followers. These governing bodies happily conform to the state's specified criteria or standards when asked to do so.

Sceptics. These governing bodies are hesitant or unwilling to cooperate for a variety of reasons, and therefore delay or obfuscate child protection work. They usually come around eventually but require a lot of policy support and advice along the way.

Resisters. These governing bodies object, complain or actively refuse to cooperate with state child protection requirements. They may have their own internally developed policies and procedures but are often reluctant to discuss them with outside agencies, funders or scrutineers.

For the purposes of this study, the stakeholders' responses were aggregated to provide organizational activation profiles that determined their position in the conceptual model. Of course, this model is not an accurate portrayal of the circumstances of all governing bodies but acts as a device for analysing the relationship between the governing body and its funder.

The aim of the study was to assess the effectiveness of the child protection programme with SGBs – in short, to assess whether they perceived it as a burden or a benefit. Twelve of the 15 SGBs approached agreed to participate in the study, which was conducted by face-to-face and telephone interviews. The findings of the study are summarized in figure 4.

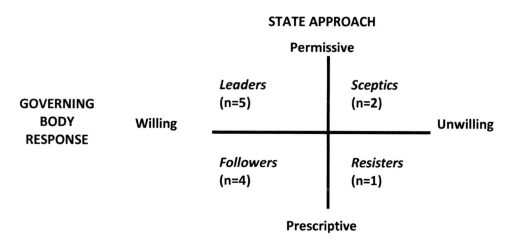

Sample: 12 governing bodies out of 15 approached.
See figure 3 for an explanation of leaders/sceptics/followers/resisters.

Figure 4. Governing body responses to child protection in sport

Key Findings

Almost all of those interviewed were positive about the child protection programme and complimentary about the helpfulness, communication and advice given by the workers who had implemented it. The interviewees varied, however, in their degree of activation. Five were clearly 'leaders', comparatively well ahead in the development of child protection and confident and committed to this work. Most of the SGB personnel interviewed said they would welcome a more prescriptive approach, especially with respect to policy development. Two interviewees were generally sceptical about the work, one of whom was especially vociferous in his views against the need to lay down rules, criteria or other markers.

The SGBs viewed sportscotland as having taken a relatively permissive approach to child protection. Several interviewees commented that delivering child protection was 'not our job' and that they would welcome greater intervention from specialists. The danger of moving to such a prescriptive approach, however, is that sport personnel might fail to own the issue or to permeate it throughout their working practices, instead regarding child protection as simply a bolt-on to their day-to-day activity. These were the 'followers' who accepted the need for child protection but did not take the initiative. Given the heavy demands of running governing bodies and the pressures of modernization and governance, it would not be surprising if these sports sought short cuts in the future in order to fulfil their obligations.

Some of the SGBs were 'sceptics' about child protection because they felt it created a large workload and bureaucracy for little need. Indeed, several mentioned that they knew of no child protection referrals at all within their sport in Scotland. The sceptics also expressed reservations about the time and effort involved in background checking, although many had registered with Disclosure Scotland[7] and viewed the checking system as functioning relatively smoothly.

Another important bias was found in the discussion with interviewees about child protection: They focused almost exclusively on sexual abuse, which is probably far less common in sport than emotional and physical abuse. Well-publicized fears of 'stranger danger' may have reinforced this myth.

Many governing bodies said they would welcome more guidance on the distinction between abuse and poor practice and on their legal responsibilities, especially where cases were sent back from the legal system for them to deal with as internal disciplinary matters.

In the main, individual stakeholders from the SGBs revealed active feelings about child protection, but with few exceptions showed low levels of knowledge about the subject and had engaged in relatively little action. For example, few had personally attended training workshops. Only one sport could be categorized as a 'resister', although this might well have reflected the strong views of its spokesperson, the chief executive.

Previous research exposed a child protection policy vacuum between governing body and club level that was also apparent in the study.[6,7,8] Though it is unlikely that this vacuum applies only to work on child protection, it nevertheless presents a particular challenge to SGBs and also to Children 1st and sportscotland. After all, it is clubs that engage directly and regularly with young people, so, in an important sense, the child protection chain is only as strong as its weakest (i.e. club) link.

Reflections

An important test of the Scottish child protection programme in the future will be its comprehensiveness, since leaks in one area will have repercussions for others. For example, supervision and monitoring of coaches are undermined if proper background checks are not undertaken prior to appointment. It is thus worth evaluating the effectiveness of progress by the pace of the slowest as well as the quality of the best governing body.

---

[7] The Scottish government's agency for checking the criminal histories of job applicants and volunteers.

Overall, one-third of those who responded to the invitation to participate in this study saw child protection responsibilities as a burden, but even the sceptics expressed some positive views about the work. For the majority it had most certainly been a benefit, and one in which sportscotland had played an important and welcome role. As a result of this study, sportscotland decided to take a more prescriptive approach with SGBs and the services of the Children 1st Child Protection in Sport Service were subsequently expanded to meet their increased support needs.

Notes

1. This chapter is based on the paper, 'Measuring the implementation of an ethics initiative: Child protection in Scottish sport', presented by the author to the symposium 'Safeguarding the Child in Sport' at the Commonwealth Games Conference, Melbourne, Australia, March 2006.
2. Boocock, S., 'The Child Protection in Sport Unit', Journal of Sexual Aggression, 2002:8, 2, pp. 99-106.
3. Sportscotland, *Sportscotland Child Protection: Objectives, programmes and targets for 2002-2005,* Edinburgh, sportscotland, 2002.
4. Children 1st, *More child protection in sport*, press release, 11 February 2004, Glasgow.
5. Brackenridge, C.H., Z. Pawlaczek, J.D. Bringer, C. Cockburn, G. Nutt, A. Pitchford and K. Russell, 'Measuring the impact of child protection through activation states', *Sport, Education and Society*, 2005:10, 2, pp. 239-256.
6. Malkin, K., L.H. Johnston and C.H. Brackenridge, 'A critical evaluation of training needs for child protection in UK sport', *Managing Leisure – An international journal*, 2000:5, pp. 151-160.
7. Summers, D., 'Organisational responses to child protection in voluntary sector sport', unpublished doctoral thesis, Bristol University, 2000.
8. Brackenridge, C.H., 'So what? Attitudes of the voluntary sector towards child protection in sports clubs', *Managing Leisure – An international journal*, 2002:7, 2, pp. 103-124.

CHAPTER 12. THE IMPACT OF CHILD PROTECTION ON THE BRITISH RUGBY LEAGUE

Phil Prescott and Mike Hartill

In recent decades, concern has emerged over child abuse outside family settings.[1] Gradually, these concerns have spread to sport organizations, which has led to some dramatic changes in the British Rugby League. This chapter outlines and critiques some of the key changes.

The Rugby Football League (RFL), the organization for amateur rugby in the United Kingdom, emerged from a clash of cultural values and attitudes between, on the one hand, "southern gentlemen educated to public school sporting values of play for its intrinsic benefits and character building" and, on the other, northern working-class communities and middle-class industrialists "that placed a premium on victory".[2] The breakaway 'Northern Union' resulted from this clash.

In contrast with these origins, a recent RFL guide for coaches states, "the welfare and safety of the child is the primary concern. Winning is less important than these".[3] At least rhetorically, this suggests a major shift, not just in terms of children's participation in rugby league but in the very nature of the sport itself. In this respect, the RFL's marketing tag line, 'It's a whole different ballgame', may reflect more than simply its desire to highlight the sport's distinctive character.

The focus on child protection has continued to grow in society as a whole. Public inquiries into child deaths have played major roles in the development of reactive policy measures for the protection of children.[4,5,6] To some degree sport appears to have followed suit. The case of British Olympic swimming coach Paul Hickson, imprisoned in 1995 for sexual crimes against swimmers, attracted considerable media attention and proved to be an important catalyst for the implementation of child protection policy in United Kingdom sport.

The Child Protection in Sport Unit (CPSU), established in 2001, was the significant outcome of pressure for change (see chapter 9). Under the responsibility of the government's Department for Culture, Media and Sport, the CPSU was the most significant political response to concerns over child maltreatment in international sport.[7] Ten fundamental standards for child protection, a three-tiered accreditation system for clubs (preliminary, intermediate, advanced) and a clear timetable for implementation of child protection policies are now linked to central funding for sport governing bodies (see chapter 25).[8,9,10] Government investment in any sport is contingent on it meeting the standards: the RFL has achieved the preliminary and intermediate levels, which helped to assure funding of over £4 million in 2007.[11]

In 2003 the British Amateur Rugby League Association (BARLA), for the amateur game, united with the Rugby Football League, the professional arm of the game, to form an umbrella organization responsible for all levels of the sport. Following recommendations made by Sport England, the Rugby League Policy Board established a child protection working group comprising league administrators, coaches and development officers as well as the director of the CPSU and the authors of this chapter. A draft policy was developed and then piloted to local clubs via a training seminar in the northwest of England. The two organizations, BARLA and the RFL, launched their child protection policy and guidelines in December 2003. The policy is binding for the game as a whole and provides guidelines to everyone in the league, whether a professional or volunteer.[12] The early implementation of the policy was the focus of the research reported here.

Research conducted in 1999 showed that 39 per cent of voluntary sport clubs in one English county had a child protection policy, from a sample of 130 clubs across 19 different sports.[13] In 2004, 85 per cent from a sample of 75 English Rugby League clubs, voluntary and professional, had a (newly appointed) child protection officer (CPO).[14] As Brackenridge predicted:

> "The introduction of a set of NGB [national governing body] standards for child protection by Sport England should have a considerable impact on the future uptake of both codes of practice and policies for child protection at club level."[15]

Each CPO is only as effective as the individual who fills the job, and each policy is only as effective as the people who implement it; this was the impetus for our research.

Research Findings

The project involved collaborative research designed to provide an ongoing evaluation of the British Rugby League's child protection strategy as it was rolled out nationally from December 2003. Other than funds for some data collection, the Rugby Football League provided no funding, to ensure objectivity.

The league stated: "All clubs must identify a designated person to be titled the Club Child Protection Officer to handle child protection issues."[16] Although 15 per cent of clubs had not appointed a CPO 12 months after the launch of the policy, findings indicated that clubs had generally responded positively. However, one club CPO illustrated some of the difficulties faced by those in the Rugby League sensitive to child protection issues:

> "I am regularly dismayed to hear comments that such policies are the thoughts of 'do gooders' and there are no such problems in junior rugby league."

The manner and format of presenting policies and guidelines to club members is crucial in determining whether or not child protection is seen as legitimate and important. A key concern was that it should not be 'slipped' into broad agendas, like an unwanted secret, through misplaced fear of creating panic and frightening away potential players and volunteers.[17] Such an approach reduces the policy to only one of a number of competing issues in an environment that has no history of considering child abuse.

'Specialist' meetings about child protection for selected personnel in the sport were common, yet these did not encourage ownership of the policy by all members of the club and, importantly, kept children at some distance from it. The use of such 'gatekeepers' who do not facilitate the dissemination of knowledge is thus problematic. For child rights to be realized, children's individual and collective voices should be included in all processes affecting them,[18, 19] and the promotion of participation is underpinned by such initiatives as Every Child Matters and Youth Matters.[20, 21] It is awareness at this club/ground level that is so crucial for securing children's rights, in any (sporting) context.

Increasing awareness and knowledge of child protection issues is a key feature of the policy process, and the impact of the Rugby Football League policy on the knowledge of its CPOs was clearly important. The research revealed that CPOs' awareness and knowledge of child abuse had either been increased or reinforced through the introduction of the child protection policy. The following examples are indicative:

"Opened my eyes to the different ways children could be abused even without violence."

"Some people think child abuse is sexual, it has made them more aware of other types of abuse, e.g. shouting and name calling – bullying."

Though much less frequent, there were also dissenting voices:

"Don't think it has impacted on our knowledge in any way."

"[The policy has] increased awareness but I do feel this is a bit of a sledgehammer to crack a nut situation in Rugby League."

Table 2. The impact of child protection policy on rugby clubs: Impressions of child protection officers[22]

Type of response (N = 75)	Total per cent (N)
Positive	64% (48)
No impact	20% (15)
Negative	7% (5)
Other/ambiguous	5% (4)
No response	4% (3)

As 'gatekeepers', the designated CPOs were in a strong position to determine whether the policy had been well received by club officials and members. Such information is crucial when considering relatively 'closed' environments, such as private sports clubs, and is especially vital for academics interested in sport. The majority of responses from individual clubs were positive (table 2).

Reflections

Embedding knowledge, awareness and policy concerning child protection into practice with children and young people in sport clubs has to be seen as a significant venture. The Rugby Football League's written policy is clear about procedures to follow after the disclosure of abuse, and the duty to inform local statutory bodies is pre-eminent. The CPSU identifies partnerships as a key strategy in its approach to safeguarding children.[23] However, this research suggests that, in general, clubs did not develop 'early' relationships with child protection professionals in preparation for the initial introduction of a club policy. Further research is clearly needed here.

During policy planning, more attention might have been given to the more subtle effects that shape policy processes. For example, key messages on awareness of child abuse and the means to safeguard children may be diluted or distorted through weak communication systems. Elsewhere we have suggested that a means to develop a deeper 'communication competence' could be explored by future child protection policy planners.[24] This could be facilitated through a club policy process model, participatory processes that embrace children's councils and development of clear relationships with local authorities.[25]

The development of relationships between clubs and child protection professionals would be a robust response to Sport England's commitment to work in partnership with parents, guardians and others to increase their knowledge of the theory and practices of safeguarding children.[26] The Rugby League community has begun to accept child protection issues as part of the fabric of their sport, and in some cases to embrace them. This is an encouraging step forward, representing something of a break from the silence that has shrouded child abuse in sport, perhaps particularly in male-dominated, 'manly' sports.[27] That said, the case-management history of the Rugby League does not include any incidents of sexual abuse or anything considered to be serious abuse, and the current caseload is largely comprised of child-on-child issues.[28] Thus, how resounding the breaking of the silence actually is, and whether agendas relating to children's rights are equally welcome, remains to be seen.

Notes

1.   Corby, B., *Child abuse: Towards a knowledge base* (3rd ed.), Open University Press, Buckingham, England, 2005.
2.   Martens, J.W., 'Rugby, class, amateurism and manliness: The case of rugby in northern England, 1871-1895', in: J. Nauright and T.J.L. Chandler (eds.) *Making Men: Rugby and masculine identity*, Frank Cass, London, 1996, p. 36.

3. Rugby Football League, *A Rugby League Coaches Guide to Child Protection*, Rugby Football League Coach Education Programme, Leeds, 2005, p. 4.
4. Butler-Sloss, Lord Justice E., *Report of the Inquiry into Child Abuse in Cleveland 1987*, Cmnd. 412, London, HMSO, 1988.
5. Department of Health/Welsh Office, *Lost in Care – The report of the tribunal of inquiry into the abuse of children in care in the former county council areas of Gwynedd and Clwyd since 1974 (The Waterhouse Report)*, London, HMSO, 2000.
6. Laming, Lord, *The Victoria Climbie Inquiry: Report of an inquiry by Lord Laming*, Crown Copyright/HMSO, Norwich, 2003.
7. David, P., *Human Rights in Youth Sport: A critical review of children's rights in competitive sports*, Routledge, London, 2005.
8. 'Advanced' level was to be achieved by March 2008.
9. CPSU, 'Standards for safeguarding and protecting children in sport', CPSU, Leicester, 2003.
10. CPSU, 'Standards for safeguarding and protecting children in sport' (2nd ed.), CPSU, Leicester, 2007.
11. Rugby Football League, 'Annual report and accounts 2006', Leeds, 2006.
12. Rugby Football League, 'Rugby League child protection policy and implementation procedures', League Publications, Leeds, 2003.
13. Brackenridge, C.H., '"… So what?' Attitudes of the voluntary sector towards child protection in sports clubs', *Managing Leisure*, 2002:7, 2, pp. 103-123.
14. Hartill, M. and P. Prescott, 'Researching the implementation of child protection in Rugby League', paper presented to the 13th Commonwealth International Sport Conference: People, Participation and Performance, 9-12 March 2006, Melbourne, Australia.
15. Brackenridge, C.H., op. cit.
16. Rugby Football League, *Rugby League Child Protection Policy and Implementation Procedures*, Leeds, League Publications, 2003.
17. Hartill, M. and P. Prescott, 'Safeguarding children in sport: Some theory, policy and practice issues in UK Rugby League', presentation for the European Sociological Association bi-annual conference, Murcia, Spain, September 2003.
18. United Nations, *Convention on the Rights of the Child*, New York, 1989.
19. Department for Education and Skills, *Every Child Matters*, available at: <www.everychildmatters.gov.uk/publications-and-resources>, 2003, retrieved 7 December 2007.
20. Department for Education and Skills, *Youth Matters*, Cmd 6629, Norwich, HMSO, 2005.
21. Department of Health, *Children Act 1989*, London: HMSO, 1989.
22. Hartill, M. and P. Prescott, 'Serious business or 'Any other business'? Safeguarding and child protection policy in British Rugby League', *Child Abuse Review*, 2007:16, 4, pp. 237-251.
23. Child Protection in Sport Unit, *Strategy for Safeguarding Children and Young People in Sport, 2006-12*, Leicester, 2006.
24. Hartill, M. and P. Prescott, 'Serious business or 'Any other business'? Safeguarding and child protection policy in British Rugby League', *Child Abuse Review*, 2007:16, 4, pp. 237-251.

25. Prescott, P. and M. Hartill, 'Safeguarding children in sport: A view from Rugby League – The policy process, participative cultures and local relationships', *Research, Policy and Planning, The Journal of the Social Services Research Group,* 2008:25, 2/3, pp. 129-141.
26. Child Protection in Sport Unit, 2006, op. cit.
27. Kirby, S.L., L. Greaves and O. Hankivsky, The Dome of Silence: Sexual harassment and abuse in sport, London, Zed Books, 2000.
28. Rosewarne, E., Acting Lead Child Protection Officer, The Rugby Football League, personal communication, December 2007.

CHAPTER 13. THE IMPACT OF CHILD PROTECTION ON HIGH-PERFORMANCE BRITISH GYMNASTICS

Tristan Collins

This chapter reports on the interim findings from a study of the impact of the British Gymnastics Child Protection Policy.[1] The policy, developed in response to legislation enacted to protect children and vulnerable adults from abuse, was re-launched in January 2004. It reflects 11 pieces of relevant legislation enacted in England, Wales, Scotland and Northern Ireland since The Children Act 1989. Through implementation of the policy, British Gymnastics recognizes that all young people and vulnerable adults have a right to be protected from abuse, regardless of age, gender, disability, racial origin, religious belief or sexual orientation. The policy also reflects the organization's commitment to ensuring the safety and welfare of all participants.

As of February 2005, approximately 100 complaints pertaining to 'poor practice' and 10 complaints of serious abuse had been filed by British Gymnastics. Abuse was categorized as emotional, physical and sexual. Some of the complaints required no formal action, some required disciplinary action and some required police intervention.

Previous research has revealed that worrying numbers of athletes coming out of high-performance programmes report have experienced abuse. The data from British Gymnastics and findings from other research demonstrate that gymnastics is not exempt from child protection issues. In fact, the sport may well be over-represented in abuse cases compared with society as a whole because of the youth of most gymnasts. This emphasizes the seriousness of the threat, both to those being abused and to the sport. It is the responsibility of the national governing body to respond to this threat.

Providing an effective response requires a detailed understanding of the issues. Developing the policy required identifying and reviewing key considerations and developing workable solutions.

Research Design

The first stage of the project was one-on-one interviews with coaches and staff members from British Gymnastics' Performance, Potential and Start programmes. These sessions aimed to establish whether the respondents perceived that child protection policy and practice in gymnastics were in conflict and, if so, to identify the areas where conflicts might exist. Two questions were asked:

1. Are there any aspects of current coaching practice in the high-performance environment that might be perceived by parents or child protection officers as conflicting with the child protection policy?
2. Are there any areas of child protection policy that are in conflict with coaching performers to optimal performance?

Key Findings

Respondents identified a number of areas in which child protection and current practice in gymnastics might conflict. These fell into four categories, each including a range of practices described by respondents:

1. Weight management:
   a) "There is a lot of positive reinforcement for weight loss, which just promotes a culture of not eating."
   b) "Coaches are constantly weighing gymnasts in public."
   c) "I think there's a general lack of knowledge about nutrition, even at the high performance end of the sport."
   d) "We use the English Institute of Sport nutritionist to help us develop the right diets for the gymnasts."

2. Verbal communication:
   a) "Shouting is part and parcel of the environment but I don't do it to humiliate."
   b) "I raise my voice but not often – only when safety is an issue."
   c) "You hear quite a lot of sarcasm and sometimes some innuendo – I don't think they know they're doing it though."
   d) "Language can sometimes be an issue. I had to speak to a Russian coach who was working in the gym – he just walked up to a girl and told her she was fat – you just can't do that."

3. Physical contact:
   a) "Pain is part of gymnastics – when you stretch them it hurts, and sometimes there are tears."
   b) "It comes down to the skill of the coach – when they are stretching I talk to them, ask them questions, ask if they want my help and then keep asking and trying to feel for myself when it is enough."
   c) "The gymnast for me is like paint and brushes for the painter or clay for the sculptor. I must be able to use my hands to mould them into the positions that are required."
   d) "Child protection must happen all the time. You keep them safe from people who might hurt them and you keep them safe when they are doing dangerous work in the gym. *That* is child protection."

4. Situations of isolation:
   a) "I have a 1:1 morning session with a gymnast every week. I'm very aware of the situation and how vulnerable I am when no one else is really around, but that's just the way it has to be."
   b) "Parents are often late picking up. You have to wait around even if it's just you with one gymnast."
   c) "Parents can be a problem in the gym. They wind each other up. They distract the gymnasts. It can be dangerous."

d) "We have an open gallery so parents can come any time. You just get used to it. It doesn't make much difference really."

The interviews were designed to give a general overview of child protection in the sport, rather than to produce detailed quantifiable data. While every individual interviewed was aware of the policy document, their answers revealed that each individual appeared to be at a different point in their knowledge and practice of child protection. This suggested that each policy area had been internalized and integrated at different levels. The range of views identified can be illustrated within a general theoretical framework representing to what degree an individual has adopted externally imposed regulations. For each interviewee a policy area could be:

- Internalized and integrated;
- Internalized but not integrated;
- Not internalized but integrated;
- Neither internalized nor integrated.

Accordingly, the first group appeared to provide models of best practice. They expressed a complex, holistic understanding of the issues and appeared to have made it personally meaningful and embedded in their value and belief systems. This was reflected in their practice.

The second group appeared broadly to engage in good practice. They expressed a good understanding of the issues but rationalized poor practice, seeing it as a practical necessity.

The third group also appeared broadly to engage in good practice. They did not express a sophisticated understanding of the issue, however, but followed the policy because they had been told it was important to do so.

The fourth group appeared more likely to be engaged in poor practice. They expressed an inability to rationalize child protection as an issue. As a result, they had no reference point for reflection on their own practice. In some cases they expressed denial that abuse and neglect occurred at any level in the sport or in society.

These theoretical 'groupings' are used for illustrative purposes only. In other words, it would be difficult to accurately place every individual interviewed into one of the groups. We also found that it was difficult to draw general conclusions about sub-groups within the sample. This is shown in the following observations:

- Those who had had extensive training in and experience of child protection did not necessarily present as the best practitioners in every area.
- Those who had been trained in former Eastern bloc countries, where it could be hypothesized that performance climates were harsher, did not necessarily present as the worst practitioners in every area.
- Neither age nor technical discipline were necessarily useful differentiating factors in the responses.

Our central observation was that views on child protection are highly individualized. This may be attributable to limitations in data collection and analysis, but in our judgement this is not the case. Those interviewed had highly differentiated and complex views on the issue and appeared to be at different stages in terms of internalizing and integrating child protection information into their practice.

Encouragingly, almost all interviewees said they were more aware of the issue and had thought more about their practice since introduction of the policy and training. This signalled that change was occurring, at least in terms of awareness. This was mediated, however, by a number of factors. Views on the policy were polarized where it was perceived not to provide definitive practice guidelines. For example, it was pointed out that the policy called for avoiding 'over-handling' of gymnasts. This led to concern that coaches could not handle gymnasts and therefore would be unable to keep them safe. Similar views were expressed in defining shouting as emotional abuse since some regarded it as a necessary technique for controlling dangerous behaviour in the training environment.

There was similar confusion about situations in which the coach ended up alone with a gymnast, perhaps waiting for a parent to pick them up or when other gymnasts had not turned up for sessions. In short, perceived 'grey areas' in the policy led interviewees to question its practical realism. Typically, the interviewees initially took an extreme view, suggesting that they would have to 'work to rule', give up coaching, or just practice as they thought was right, regardless of the specifics of the policy and the implied consequences. Child protection was not seen holistically, which led to a polarization of responses to it. Views were oriented around the detail of the policy document rather than the wider intention of keeping children free from abuse and neglect.

Reflections

Information gathered in the first stage of the project suggests that each individual is at a different stage in their understanding and practice of child protection. Understanding and good practice will accelerate when training is individualized and tailored to the needs of the learner. At a strategic level, impediments to improving internalization and integration include:

- Resources: More funding is needed for additional child protection personnel, transportation, etc.
- Planning: Training and logistics should be planned with child protection issues in mind.
- Motivation: Coaches will change only when they understand issues in the 'real world' context of training and competition for high-performance gymnasts.
- Knowledge: Child protection training should facilitate learning in context and reflecting individual learners' needs.

Clearly, the implementation of child protection policies and standards is important in changing sport culture. But change is a complex, multidimensional process, not an event. The adoption of new, desirable behaviours, or best practice, does not occur in a vacuum; it must be generated using a range of methods. Once new behaviours have been modelled they will, in supportive conditions, develop into norms. With a new culture established, new members will adopt best practice because it is 'normal' and 'right' and not simply because they are instructed or compelled to do so.

Notes

1. With kind thanks to British Gymnastics for permission to reproduce this slightly abridged version of a commissioned report, first presented to them by the author in October 2005.

Part 3
GLOBAL ISSUES: HARASSMENT AND ABUSE RESEARCH

CHAPTER 14. SEXUAL HARASSMENT AND ABUSE IN CANADIAN SPORT

Sandra Kirby

The first nationwide quantitative research study of sexual harassment and abuse of high-performance athletes was reported in 1996. But the research in Canadian sport actually began with earlier anecdotal reports from, for example, 'Unsafe at home base: Women's experiences of sexual harassment in university sport and physical education' (1992),[1] 'Sexual harassment in athletics: Listening to the athletes for solutions' (1994)[2] and 'Not in my back yard: Sexual harassment and abuse in sport' (1994).[3] The purpose of the latter was the political contextualization of women, sport and physical activity within the patriarchal system. That work provided some descriptions and explanations of harassment and abuse experiences of girls and women within the sport setting. Also addressed were the privileged relationship between athlete and coach, the power relationship inherent in harassment situations and the negative relationship between sexual harassment and excellence in sport. Kirby concluded with strategies for bringing about progressive change to sport.[4]

In the United Kingdom, Celia Brackenridge was writing about the need for codes of practice for coaching as early as 1986.[5] Mariah Burton Nelson wrote about sexual harassment and abuse in her 1991 book *Are We Winning Yet? How sports are changing women and women are changing sport.*[6] Like other researchers in the harassment and abuse field, she had begun receiving telephone calls from people wanting to tell their stories, not so much to have them included in research but to get them heard. The stories were and are haunting for two reasons: one, the random damage caused to sport and all of its participants, particularly to talented individuals who dedicated themselves to sport career paths; and two, the evasion of censure by so many of the persons who did the abusing.

About the time of these early publications, reports and stories, the 1994 Commonwealth Games Conference (Victoria, B.C., Canada) presented perhaps the first opportunity to take these issues to an international academic sport audience. In late 1993, following the disclosure of sexual harassment and sexual abuse cases in Canada and the United Kingdom,[7] Kirby and Greaves applied for funding from Sport Canada (the government agency that promotes sport) to research sexual harassment and abuse in sport. Although the data from this research were not ready in time for the 1994 conference, the researchers were able to identify the nature and scope of sexual harassment and abuse from the perspective of high-performance athletes. These findings were presented at the 1996 Pre-Olympic Games Scientific Congress (Dallas). That presentation broke new ground. As Celia Brackenridge wrote in the preface to the subsequent book on the study, the statistical data were "linked to the wider debates on the prevalence of sexual violence in modern life".[8]

Research Design

With the financial assistance of Sport Canada and support of Athletes CAN (the association of national team athletes), a Canada-wide survey of current and recently retired national team athletes was completed in 1996.[9] This was the first national, quantitative study addressing the nature and scope of the problem among high-performance athletes. Although studies outside sport had indicated the kind of sexual violence experienced by women and children, none had specifically addressed such violence to females and males in the sport context.[10]

Using a design based on and tested for validity in the 1993 Canadian Women's Safety Project, a four-part, bilingual sport survey was constructed for athletes. The first part addressed athletes' concerns, or lack of concerns, about sexual harassment and abuse. The second tackled the 'rumour mill' – what athletes had seen and heard in sport. The third consisted of questions about athletes' experiences in the sport context, focusing on what experiences had been most upsetting. Finally, athletes were asked what, if anything, they had done about such experiences. Their additional qualitative descriptions helped to complete part of the picture.

Key Findings

Presented here is a summary of the statistical and qualitative information provided. Given that the athletes were asked to describe only the most upsetting sexual harassment and abuse experiences, the number of athletes reporting such experiences is known, but the number or frequency of such experiences is not. This is the 'tip of the iceberg' (or threshold) approach common to many harassment and abuse studies.

About 80 per cent of the 266 responding athletes (55 per cent female and 45 per cent male) indicated that harassment and abuse were issues of concern to them. Despite the high awareness levels, only one in seven felt personally vulnerable to sexual violence, and females felt more vulnerable than did males (statistically significant at the $p < 002$ level). Additionally, female athletes were more afraid than males of rape/sexual assault (39 per cent compared with 17 per cent) and sexual harassment (29 per cent versus 10 per cent), while males were more afraid than females of physical harassment (20 per cent against 8 per cent) and child sexual assault (32 per cent versus 7 per cent, $p < 000$).[11] This latter finding was quite startling because it foreshadowed the revelations by Sheldon Kennedy and other males in sport about the sexual abuse they had experienced.[12]

When asked if they could recall a specific sexual harassment or abuse event, about 20 per cent of the respondents (more females than males) provided a description of an event or experience. This revealed three things: that there was a thriving sexist environment in sport; that the perpetrator of abuse was most often a person in a position of authority or power over the athletes, usually the coach; and that those athletes did not always feel safe with other athletes. Both females and males were victimized, although the athletes were much more aware of the victimization of women. Females were more likely to be harassed and/or abused, mostly by males. The reports were extremely disturbing, revealing patterns of systematic sexual harassment and abuse of athletes, often by sport authority figures.

Although sexual harassment/abuse was often regarded as an issue for girls and women, the study also revealed concern among boys and men. Though the harasser is most often male and the victim female, there was also evidence of harassment by a member of the same sex or of a female harassing a male. The types of harassment and abuse experienced were varied, including put-downs and insults, sexually suggestive comments, being made afraid (of losing a place on the team, of being identified as of sexual interest and of having to give sexual access to another). Perhaps the most disturbing finding was that 21.8 per cent of athletes reported having had sexual intercourse with a person in a position of authority over them. Most authority figures were older than the athletes; 8 per cent of these older people were more than 20 years older than the athlete in question. On this point, it is important to underline the all-important issue of consent: It is *not* consent if an athlete agrees to sexual activity with someone who is in authority over them.

Athletes reported other unwanted sexual experiences in sport, such as behaviours that occurred in a poisoned or 'chilly' climate. These included coaches' and other athletes' use of profanity or trash talk; constant attention being paid to one's physical, social or sexual attributes; and/or a homo-negative environment for gays and lesbians. Additionally, athletes reported receiving obscene phone calls (4.1 per cent of athletes; to younger athletes [p.<01]; from opposite sex [p.<02]), sexual comments or advances (19.2 per cent; more females than males [p.<000]), stalking (6.4 per cent) and flashing (to younger age [p.<03]; opposite sex [p.<001]). Most found it easier to ignore such experiences than to resist, challenge or report since there was no apparent mechanism to stop these forms of harassment or abuse.

Among the most disturbing of findings was that 8.6 per cent of the athletes reported experiencing forced sexual intercourse (oral, vaginal, anal). Of these athletes, more than one in five (21.7 per cent) were under the age of 16 years when this occurred, and more males than females reported such abuse. Above age 16 this trend reversed, with males reporting only 22 per cent of such incidents. However, 40 per cent of the perpetrators against males were reported to be 5 to 27 years older than the athlete they abused.

Finally, few athletes made an official complaint, and those who did were generally unsatisfied with the process or the outcome. The athletes avoided complaining because either they did not have faith in the complaint process or they felt that too much was at risk if they spoke out. Whatever the case, the great majority felt pressure to be silent, hence the name of the subsequent research report ('The Dome of Silence: Sexual harassment and abuse in sport').[13]

Coaches, generally males, were most likely to be identified as perpetrators of sexual harassment and abuse, and those they abused were more likely to be physically and socially isolated from other athletes or from social supports. This made them not only more vulnerable to abuse but also less likely to disclose it. Many of the sexual abuse incidents were described or 'framed' as relationships,[14] although they involved athletes sometimes much younger than the abusers. The abuse continued over extended periods of time and, most likely, remains unreported to this day.

Among high-performance athletes, the experiences were of concern to athletes and were gendered in nature. The experiences ranged from unwanted comments and sexual touching to violent rape. The harassment or abuse occurred on playing fields, tracks, ice rinks, pools/waterways and in locker rooms, buses, cars, hotel rooms and elevators. It happened on team trips and training courses and at conferences and team parties. It happened to members of the public and sport participants in sport facilities before, during and after sport events. It usually happened repeatedly, over a short or sometimes long period of time. Most often it happened in private.

The survey revealed a considerable amount of sexual abuse in sport, though as an institution sport generally resisted acknowledging both the problem and its severity. At the time the Canadian sport world was still characterized by a lack of awareness about equality, diversity and discrimination issues, and the issue of sexual abuse was still covered by 'the dome of silence'.

However, the picture was coming into focus. Information from other studies on violence in the family, the church, the military and schools was used to shed light on the dynamics of athletes' experience of violence in the sport context. It was also used to help athletes and others overcome the overwhelming silence about abuse within the sport world. Amid sensational reports of abuse in hockey, gymnastics and other sports, "some sport organisations in Canada and in Great Britain [began] the painful process of looking in the organisational mirror, analysing and reviewing their behaviour then changing their methods and practices," according to Celia Brackenridge.[15]

Reflections

The results of this study have received attention worldwide, and subsequent studies have looked at other populations and used other methods. Since the earliest research – by Todd Crosset, in 1985 – empirical studies have taken place in a number of countries.[16] These have taken a variety of forms. First are the 'nature and scope' studies on (a) types of harassment and abuse (e.g. victims, perpetrators and outcomes), (b) types of sports and (c) types of athletes (e.g. populations with special risks). Second are the prevalence studies assessing the proportion of athletes experiencing harassment and abuse (e.g., the reported and/or estimated rates of abuse). More recently, comparative studies have begun to emerge addressing, for example, athletes and non-athletes and those with and without disabilities. A complete list of research through 2000 can be found in Brackenridge's comprehensive publication on sexual harassment and abuse.[17]

Several other studies have spun off the original 'dome of silence' research, including those on harassment and bullying and on hazing and initiation in sport.[18, 19] In another article, Brackenridge and Kirby have proposed the 'stage of imminent achievement' as the period of peak vulnerability to sexual abuse for young athletes.[20] Research is also being conducted to address the role of programmes to prevent sexual harassment and abuse in sport in Canada, specifically in the province of Quebec. It first describes the international sport context of sexual harassment and abuse and then considers the needs of disabled and gay athletes.[21, 22] There are few if any data on the vulnerabilities of disabled or lesbian, gay, bisexual or transgendered athletes, or on specific prevention measures aimed at them. Such gaps in the literature make it difficult to evaluate the effectiveness of sexual harassment and abuse intervention programmes. There is a pressing need for research and policy advocacy to ensure protection is offered to all athletes, not just 'mainstream' athletes.

In sum, the dangers of sexual predation for athletes in the sport world are difficult to determine both nationally and internationally, given that the definitions chosen both determine relative frequencies of various forms of abuse (to some degree) and also influence our understanding of the nature and scope of the problem.[23] This is exacerbated by the need for sport researchers to 'make sense' of a variety of objectively defined sexually abusive activities that athletes experience in a subjective manner.[24] We still have to clarify key terms used to describe sexual harassment and abuse across cultures and across sports.

Notes

1. Lenskyj, H.J., 'Unsafe at home base: Women's experiences of sexual harassment in university sport and physical education', *Women in Sport and Physical Activity Journal*, 1992:1, 1, pp. 19-34.
2. Holman, M., 'Sexual harassment in athletics: Listening to the athletes for solutions', unpublished paper presented to the annual conference of the North American Society for the Sociology of Sport, 1994.
3. Kirby, S.L., 'Not in my back yard: Sexual harassment and abuse in sport', Proceedings of the Commonwealth Games Conference, Victoria, B.C., Canadian Woman Studies/Les Cahiers de la Femme, 1994:15, 4, pp. 58-62.
4. Kirby, ibid.
5. Brackenridge, C.H., 'Problem? What problem? Thoughts on a professional code of practice for coaches', unpublished paper presented to the Annual Conference of the British Association of National Coaches, Bristol, England, December 1986.
6. Burton N.M., *Are We Winning Yet? How sports are changing women and women are changing sports*. New York, Random House, 1991.
7. Kirby, op cit.
8. Kirby, S.L. and L. Greaves, 'Foul play: Sexual abuse and harassment in sport', paper presented to the Pre-Olympic Scientific Congress, Dallas, Texas, USA, 11-14 July 1996.
9. Kirby and Greaves, ibid.
10. Kirby, S.L., L. Greaves and O. Hankivsky, *The Dome of Silence: Sexual Harassment and Abuse in Sport*, Halifax, Fernwood, 2000.
11. Kirby, Greaves and Hankivsky, ibid., p.29.

12. Kennedy, S., *Why I Didn't Say Anything: The Sheldon Kennedy story,* Canada, Insomniac Books, 2006.
13. Kirby, Greaves and Hankivsky, op.cit.
14. Kirby, Greaves and Hankivsky, op cit., p.29.
15. Brackenridge cited in Kirby et al., op cit., p. 9.
16. Crossett, T., 'Male coach/female athlete relationships: A case study of the abusive male coach', unpublished paper, 1985.
17. Brackenridge, C.H., *Spoilsports: Understanding and preventing sexual exploitation in sport,* London, Routledge, 2001.
18. Kirby, S.L. and G. Wintrup, 'Running the gauntlet: An examination of initiation/hazing and sexual abuse in sport', *Journal of Sexual Aggression,* 2002:8, 2, pp. 49-68.
19. Johnson, J. and M. Holman (eds.), *Making the team: Inside the world of sports initiations and hazing,* Toronto, Canadian Scholars Press, 2004.
20. Brackenridge, C.H. and S.L. Kirby, 'Playing safe? Assessing the risk of sexual abuse to young elite athletes', *International Review for the Sociology of Sport,* 1997:32, 4, pp. 407-418.
21. Demers, G., S. Parent, S. Kirby and J. Malo, 'Le harcèlement et les abus sexuels dans le sport: Situation des athlètes ayant une incapacité' (Sexual harassment and abuse in sport: The situation of athletes with disabilities), paper presented at Rehabilitation International: International Congress, Quebec City, 24-27 August 2008.
22. Kirby, S.L., G. Demers and S. Parent, 'Vulnerability/prevention: Considering the needs of disabled and gay athletes in the context of sexual harassment and abuse', *International Journal of Sport and Exercise Psychology,* in press,
23. Kelly, L., R. Wingfield, S. Burton and L. Regan, *Splintered Lives: Sexual exploitation of children in the context of children's rights and child protection,* Ilford, Essex, Barnado's, 1995.

CHAPTER 15. EMOTIONAL ABUSE IN CANADIAN SPORT

Ashley E. Stirling and Gretchen A. Kerr

Focus on child maltreatment began during the first and second world wars based on moral concern for orphaned children and children in impoverished families. It grew to include concern about abusive and neglectful behaviours directed at children.[1] Since then, various definitions and classifications of child maltreatment have been proposed. In general, forms of maltreatment can be roughly categorized as relational (perpetrated by a person the victim knows and trusts) and non-relational (perpetrated by anyone else).[2]

Much maltreatment, both relational and non-relational, takes place within relationships of differential power. Thus it is the nature of the relationship in which the maltreatment occurs that differentiates various forms of maltreatment in sport. The major recognized forms of relational child maltreatment include neglect, emotional abuse, sexual abuse and physical abuse. Crooks and Wolfe refer to these maltreatments as 'relational disorders' as they "occur within the context of a critical relationship role" in which the relationship has significant influence over the child's sense of safety, trust and fulfillment of needs.[3] Forms of maltreatment that occur outside critical relationships are referred to as non-relational maltreatment. These include child corruption/exploitation, sexual exploitation/prostitution, child labour, abuse/assault by persons not known closely by the child, harassment, bullying and institutional child maltreatment.[4]

Child protection in the societal context has evolved. Likewise the advancement of athlete protection initiatives and research on athletes' experiences of maltreatment must be examined within the greater societal and cultural context. Earlier advances in sport – such as the development of children's and athletes' rights, increased scrutiny of the coaching profession and endorsement of positive athlete development models – have all encouraged the development of athlete protection initiatives. Yet it is apparent that more is required to protect athletes from maltreatment.

Research clearly indicates that relational athlete maltreatment remains a significant problem.[5-11] To date, sexual abuse in sport has been the focus of most of this research, with emotional abuse receiving far less attention. As such, a series of studies was carried out on athletes' experiences of relational abuse, specifically emotional abuse in sport. These studies are reviewed below.

Research Design

Each study used a qualitative research design. All participating athletes had competed previously at the junior national, senior national or international level. All were females from the individual sports of swimming and gymnastics, in which athletes tend to specialize and reach professional maturity at a young age. Semi-structured interviews were conducted individually with elite and sub-elite female athletes.[12] Participant samples ranged from 9 to 14 athletes. Interviews were digitally recorded and transcribed verbatim, and data were analysed inductively using open, axial and selective coding techniques.

Key Findings

Power of the coach

The coach has immense power over the athlete, which often extends to non-sport areas of the athlete's life, including academics, social life and diet. Specific aspects of their coaches' power made the athletes susceptible to physical, sexual or emotional abuse. These included the closeness of the relationship and the coach's legitimate authority, expertise, success and ability to control access to the athletes. As a consequence of the coach's power, the athletes experienced fear and often normalized abusive behaviours. They perceived their coaches' power as inhibiting their ability to report abuse.

Definition of emotional abuse in sport

A strong criticism of the work conducted to date on emotional abuse, both generally and in sport specifically, is the lack of a standardized definition and classification structure for emotional abuse. Definitions of emotional maltreatment often differ depending on whether the occurrence is defined by the behaviour itself[13] or by the outcome of a particular behaviour.[14] This discontinuity may be explained by examining the purpose of the definition or classification.[15] For clinical purposes, emotional abuse may be best defined based on the degree and/or type of harm experienced. But from the perspective of applied research and intervention, these definitions are not sufficient. To advance the identification and prevention of emotional abuse in sport, the definition must include criteria for the behaviour perpetrated. Thus, the following definition of emotional abuse was adopted for this research:

> A pattern of deliberate non-contact behaviours by a person within a critical relationship role that has the potential to be harmful. Acts of emotional abuse include physical and verbal behaviours and acts of denying attention and support. These acts have the potential to be spurning, terrorizing, isolating or exploiting/corrupting or to deny emotional responsiveness, and they may be harmful to an individual's affective, behavioural, cognitive or physical well-being.

This definition of emotional abuse is the first derived from the experiences of emotional abuse within an athletic environment. It combines previous definitions of emotional abuse and attempts to include both the syndrome of the abuse and criteria for identifying emotionally abusive behaviour.

Types of emotional abuse in sport

Coaches perpetrate emotionally abusive behaviours in three ways: through physical behaviours, verbal behaviours and denial of attention and support. Physical behaviours reported included acts of aggression such as hitting and throwing objects at the athlete or in the athlete's presence. Study participants reported that coaches repeatedly threw objects following an athlete's inadequate performance, including swimming kickboards, soft-drink cans, flag poles, chairs, pool toys, markers, pylons, blocks, erasers and water bottles. Verbal behaviours consisted of yelling and shouting at an athlete or group of athletes, belittling, name-calling and degrading, humiliating or intimidating comments. Finally, the third category of emotionally abusive behaviour included the intentional denial of attention and support that would be expected from a coach.

Effects of various types of emotional abuse on athletes

Athletes' reactions differed depending on the type of emotional abuse. Participants reported that denial of attention and support had the most negative effect, followed by verbal behaviours. Interestingly, physical behaviours had the least negative effect.

One potential explanation for these different responses is the degree to which each behaviour threatens the athlete's self-esteem and her relationship with her coach. Physical behaviours can be intimidating but they do not compromise an athlete's self-esteem to the same degree as verbal behaviours and the denial of attention and support. Also, despite the aggressive nature of physical behaviours, the relationship is still intact; the coach and the athlete are still interacting with one another. But verbal behaviours such as belittling and degrading comments can be internalized, damaging the athlete's self-esteem and athletic identity. However, as with physical behaviours, the coach is still providing the athlete attention; even though it not necessarily positive, it preserves the coach-athlete relationship.

The denial of attention and support is the most threatening because it compromises both the athlete's relationship with her coach and her sense of identity, which is immersed in this domain. According to the athletes, coaches use denying attention and support as a form of punishment that compromises the closeness of the relationship and tells the athlete that she is not worthy of attention. This has the result of degrading the athlete's sense of self-worth and reducing her ability to cope with the emotional abuse.

Experiences across time

Not only do athletes experiences the various types of emotional abuse differently, but they experience the same behaviours differently at different stages of their career. Interestingly, athletes' responses to emotional abuse seem to be entwined with their self-perceptions of athletic performances and acquiescence to the culture of sport as reflected in the phases of normalization and rebellion. During the bulk of their careers, athletes' experiences of emotional abuse are normalized or accepted as part of the elite sport culture. At this stage, emotionally abusive coaching practices are accepted as a required part of the training process, and feelings about emotional abuse are low. But there is generally a point at which the athlete's perceptions of her performance shift from positive to negative. An associated shift is seen in the athletes' responses to emotional abuse, with negative feelings increasing as perceptions of performance become more negative.

At this time, even though the athletes still view the emotionally abusive behaviours as a normal part of the training process, the behaviours have a significant negative effect on them. Near the end of their careers, many start to question the normalization of their coach's deviant behaviours and question the culture of elite sport in which the emotionally abusive behaviours occur, ultimately rebelling against these behaviours. In this phase, athletes are significantly and negatively affected by their experiences of emotional abuse.

In addition to general unhappiness during the latter stages of their careers, many participants also recalled experiences of depression, eating disorders and social withdrawal as a result of their emotionally abusive experiences (see figure 5).

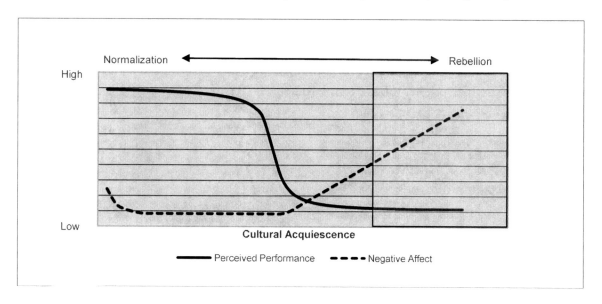

Figure 5. Athletes' experiences of emotional abuse

Reflections

Given that research on emotional abuse in sport is relatively new, many important theoretical and practical questions remain. Interestingly, both male and female coaches used emotionally abusive behaviours. As no previous studies have examined the influence of the coach's gender on athletes' experiences of emotional abuse, this would be a fruitful line of research. Future questions of interest include: Does the frequency or form of emotional abuse differ between male and female coaches? Do athletes who train with male versus female coaches differ in their experiences of emotional abuse?

As the reviewed studies looked solely at female athletes, an investigation of male athletes' experiences and potential gender differences in the experience of emotionally abusive behaviours is warranted. Moreover, it would be interesting to explore the process by which individuals may experience emotional abuse in other potentially critical sport relationships such as between athletes and between parents and athletes.

The findings presented also highlight the importance of context. The coaches' behaviour would not be allowed in other instructional settings: Teachers, for example, would incur serious consequences for name-calling and throwing objects at students. The contextual factors that contribute to the occurrence of emotional abuse in sport require further investigation. Future research is also required on the incidence, prevalence and types of emotionally abusive behaviours in sport. The authors assume that positive non-abusive coaching practices exist in sport. Thus, research demonstrating the success of non-abusive coaching methods is warranted – given that emotionally abusive behaviours are often justified as a means to produce successful sport performance.

Notes

1. Giovannoni, J., 'Definitional issues in child maltreatment', in: D. Cicchetti and V. Carlson (eds.), *Child Maltreatment: Theory and research on the causes and consequences of child abuse and neglect*, New York, Cambridge University Press, 1989, pp. 3-37.
2. Crooks, C.V. and D.A. Wolfe, 'Child abuse and neglect', in: E.J. Mash and R.A. Barkley (eds.), *Assessment of childhood disorders* (4th ed.), New York, Guilford Press, 2007.
3. Crooks and Wolfe, op. cit., p. 17.
4. Wachtel, A., *The State of the Art in Child Abuse Prevention, 1997*, Health Canada, 1999.
5. Brackenridge, C.H., '"He owned me basically…" Women's experience of sexual abuse in sport', *International Review for the Sociology of Sport*, 1997, 32:2, pp. 115-130.
6. Brackenridge, C.H., 'Dangerous sports? Risk, responsibility and sex offending in sport', *Journal of Sexual Aggression*, 2003:9, 1, pp. 3-12.
7. Brackenridge, C.H., 'Women and children first? Child abuse and child protection in sport', *Sport in Society*, 2004, 7:3, pp. 322-337.
8. Fasting, K. and C.H. Brackenridge, 'The grooming process in sport: Case studies of sexual harassment and abuse', *Auto/biography*, 2005, 13:1, pp. 33-52.
9. Kirby, S. and L. Greaves, 'Foul play: Sexual harassment in sport', paper presented at the Pre-Olympic Scientific Congress, Dallas, Texas, 11-15 July 1996.
10. Stirling, A.E. and G.A. Kerr, 'Elite female swimmers' experiences of emotional abuse across time', *Journal of Emotional Abuse*, 2007:7, 4, pp. 89-113.
11. Stirling, A.E. and G.A. Kerr, 'Defining and categorizing emotional abuse in sport', *European Journal of Sport Science*, 2008:8, 4, pp. 173-181.
12. For more details on these studies, please refer to: A.E. Stirling and G.A. Kerr, 'Abused athletes' perceptions of the coach-athlete relationship', *Sport in Society*,

in press; A.E. Stirling and G.A. Kerr, 'Defining and categorizing emotional abuse in sport', *European Journal of Sport Science*, 2008:8, 4, pp. 173-181; A.E. Stirling and G.A. Kerr, 'Elite female swimmers' experiences of emotional abuse across time', *Journal of Emotional Abuse*, 2007:7, 4, pp. 89-113. .

13. Paavilainen, E. and M. Tarkka, 'Definition and identification of child abuse by Finnish public health nurses', *Public Health Nurses*, 2003:20, 1, pp. 49-55.

14. Iwaniec, D., 'Identifying and dealing with emotional abuse and neglect', *Child Care in Practice*, 2003:9, 1, pp. 49-61.

15. Porter, M.R., J. Antonishak and N.D. Reppucci, 'Policy and applied definitions of child maltreatment', in: M.M. Feerick, J.F. Knutson, P.K. Trickett and S. Flanzer (eds.), *Child Abuse and Neglect: Definitions, classifications, and a framework for research,* Brooks Publishing, Baltimore, Maryland, 2006.

CHAPTER 16. SEXUAL HARASSMENT AND ABUSE IN NORWEGIAN SPORT

Kari Fasting

Sport is very popular in Norway – of its approximately 4.5 million people, over 2 million are members of sport clubs. More than 800,000 of them are under the age of 20,[1] making sport clubs a significant socialization arena for children and youth. It is therefore important to ask how safe children and youth are in Norwegian sport. Very few empirical studies concerning sexual harassment of adults and abuse of children in sport have been carried out in Norway: none have focused particularly on children or youth. Only two projects have provided empirical data. The first was part of the 2000 Norwegian Women Project, administered by the Norwegian Olympic Committee.[2] The other was a comparative study among female sport students in Czech Republic, Greece and Norway from 2005. This chapter describes findings from these two studies.

Research Design – Norwegian Women Project

The main goal of the Norwegian Women Project was to produce practical knowledge useful for athletes and sport organizations, particularly in relation to prevention of harassment and abuse. The first part of the two-part study consisted of a survey of all female elite athletes. Its aim was to establish an overview of sexual harassment, the degree to which it existed and the degree to which it could be characterized as a problem for Norwegian sport. Part two consisted of interviews with elite athletes who had experienced one or more forms of sexual harassment. The purpose was to obtain more knowledge about risk factors, reactions to sexual harassment and the consequences of these experiences for the athletes.[3]

A total of 660 elite female athletes aged 15 to 39, representing 58 sport disciplines, were invited to participate in the study. Three age groups were studied: 15-18 years, 19-22 years and 23-39 years. The athletes were defined as members of a junior, development or senior national team. As a control the same questionnaire was administered to a representative sample of 785 girls and women of the same age group who were not elite athletes. A total of 572 athletes (87 per cent) and 574 controls (73 per cent) answered the questionnaire. The average age of the athletes was 21.4 years; the control group was somewhat older, with a mean age of 24.8 years. About one third of the athletes and 23 per cent of the controls were 18 years old or younger.

Eleven questions measured the experiences of sexual harassment. These ranged from light harassment, such as 'repeated unwanted sexual remarks concerning one's body, private life, sexual orientation etc.' to severe sexual harassment, defined as 'attempted rape or rape'. For each question, respondents were asked to mark whether they had experienced it or not, and whether it had been perpetrated by a man or a woman. The elite athletes were asked to indicate if the perpetrator(s) had been an authority figure in sport, a peer in sport or someone outside sport. The equivalent perpetrator categories for the controls were a supervisor at work or a teacher at a school, a fellow worker or student, or someone outside these settings.

Key Findings

Quantitative findings

The most important results from the survey were:

- Among the athletes, 28 per cent had experienced sexual harassment or abuse in sport, perpetrated either by an authority figure in sport and/or by other athletes.

- There was no difference between the different age groups, but younger subjects had experienced more sexual harassment than older ones, an unexpected trend.

- The athletes had more often been harassed or abused by peer athletes than by authority figures in sport.

- A higher percentage of athletes with eating disorders (34 per cent), compared with those without (26 per cent), reported experiencing sexual harassment by someone in sport.[4]

- Female elite athletes who participated in masculine sports experienced more harassment and abuse than other women, perpetrated especially by peer athletes, when the sport disciplines were grouped according to the following variables:

  1) Formation of the sport (team or individual);
  2) Amount of clothing coverage required for competition (a little, a moderate amount or a lot);
  3) Gender structure (male or female dominated);
  4) Gender culture (masculine, gender-neutral or feminine).[5]

- Performance level also seemed to be related to sexual harassment: Athletes who had participated in a world championship and/or the Olympic Games had experienced more sexual harassment than those who had not. This was true primarily for those above 18 years of age.

- There was no difference between the athletes' experiences of sexual harassment/abuse in sport and the controls' experiences of sexual harassment in school/at work.

- There was a distinct difference between the proportion of athletes (15 per cent) who had experienced sexual harassment perpetrated by an authority figure in sport compared with the control group's experience of harassment by authority figures at work or school (9 per cent). This percentage was higher among the older sport respondents.

- The forms of sexual harassment most commonly experienced by the athletes were:

  o 'Ridiculing of your sport performances and of you as an athlete because of your gender or your sexuality (for example, 'Soccer is not suitable for girls').'

  o 'Unwanted physical contact, body contact (for example, pinching, fondling, being kissed against your will, etc.)'

  o 'Repeated unwanted sexually suggestive glances, comments, teasing and jokes about your body, your clothes, your private life, your sexual orientation etc.'

  o 'Being the subject of humiliating treatment or situations which have undermined your self-respect and/or had a negative influence on your sport performance.'

Authority figures in sport were perpetrators of the last two forms of harassment more often than were peer athletes. The opposite was true for the first two categories. As many as 62 per cent of athletes who had experienced sexual harassment or abuse from peer athletes had experienced ridicule. In addition, only ridicule had been experienced more often by athletes than by the controls. However, the controls had experienced much more serious forms of sexual harassment than the athletes, such as "forced into sexual behaviour" and "rape and attempted rape".[6]

The survey results revealed that two groups had experienced the most abuse/harassment: these were, first, the oldest athletes who had participated in world championships and/or Olympic Games and, secondly, those athletes with eating disorders. Among the older group as many as 39 per cent had experienced sexual harassment and abuse in a sport environment, while 30 per cent of the youngest athletes with eating disorders had experienced sexual harassment perpetrated by authority figures in sport.

Qualitative findings

Qualitative interviews were undertaken with 25 female athletes who had indicated that they had been sexually harassed by an authority figure in sport. They represented 15 different sports. More than half practised for at least 16 to 20 hours per week, and 15 of them had competed in the Olympic Games, world championships or world cup. The interviews revealed that most had been harassed or abused by a coach. Though they were 15 to 33 years of age when interviewed, their experiences of sexual harassment/abuse typically had taken place when they were around 14 to 16 years of age. The findings from these interviews can be summarized as follows:

- The athletes' emotional reactions were 'disgust', 'fear', 'irritation' and 'anger' when the sexually harassing incidents occurred. Their behavioural responses had been 'passivity', 'avoidance', 'direct confrontation' and 'confrontation with humour'. They therefore demonstrated individual, internally focused responses to the harassment rather than collective, externally focused ones.[7]

- The reported consequences of the sexual harassment were generally negative, but some reported that their experiences had had no consequences for them. The most negative consequences mentioned were 'thinking about the incidents', 'a destroyed relationship with the coach', and 'more negative view of men in general'. In addition, several had chosen to move to a different sport or to drop out of elite sport altogether because of the harassment.[8]

The qualitative part of the study also addressed the characteristics of the harassing coach. It questioned how harassing coaches are characterized by their victims and whether they demonstrate specific behaviours. An article that resulted from these interviews presented a three-part typology: (1) the flirting-charming coach, (2) the seductive coach and (3) the authoritarian coach. The data further suggest that sexually harassing coaches were not exclusively one type; they varied their behaviour according to the situation.

Key Findings – Study of Female Sport Students in Czech Republic, Greece and Norway

The comparative study of female sport students in Czech Republic, Greece and Norway aimed to develop knowledge about the influence and meaning of gender relations in their lives.[9] A total of 616 women who were studying in sport departments of academic institutions participated in this study, all answering the same questionnaire. The women were aged 17 to 45 years with a mean of 21.75. All but 7 participants reported that they exercised regularly. In addition to this sample, 10 Norwegian sport students who had been harassed by a coach were interviewed.

To avoid subjective opinions about what constitutes sexual harassment, the students were asked if they ever had experienced the following situations:

a) Unwanted physical contact, such as pinching, hugging, fondling, being kissed against your will, etc.
b) Repeated unwanted sexually suggestive glances, comments, teasing and jokes about your body, your clothes, your private life, etc.
c) Ridiculing of your sport performance and of you as an athlete because of your gender or your sexuality (for example 'Soccer is not suitable for girls').

For each question, participants were asked to indicate whether they had experienced the behaviour perpetrated by a male or female coach, a male or female peer-athlete, a male or female member of the sport management team, a male or female teacher, a male or female peer-student, a male or female family member, and/or by other males or females outside sport/family.

Thirty per cent of the students overall reported sexual harassment perpetrated by men in sport. Differences between the countries were large, however: 20 per cent of the Norwegian students had experienced sexual harassment, compared with 32 per cent among the Greek respondents and 35 per cent among those from Czech Republic.[10] When asked about the forms of sexually harassing behaviours, the most common (20 per cent) was 'unwanted sexual glances, etc.', followed by 'ridicule' (15 per cent) and 'unwanted physical contact' (14 per cent).

Looking at differences by country, there were no statistical differences concerning the students' experiences of ridicule. However, the other forms of sexual harassment yielded significant differences between countries. The Czech students reported experiencing the most unwanted sexual glances, and the Greek female students experienced the most unwanted physical contact. Norwegian students had experienced the least on all three types.[11]

The study also revealed that 19 per cent of these female students had been harassed by their coaches. Those who had experienced sexual harassment by a coach had also experienced more authoritarian coaching.[12]

Reflections

Based on these results, there is no reason to conclude that sexual harassment is worse in sport than in other arenas. As a societal problem, it occurs in sport, but it does not seem to occur there more often than in other settings.

These results should influence the development of policies and procedures for preventing sexual harassment and abuse, for the education of coaches and athletes, and for sport psychology consultants and other support personnel.

Also noteworthy is the lack of studies on children's experiences of violence in sport. In Norway many studies have been conducted on children in sport, but none has focused on sexual harassment and abuse. Both quantitative and qualitative studies are therefore needed about young people's and children's experiences and reactions to violence in different sport settings as well as the consequences.

Notes

1. Norwegian Confederation of Sports, *Årsrapport 2006 – Norges Idrettsforbund og Olympiske Komitè (Annual Report 2006 – Norwegian Sports Federation and Olympic Committee)*, The Norwegian Olympic Committee and Confederation of Sports, Oslo, 2007.
2. The project was carried out by Professor Kari Fasting, in cooperation with Professors Celia Brackenridge and Jorunn Sundgot Borgen.

3, Fasting, K., C.H. Brackenridge and J. Sundgot Borgen, *The Norwegian Women Project – Females, elite sports and sexual harassment*, the Norwegian Olympic Committee and Confederation of Sports, Oslo, 2000.

4. Sundgot-Borgen, J., K. Fasting, C.H. Brackenridge, M. Klungland and B. Bergland, 'Sexual harassment and eating disorders in female elite athletes: A controlled study', *Scandinavian Journal of Medicine & Science in Sports*, 2003, 13:5, pp. 330-335.

5. Fasting, K., C.H. Brackenridge and J. Sundgot Borgen, 'Prevalence of sexual harassment among Norwegian female elite athletes in relation to sport type', *International Review for the Sociology of Sport*, 2004:39, 4, pp. 373-386.

6. Fasting, K., C.H. Brackenridge and J. Sundgot Borgen, 'Sexual harassment in and outside sport. Forms of sexual harassment experienced by female athletes and non-athletes', *International Journal of Psychology*, 2000, 35, 3/4, p. 215.

7. Fasting, K., C.H. Brackenridge and K. Walseth, 'Women athletes' personal responses to sexual harassment in sport', *Journal of Applied Sport Psychology*, 2007:19, 4, pp. 419-433.

8. Fasting, K., C.H. Brackenridge and K. Walseth, 'Consequences of sexual harassment in sport', *Journal of Sexual Aggression*, 2002:8, 2, pp. 37-48.

9. This project is chaired by Kari Fasting in cooperation with Nada Knorre and Stiliani Chroni.

10. Fasting, K., et al., 'The experiences of male sexual harassment among female sport students in the Czech Republic, Greece and Norway', paper presented at the FEPSAC 12th European Congress of Sport Psychology, 4-9 September 2007.

11. Chroni, S., et al., 'Forms of sexual harassment experienced by female sport students in the Czech Republic, Greece and Norway', paper presented at the FEPSAC 12th European Congress of Sport Psychology, 4-9 September 2007.

12. Sand, T.S., et al., 'Authoritarian coaching behaviour and experiences of sexual harassment among sport students in three different European countries', paper presented at the FEPSAC 12th European Congress of Sport Psychology, 4-9 September 2007.

CHAPTER 17. SEXUAL ABUSE IN COMPETITIVE SPORT IN AUSTRALIA

Trisha Leahy

Studies from around the world have consistently documented the occurrence of sexual abuse in sport.[1-3] This chapter summarizes a study assessing the occurrence and long-term traumatic impact of childhood sexual abuse of athletes in the competitive sport system in Australia.

Research Design

The study was based on a survey distributed to athletes at the elite (national) and club (local) levels, both males and females. An age-based matched control group was also included. A sub-sample from the larger group comprising 90 athletes (45 men and 45 women) was selected to balance the distributions of male and female participants and reported childhood sexual abuse across the sample. The study used a cross-sectional, retrospective investigation, standardized, self-report questionnaires and a semi-structured interview.

Sexual abuse was defined as any sexual activity between an adult and a child (under 18 years old) regardless of whether it involves deception or whether the child understands the sexual nature of the activity. This includes sexual contact accomplished by force or the threat of force, regardless of the age of the victim or perpetrator. Sexual abuse may include acts not involving contact (such as exhibitionism, involving a child in sexually explicit conversation, engaging a child in pornographic photography), acts involving contact (sexual touching, masturbation) and penetrative acts (oral, vaginal, anal).

Key Findings

With responses from 370 male and female athletes, both elite and club, 31 per cent of female athletes and 21 per cent of male athletes reported having experienced sexual abuse before the age of 18.[4] Environment-specific sexual abuse rates were particularly high; 41 per cent of the sexually abused females and 29 per cent of the sexually abused males indicated the abuse was perpetrated by sport personnel.[4] The sport-related abuse was largely perpetrated by those in positions of authority or trust with the athletes. Primarily these were coaches; less frequently they were support staff and other athletes. The vast majority (over 96 per cent) of perpetrators were men.

Long-term impact of sexual violence on child athletes

The study examined the long-term traumatic results associated with childhood sexual abuse, taking into account both childhood physical and psychological abuse experiences and more recent adult trauma. These variables were included because other research indicates that results are confounded when there is no control for the interaction of different forms of childhood abuse, or for the effect of trauma about such experiences emerging only in adulthood, when assessing related long-term post-traumatic symptomatology.[5] Additionally, while individual forms of child abuse are unlikely to be experienced unidimensionally,[6] some researchers have suggested that the main harm of sexual and physical abuse arises from the psychological abuse associated with these experiences.[7-8]

The results revealed that childhood sexual, physical and psychological abuse were strongly correlated. As predicted, childhood psychological abuse was more related to sexual and physical abuse.[9] This may relate to the sociocultural context of competitive sport in Australia (and in some other industrialized countries), which has been criticized as normalizing psychologically abusive coaching behaviours as part of the winning strategy.[10-12] It may also specifically relate to the particular strategies that appear to be used by perpetrators within the athlete's environment, as described below.

Perpetrator methodology

The interview transcripts of 20 athletes were analysed. The group was selected to balance male and female participants with similar sexual abuse experiences, half of whom were clinically traumatized. Two general aspects of perpetrator methodology were revealed, apparently designed to make the athlete feel powerless and, conversely, to make the perpetrator seem omnipotent. First, and particularly obvious in cases of prolonged and repeated abuse, the perpetrator imposed his version of reality on the athlete and isolated the athlete within that reality. Second, the perpetrator successfully maintained that reality by controlling the psychological environment. In addition to dominating the athlete's public or outer life, the perpetrator controlled her/his inner, psychological life through direct emotional manipulation and psychological abuse.[13]

The psychological literature demonstrates that a victim can become entrapped in a powerful perpetrator's viewpoint when the perpetrator repeatedly imposes his world view and the victim lacks alternative reference points due to the perpetrator's ability to isolate and silence the victim.[14] This can be seen in the following statement from a male athlete abused by his coach:

> "... although at the time ... I suppose I did wonder how he could get an erection in front of me, but ... I didn't really think that he was getting off on it, because it was always presented as education, and that sort of thing."

The athletes' reports described a sport environment pervaded by an unpredictable, volatile and emotional reward-punishment cycle. This cyclical repetition of fear and reprieve, punishment and reward, in the closed context of a competitive sports team, can result in a feeling of extreme dependence on the perceived omnipotent perpetrator.[14] As reported by one female athlete sexually abused by her coach: "To us at that time, his word was like gospel." The psychology literature explains this state as a traumatized attachment to the perpetrator. Under these conditions, disclosure simply does not happen. Silencing is an integral, not separate, part of the experience; these aspects of the perpetrator's methodology target the individual's emotional life as a method of keeping that person in a state of confusion, fear and entrapment. This is illustrated in the statements below by three athletes sexually abused by their coaches.

Confusion

"It was more emotional, everything he did ... he'd put me down, he'd really put me down as an athlete and then build me up with his affection and then it got really confusing and I didn't know the difference, if he was a coach or somebody who was just playing with my emotions." *(Female athlete)*

Fear

"I didn't feel like I could tell ...'cause not only would I lose my sport, but I was scared of what would happen. I think, you know, I wasn't thinking that logically ... at the time I was just so confused. I was just really confused..." *(Female athlete)*

Entrapment

"... so what do you do when you trusted this person, and you've got all this at your feet like your sport and a whole bunch of new friends, so what are you going to do? ... it's just your word against his ... and you don't know, maybe it happens to everybody? Maybe this is the way it goes ...? *(Male athlete)*

The bystander effect

The prevalence of the 'bystander effect' compounded long-term psychological harm for sexually abused athletes. The bystander effect refers to a situation in which the victim perceives that others knew about or suspected the sexual abuse but did nothing about it. A female athlete sexually abused by her coach, who was simultaneously abusing others in the team, provides a distressing account of the bystander effect:

"They saw things that were wrong, and they didn't do anything about it ... this is very bad, not only the fact that I fell out of a sport that should have protected me... I lost so ... I lost my relationship with my family ... I could have saved a few years of my life." *(Female athlete)*

Athletes' experiences of the bystander effect make clear the distress-amplifying impact of abandoning the victim to isolation and silence. The apparent lack of systemically sanctioned accountability in relation to the power of the coach-perpetrator appeared to influence other adults in the competitive sport environment, preventing them from speaking out. These included coaching and other support staff or volunteers who were less senior than the perpetrator. This silence was especially notable in the elite sport context, in which it is unusual to challenge authority ("... we were so elite and no one ever questioned what we were doing."). When other adults fail to intervene, the young person is likely to presume that they are also powerless in relation to the perpetrator.

Children may keep the abuse secret if they believe or know that other adults are aware of it.[15] If observing adults take no action, the child may assume the behaviour is socially acceptable; older children may accept the perpetrator's message that he is omnipotent, leaving them to feel truly trapped.[16]

Reflections

Particularly evident from this study was how the culture of competitive sport facilitates, rather than inhibits, the sexually abusive strategies of people in positions of authority and trust. One of the more urgent implications of this study is the need to eliminate the acceptance of psychologically abusive coaching styles. Psychological abuse was clearly and uniquely implicated in long-term traumatic outcomes in the athletes who participated in this study, even where no sexual abuse had occurred. Psychological abuse also effectively masks sexual offences that rely on psychological abuse and emotional manipulation.

To overcome the bystander effect, comprehensive and ongoing sexual abuse awareness education is imperative for all those involved in organized sport in Australia, including athletes, parents and all associated support personnel. The adults in the system have particular responsibility to ensure children's safety; it should not be relegated to the children themselves. It is important to understand that silencing is an integral part of the sexual abuse experience; non-disclosure is the norm. Every person in the athletes' entourage has a right to be informed and specifically empowered to act to safeguard athletes' welfare through clear guidelines and procedures.

Realistically the sports sector, like all sectors of the community, cannot prevent serial offenders gaining entry into the system. But it is possible to increase deterrence by empowering all adults in the system with the specific knowledge and resources to act to protect children.

Notes

1. Brackenridge, C.H., 'Dangerous relations: Men, women, and sexual abuse in sport', report of unpublished inaugural professorial lecture, Cheltenham & Gloucester College of Higher Education, United Kingdom, 1997.
2. Fasting, K., C.H. Brackenridge and J. Sundgot Borgen, *Sexual harassment in and outside sport,* Oslo, Norwegian Olympic Committee, 2000.
3. Kirby, S., L. Greaves and O. Hankivsky, *The Dome of Silence: Sexual harassment and abuse in sport,* Halifax, Nova Scotia, Fernwood Publishing, 2000.
4. Leahy, T., G. Pretty and G. Tenenbaum, 'Prevalence of sexual abuse in organised competitive sport in Australia', *Journal of Sexual Aggression,* 2002:8, 2, pp. 16-35.
5. Higgins, D.J. and M.P. McCabe, 'Multiple forms of child abuse and neglect: Adult retrospective reports', *Aggression and Violent Behavior,* 2001:6, pp. 547-578.

6. Higgins, D.J. and M.P. McCabe, 'Relationships between different types of abuse during childhood and adjustment in adulthood', *Child Abuse*, 2000:5, pp. 261-272.

7. Hart, S., M. Brassard and H. Karlson, 'Psychological abuse', in: J. Briere, L. Berliner, J. Bulkley, C. Jenny and T. Reid (eds.), *The APSAC Handbook on Child Abuse*, Newbury Park, California, Sage, 1996, pp. 72-89.

8. Jellen, L.K., J.E. McCarroll and L.E. Thayer, 'Child psychological abuse: A 2-year study of US Army cases', *Child Abuse and Neglect*, 2001:25, pp. 623-639.

9. Leahy, T., G. Pretty and G. Tenenbaum, 'A contextualised investigation of traumatic correlates of childhood sexual abuse in Australian athletes', *International Journal of Sport and Exercise Psychology*, 2008:16, 4, pp. 366-384.

10. Brackenridge, C.H., *Spoilsports: Understanding and preventing sexual exploitation in sport*, London, Routledge, 2001.

11. Leahy, T., 'Preventing the sexual abuse of young people in Australian sport', *The Sport Educator,* 2001:13, pp. 28-31.

12. Toftgaard-Nielson, J., 'The forbidden zone: Intimacy, sexual relations and misconduct in the relationship between coaches and athletes', *International Review for the Sociology of Sport*, 2000:136, pp. 165-183.

13. Leahy, T., G. Pretty and G. Tenenbaum, 'Perpetrator methodology as a predictor of traumatic symptomatology in adult survivors of childhood sexual abuse', *Journal of Interpersonal Violence*, 2004:19, pp. 521-540.

14. Herman, J. L., *Trauma and Recovery. From domestic abuse to political terror*, 2nd ed., New York, Basic Books, 1997.

15. Palmer, S.E., R.A. Brown, N.I. Rae-Grant and M.J. Loughlin, 'Responding to children's disclosure of familial abuse: What survivors tell us', *Child Welfare*, 1999:78, pp. 259-283.

16. Leahy, T., G. Pretty and G. Tenenbaum, 'Childhood sexual abuse narratives in clinically and non-clinically distressed adult survivors', *Professional Psychology: Research and Practice*, 2003:34, pp. 57-665.

CHAPTER 18. SEXUAL HARASSMENT AND ABUSE IN SPORT IN THE NETHERLANDS

Petra Moget, Maarten Weber and Nicolette van Veldhoven

In evaluating the policy to prevent sexual harassment and abuse in sport in the Netherlands, 1996 was a crucial year: Three elite athletes announced that their coach had sexually abused them. The response from the sport world was unprecedented. Along with public repudiation of the coach's actions came a call for measures to prevent new incidents. This is remarkable because similar incidents reported in earlier years had met with little or no response. Attempts by sport organizations to create policies to prevent sexual abuse had failed due to lack of support for this specific and unfamiliar area of policy.

After the incident, the National Olympic Committee*National Sports Federation (NOC*NSF) initiated development of an abuse prevention policy for all organized sports. To create a strong foundation for the policy, research was conducted on risk factors that contribute to sexual harassment and abuse in sports, especially on relationships characterized by power differences, most noticeably the coach/athlete relationship. This was the first research into the nature and extent of sexual harassment and abuse in Netherlands' sport.

The results were published in 1997 and, together with athlete reports, became the basis of the policy developed by NOC*NSF.[1] The results of the study and the early abuse cases had a major impact on the policy development process. (It is noteworthy, however, that there has been no follow-up to the 1997 study.)

Research Design

The incidents reported in 1996 led the sports world to call for a preventive policy. Because this was a new area of research, it was decided to begin by investigating the risk factors. After a literature study, researcher Marianne Cense formulated a model in 1997 of risk factors for sexual harassment and abuse in sports,[2] based on non-sport theories, such as 'The four preconditions for abuse' by Finkelhor and 'The cycle of offending' by Wolf.[3, 4] Existing sport-specific theories from studies by Brackenridge were also used.[5-7]

Because the theoretical model was based on studies conducted outside sport, Cense tested it by interviewing 16 former athletes who had experienced sexual abuse in their sport. The results contributed to the final explanatory model, which is based on the idea that several sequential phases precede sexual abuse of children and young adults.[8] These are:

1. Motivation;
2. Overcoming internal inhibitions;
3. Overcoming external inhibitions;
4. Overcoming the athlete's resistance.

Cense identified three clusters of risk factors, associated with the coach, the sport situation and the athlete, and described the indicators for them at each stage. The indicators are the danger signals for each risk factor.

The original model was largely confirmed by the results of the interviews and informed the final version of the model for explaining sexual abuse of children and young adults in sport. Below are examples of indicators for each risk factor.[9, 10]

Key Findings

The coach as risk factor

In order to abuse someone, the potential abuser must be motivated to abuse (phase 1), but strong motivation does not automatically result in abuse. The abuser has to set aside his/her inner inhibitions (phase 2). Feelings of inferiority and disruptive sexual relationships play a part in both stages, as can socio-cultural indicators such as a lack of punitive measures within the sport.

The sport situation as risk factor

By supervising and protecting the athlete the sport environment creates external inhibitions for the abuser that have to be overcome (phase 3). The erosion of social networks and lack of social support from the environment are clear risk indicators, as is the internal culture of the sport, which tends to venerate coaches and accept their behaviour without question.

The athlete as risk factor

The last step of the process is overcoming the resistance of the child. The abuser aims to undermine the defensibility of the athlete, through actions that make the child feel insecure, helpless or abandoned. An athlete's weak social position and low self-esteem are examples of indicators that increase the risk of abuse. A clear indicator is a relationship of extreme dependence on a coach who has excessive control over the life of the athlete.

Continuation and end of the abuse

The interviews gave additional information about abusers' strategies and the process of the abuse as well as the phase after it ended. Sexual abuse may continue for several years; for 7 of the 16 interviewees it went on for two to five years, without the athlete telling anyone or doing anything else to end it. Not recognizing abuse in the early stages and shame and fear of the consequences are important reasons for the athletes' silence. In all cases the athletes had ended the abuse themselves. This was because the coach's power over them decreased or they became less involved in the sport, left home or became involved in a different intimate relationship.

Development of policy

The risk factors identified led the NOC*NSF, together with the sport world, to formulate preventive policy instruments. Victims, their parents, staff of sport organizations and those accused of perpetrating abuse can now call a 24-hour telephone hotline offering advice and support and can be referred to a counsellor, appointed by NOC*NSF.

Other policy instruments focus on the sport situation and the coach. There is an official complaint procedure, and since 2006 an independent institute for sport justice has handled complaints about sexual harassment and abuse. Soon convicted perpetrators will have to be identified on a special register. Information brochures have been published for different target groups such as athletes and clubs, explaining abuse and what to do when confronted with it. The NOC*NSE has also developed an informational website and a movie.

Actions targeting coaching focus on reducing the opportunities for sexual harassment and abuse. One component is a coach education module, 'Etiquette for Coaches'. It stimulates awareness of the relationship between a coach and an athlete, the uneven power balance between them and how teaching techniques can be used to develop athlete autonomy within a safe socio-emotional climate.[11] It is noteworthy that, in practice, sport organizations often limit themselves to the procedural side of prevention, focusing on the risk factor *sport situation* rather than the functioning of relationships between coaches and athletes.

The nature and extent of sexual harassment and abuse

During Cense's study the extent of sexual harassment and abuse in sport remained unclear, leading the NOC*NSF to initiate data gathering in 2005. But its first attempt at a quantitative study, a survey sent to 2,000 people, had a response rate of only 11 per cent, so it was not possible to draw any conclusions.

NOC*NSF now has a database with over 10 years of incident reports (table 3) from the hotline and NOC*NSF counsellors. Solid research of this database could provide a wealth of information. Preliminary analysis shows the following:

- Reports of abuse incidents fluctuate but show an upward trend. The number has ranged from a low of 48 in 2002 to a high of 104 in 2004. The fluctuations seem partly connected to media attention; more media exposure leads to more reports of incidents.

- Reports come from around 20 different sports. On average, about 70 per cent of the victims are female. The nature of the abuse varies from verbal harassment to unwanted touching such as cuddling and kissing to indecent assault, sexual abuse and rape. Over a third of the incidents cover these latter three categories, the most serious forms of sexual harassment and abuse. Over 95 per cent of the victims are below age 20. In almost all cases the alleged abusers are coaches or supervisors, and male.

Table 3. Incidents of sexual harassment and abuse reported to the NOC*NSF hotline

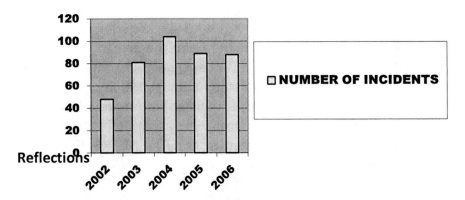

Sexual abuse in sport results from three major risk factors centred around the coach, the sport situation and the athlete. It is clear that most of the research and the prevention policy focus on the sports situation rather than the other risk elements.

To understand this imbalance, it is important to consider the strong influence of the paradigms that are the conceptual basis of the research: Wolf's 'cycle of offending', originally derived from paedophile behaviour, in combination with Finkelhor's 'four preconditions of sexual abuse'.[12] Wolf's cycle of offending suffers a conceptual limitation, specifically portraying the offender's sexual behaviour as (biologically) compulsive, thus leaving no room for socio-cultural interpretations. To overcome this, Brackenridge proposed the 'predator cycle' as an alternative.[13] It not only differs from Wolf's cycle with respect to possible socio-cultural explanations of the perpetrator's behaviour but also in its portrayal of the perpetrator – as confident, successful and power-driven, with good social skills, compared to Wolf's description of the perpetrator as withdrawn, unassertive and with low self-esteem.

The available NOC*NSF data on sexual abusers in sports coincides in many aspects with the perpetrator as a predator. Only a few exceptions resemble Wolf's concept of the paedophile. This shift in approaches makes it possible to include socio-cultural explanations of sexual aggression in sports, but it still under-emphasizes some of the major risks factors.

To understand why, it is necessary to consider a second reason for the imbalance mentioned above: the fact that both socio-cultural and socio-biological explanations are macro-level or general models. This makes them very useful for developing macro policy connected with the risky *sport situation*. But to develop a policy to address the two other major sets of risk factors, *coach* and *athlete*, requires a theory oriented to the micro-level that addresses coaching practice.

Regarding the risk factors associated with the *coach,* such a theory should be able to specify both socio-cultural and socio-biological conditions that differentiate between aggressors and non-aggressors. Such variables are physiological arousal (including both stimulus control and response control), cognitive (thought) processes, lack of impulse control, socialization experiences and personality traits.[14, 15]

A complete understanding of the abuser's behaviour must also address narratives that set out the wider life context of the coach, to explain why one coach misuses his power for sexual abuse and another does not. Such narratives could help to reveal important features of the inner processes by which abusers make decisions to abuse, such as how they overcome their own inhibitions. We suggest that this process is at least partly linked to the way the coach adjusts his moral judgements about his desire to abuse. This moral judgement is directed at (a) his intention to abuse, (b) the act of abuse itself and (c) the consequences of the abuse. Knowledge about this process could inform preventive and prohibitive measures by addressing moral reasoning explicitly.[16] For example, educating coaches about the devastating effects of sexual abuse could decrease the likelihood of them perpetrating sexually aggressive acts.[17] This line of research could, therefore, give more insight about the risk factors associated with the *coach*.

Further knowledge about the risk factors associated with the *athlete* could lead to a policy to empower athletes and thus to increase their awareness of and resistance to abuse. For example, elements of an athlete education and abuse prevention programme could include informing athletes about the risks of certain interactions, such as 'grooming' (establishing a relationship of affection and trust in preparation for abuse), about dangerous behaviours by coaches at the different stages of abuse and about how to seek help when they recognize sexual abuse.

A contingency model that addresses socio-cultural, socio-biological *and* individual (social learning) elements in abuse helps to explain all three major areas of risk. Such an approach challenges one of the assumptions of Finkelhor's model, namely the impossibility of influencing the perpetrator's sexual inclinations.

To direct future research and prevention policies, sport should develop a more sophisticated vision of the working relationship between coach and athlete or, more generally, about sport and its pedagogical responsibilities and practices. Such a model not only encompasses core values such as children's rights, children's best interests and independence, as well as the power in sport relationships, but should also provide a framework for evaluating abuse risk factors, the development of behavioural codes in sport and the development and evaluation of preventive policies.

Notes

1. Cense, M., *Rode kaart of carte blanche Risicofactoren voor seksuele intimidatie en seksueel misbruik in de sport (Red Card or Carte Blanche: Risk factors for sexual harassment and abuse in sport)*. Onderzoekrapport, 1997.
2. Ibid.

3. Finkelhor, D., *Child Sexual Abuse: New theory and research*, New York, The Free Press, 1984, and Finkelhor, D. (Ed.), *A Sourcebook on Child Sexual Abuse*, London, Sage, 1986.

4. Wolf, S.C., 'A multi-factor model of deviant sexuality', 1984, paper presented to the Third International Conference on Victimology, Lisbon, cited by D. Fisher in T. Morrison, M. Erooga and R.C. Beckett (eds.), *Sexual Offending Against Children: Assessment and treatment of male abusers*, London, Routledge, 1994.

5. Brackenridge, C.H., 'Fair Play or fair game? Child sexual abuse in sport organisations', *International Review for the Sociology of Sport*, 1994:29, pp. 287-299.

6. Brackenridge, C.H., 'Educating for child protection in sport', paper presented to the Leisure Studies Association Conference, Eastbourne, United Kingdom, 12 -14 September 1995.

7. Brackenridge, C.H., "'He owned me basically... ': Women's experience of sexual abuse in sport, *International Review for the Sociology of Sport*, 1997, 32:2, pp. 115-30.

8. The explanatory model by M. Cense (op. cit) is a continuing process – see C.H. Brackenridge, 'Researching sexual abuse and sexual harassment in sport', in: G. Clarke and B. Humberstone (eds.), *Researching Women in Sport*, London, Macmillan, 1997, and M. Cense and C.H. Brackenridge, 'Temporal and developmental risk factors for sexual harassment and abuse in sport', *European Physical Education Review*, 2001:7, 1, pp. 61-79. In this chapter terms from the latest developments are used.

9. Cense, M., op. cit.

10. Brackenridge, C.H., *Spoilsports: Understanding and preventing sexual exploitation in sport*, London, Routledge, 2001.

11. Moget, P.C.M. and M. Weber, *The independent athlete. Educational guidelines for training and coaching young athletes*, NOC*NSF, internal publication, 2007.

12. Finkelhor, D., *Child Sexual Abuse: New theory and research*, New York, The Free Press, 1984, and D. Finkelhor (ed.), *A Sourcebook on Child Sexual Abuse*, London, Sage,1986.

13. Brackenridge, C.H., "'He owned me basically...": Women's experience of sexual abuse in sport, *International Review for the Sociology of Sport*, 1997:32, 2:115-130.

14. Hall, G.C.N. and R. Hirschman, 'Toward a theory of sexual aggression: A quadripartite model', *Journal of Consulting and Clinical Psychology*, 1991:59, pp. 662-669.

15. Hall, G.C.N., D.D. Shondrick and R. Hirschman, 'The role of sexual arousal in sexually aggressive behaviour: A meta-analysis', *Journal of Consulting and Clinical Psychology*, 1993:61, pp. 1091-1095.

16. Moget, P.C.M. and M. Weber, 'Project sexual intimidation in sport, NOC*NSF: 1996-2006', *Ethic Perspectives,* 2006:3, pp. 300-311.

17. Hamilton, M. and L. Yee, 'Rape knowledge and propensity to rape', *Journal of Research in Personality*, 1990:24, pp. 111-122.

CHAPTER 19. RISKS AND POSSIBILITIES FOR SEXUAL EXPLOITATION IN THE DANISH SPORT CLUB SYSTEM

Jan Toftegaard Stoeckel

Modern sport is associated with values such as fairness, morality and courage. Historically sport has also been an important arena for teaching children and young people basic moral and societal values. However, the notion of sport as a morally pure institution stands in clear contrast to the growing documentation of critical issues such as doping, corruption and sexual harassment and abuse of athletes by their coaches. The issues of doping and paedophilia have raised questions about ethical standards in sport and caused a moral panic. This has provoked Danish sport clubs to adopt hurriedly the '10 recommendations for preventing sexual abuse', issued by the main sport organizations. Based on assumptions rather than research, these recommendations have tended to put the focus of attention on individual perpetrator pathology rather than the complex nature of interpersonal relations in sport. These recommendations are negotiated within the context of organizational structures and cultures that allow the grooming and exploitation of athletes.

Sport organizations have reacted to the problem of sexual harassment and abuse by coaches by developing case-handling procedures and brochures, fact sheets and recommendations. But the responsibility for developing adequate child protection standards has been left entirely to local sport clubs. Until now, the development of child protection strategies or action plans has not been a priority for Denmark's national governing bodies. Their justification is that initiatives should correspond to the size of the problem, which is currently perceived to be small. Before the study reported below, no empirical research had been conducted to support or challenge claims about child safety in voluntary youth sport clubs, and very little was known about the prevalence of sexual harassment and abuse in sport.

Since the mid-1980s researchers from various countries and scientific fields have sought to investigate the scope and context of sexual exploitation in sport. These studies include both qualitative investigations and quantitative surveys. While the quantitative studies mostly have been used to document the prevalence of various abusive behaviours, the qualitative studies have been used to gather descriptions of harassment and abuse experiences among athletes who experienced exploitation by their coaches, typically around puberty.[1] The focus has typically been on investigating abuse dynamics and individual risk factors, and few empirical studies have been conducted with coaches and sport clubs. This chapter presents the results of the first study on child protection issues among voluntary youth sport clubs in Denmark.

Researchers largely agree that sexual exploitation stems from power imbalances rooted in organizational cultures and structures that allow harassment and abuse. Study of risk factors has led to theories focusing on the context. According to Brackenridge's contingency model (2001), the overall risk of sexual exploitation depends on the risk level related to coach determination, athlete vulnerability and sport opportunity.[2] Sport opportunity is not only a question of situational risks, such as absence of other adults at a training session or the athlete coming to the coach in desperation or admiration. It also relates to the wider cultural practices and organizational structures found in sport.

A study undertaken among 396 sports clubs in England in 2001 addressed child protection awareness, attitudes and experiences in sport. It found that awareness of the main child protection issues varied greatly. It discovered that "there was a clear misapprehension among sport clubs that children are safest amongst those whom they know best and most at risk in relation to strangers outside the clubs".[3] It also found that "… the unwillingness of club personnel to challenge their own assumptions is causally linked to a culture of complacency about child protection in voluntary sport".[4]

A Danish study of identity in sport supports the theoretical grounding behind these findings. The study reveals sport as a cultural institution with norms and standards that differ from those found in the rest of society.[5] Mortensen found that the general purpose of sport can be summed up under the three major headings: 'voluntary work', 'comradeship' and 'getting the young people away from the street corners'. Because sport in Denmark is perceived as 'good' and based on voluntarism, it has been able to operate with a high level of autonomy, which has protected it against public interference, regulation and bureaucracy.

Traditionally, proponents have argued that participation in voluntary sport was the best way to ensure moral standards and social inclusion and teach democratic values.[6] By keeping children and young people off the streets and teaching discipline and social skills through athletics, organized sport has been seen as not only helping to prevent crime and social decay but also securing enlightenment, mental strength and physical health. Amateur sport has received massive public funding almost without conditions. Sport clubs have claimed autonomy to such a degree that national sport governing bodies find it unpleasant and difficult to introduce child protection policies, rules and procedures.

Research Design

The aim of the sport club study was to investigate awareness, knowledge, attitudes and experiences with regard to child protection and sexual abuse. A semi-structured questionnaire was conducted among 2,062 youth sport clubs along with 10 follow-up group interviews with board members from clubs that had faced allegations or formal complaints.[7] Selection criteria for the sport clubs were aimed at reaching 20 per cent of youth athletes in Denmark and creating a representative sample of small and large clubs within the 30 biggest sports. Twenty four sport clubs with previous abuse cases were included in the sample, as well as 106 sport clubs certified as 'healthy sport clubs for children'.[8]

Due to the sensitivity and complexity of sexual abuse, strict ethical procedures were followed throughout the research. Permission to conduct the survey was obtained by the Danish Sport Confederation, and the 30 different sports were notified in advance of the study. A separate note followed the questionnaire stating the exact purpose of the study along with a guarantee of full anonymity for participating clubs. On the last page of the questionnaire the clubs could indicate whether they wished to participate in a follow-up interview. Ten interviews were conducted, typically involving two or more members of the club board. All interviewees agreed to the taping and transcribing of the interviews.

A representative sample of 48 per cent (958 responses) returned the questionnaire before the deadline, a satisfactory response rate given the sensitivity of the study. The questionnaires were electronically scanned and converted to an SPSS data file. All text strings were typed into a separate spreadsheet and treated manually according to a thematic content analysis.

The 37-item questionnaire consisted of three parts. The first part contained general questions about the club and its members and coaches, followed by questions about coach recruiting procedures. The second part included questions about prior discussion of ethical norms, standards or guidelines with regard to coach-athlete behaviour. The third part contained questions about case knowledge, response procedures, handling of past allegations and complaints, and attitudes towards child protection measures.

Key Findings

Results from the questionnaires and the interviews revealed that 8 per cent of sport clubs knew of sexual abuse incidents in their own clubs. Generally, clubs agreed that preventing sexual abuse in sport was more important than the problems of eating disorders, doping and fair play. Accordingly, 60 per cent of clubs (575) said they had discussed the appropriate tone and behaviour in their clubs. Of these clubs 80 per cent (460) said that their board had involved coaches in this discussion, 25 per cent had involved members and 10 per cent had involved external experts. Forty seven per cent of all the responding sport clubs said they had informal norms, 21 per cent reported written norms and 15 per cent said they had formal ethical guidelines covering interpersonal behaviour. Further analysis showed that clubs with written norms were twice as likely to disseminate their norms to coaches, athletes, parents and others.

These findings indicated that clubs generally were aware of the risk of abuse between coaches/leaders and athletes. However, the depth of the discussions of moral behaviour and norms seemed to vary greatly between clubs. Surprisingly, 175 clubs that claimed they had discussed tone and behaviour had not had any discussions regarding the consumption of alcohol. Fifty-four per cent of the responding clubs had discussed a policy regarding alcohol consumption in or around the club domain.

Generally, the sport clubs seemed reluctant to ask for personal or formal qualifications when selecting new coaches. Only occasionally had clubs arranged formal interviews and asked for personal or educational qualifications. As shown in table 4, sport clubs generally demonstrated reluctance to hire coaches who had been involved with child abuse, drunk driving or drug possession or abuse; 87 per cent of responding clubs said they would not hire a leader or coach if he/she had a criminal record for child abuse.[9] The interviews revealed that clubs were less likely to ask about alcohol convictions and drug abuse than to ask permission to obtain a criminal record check regarding sexual offences.

Table 4. Willingness of sport clubs to overlook past offences by coach applicants

Would you hire a coach/instructor if you knew he or she had ...	Yes	No	Not sure	Missing
A criminal conviction for drunk driving	36	42	11	11
Used doping	3	64	22	11
Been in possession of drugs	2	70	17	11
				1
A criminal conviction for child abuse	>1	87	2	1

Table 5. Comparison of child protection measures among clubs with and without past abuse cases

Has your club...	Clubs with past abuse cases (78)	Clubs without past abuse cases* (767)
Discussed norms for verbal and physical behaviour?	78%	63%
Written standards for verbal and physical behaviour?	35%	21%
Verbal or written ethical guidelines for coaches/ instructors?	35%	15%
Discussed the rules for alcohol or substance use?	69%	6%
Discussed procedure for case handling (of abuse cases)?	61%	25%
Written procedures for case handling (of abuse cases)?	9%	3%
All of the above**	9%	0.5%

* This figure is entirely based on the answers given in the self-administered questionnaire and should therefore be considered a minimum figure.
** The figures in this row have been generated from calculations

Just 5 per cent of clubs reported that they would ask new, unknown coaches for permission to make criminal record checks regarding past sexual crimes. With known coaches this figure was only 2 per cent. The gap between attitude and actions underscores the widespread misapprehension that 'it' (sexual abuse) could not happen in their own club. Interviewee comments reflected this: "...we all know each other well, and have done so for years" or "...there are always other adults present during training, so it cannot happen here".

But clubs that had experienced cases of sexual abuse appeared to have a different and more rational approach. As shown in table 5, sport clubs with past case histories of abuse were much more likely to ask coaches for criminal record checks and personnel recommendations and to ask about formal qualifications than were clubs without previous cases. Furthermore, clubs with previous abuse cases were less worried that asking for permission to obtain a criminal record check would scare away voluntary coaches.

Reflections

The findings reflect a paradox: While 8 per cent of sport clubs knew of sexual abuse cases, and more than 9 out of 10 agreed that preventing it was the most important prevention field in sport, only 15 per cent of these clubs had written guidelines for coaches. This incongruence between attitudes and actions may indicate that many sport clubs avoid child protection initiatives due to complacency and ignorance about abuse dynamics. The fact that 70 per cent of the responding clubs had informal norms about interpersonal behaviour and only 60 per cent said they had discussed such norms may indicate that sport clubs prefer to have informal agreements rather than written regulations and to leave things unsaid, thinking such measures are unnecessary or even expressions of distrust. The differences between the clubs that had experienced previous cases and those that had not was remarkable; the former were twice as likely to have written guidelines and three times as likely to have written case procedures.

The results replicate past findings by Brackenridge in a smaller English sample, indicating that results can be generalized to other countries or at least serve as a benchmark. Since completion of this study, Denmark has instituted rules requiring criminal record checks for all new staff in all sectors of society where adults work with children. This legislation has been approved and recommended by the national governing bodies of sport: the majority of clubs now comply with this procedure, in contrast to less than 5 per cent in 2003. This may reinforce the need for sport organizations to have clear child protection policies for guiding youth sport clubs, especially given that members generally have little knowledge about how to develop effective child protection measures. It is unfair that children should pay the price of adult vanity and complacency. This research underscores the fact that all parts of organized sport have an important role to play in developing safe and healthy sport environments.

Notes

1. Fasting, K., C.H. Brackenridge and K. Walseth, 'Consequences of sexual harassment in sport for female athletes', *Journal of Sexual Aggression*, 2002:8, 2, pp.37-48.
2. Brackenridge, C.H., *Spoilsports: Understanding and preventing sexual exploitation in sport*, 2001, pp. 135-145.
3. Brackenridge, C.H., '"… so what?" Attitudes of the voluntary sector towards child protection in sports clubs', *Managing Leisure*, 2001:7, 2, pp. 103-124.
4. Brackenridge, C.H., ibid.
5. Mortensen, M., *Idræt som kommunal velfærd, Mentalitet, velfærd og idrætspolitik i København, 1870-1970* (Sport as public welfare, mentality, welfare and sports policy of Copenhagen, 1870-1970), Ph.D., Institut for Idræt (Institute of Sport Sciences), Københavns Universitet (University of Copenhagen), 2004.
6. Jørgensen, P., 'Ikke at more, men at opdrage (not to amuse but to bring up)' in: I. Sørensen and P. Jørgense., (eds.) *Een time dagligen – skoleidræt gennem 200 år (One hour a day – school sport through 200 years)*, Odense Universitetsforlag, 2000.
7. A total of approximately 6,500 clubs offer children's sports, according to the National Sport Confederation (Danmarks Idræts-Forbund).
8. Certification called "Et godt idrætsmiljø for born" (a good sport environment for children), made by the National Sport Confederation (Danmarks Idræts-Forbund) in the period 1998-2003.
9. The criminal record checks available for sport clubs only cover sexual offences committed against children under 15 years of age.

CHAPTER 20. SEXUAL HARASSMENT OF FEMALE ATHLETES IN THE CZECH REPUBLIC

Kari Fasting, Trine Thoresen and Nadia Knorre

This chapter presents results extracted from a study of female athletes in the Czech Republic. Since gender relations in society may influence women's participation and experiences in sport, it first presents statistics about gender relations in the Czech Republic as well as some of the legislation concerning equal rights and sexual harassment. We think it is important to interpret and understand the results of the study within this wider context.

The Czech Republic of today is a very young state, founded in 1993. From 1948 until the 'velvet revolution' in 1989 it was a totalitarian communist state under the Soviet Union. In this period the emancipation of women became a part of the political doctrine. This is perhaps the most significant reason why many people today do not see the need to actively pursue equal opportunities for girls and women.

Research shows conclusively that women and men do not have equal opportunities, either in sport or in society at large, yet still many believe that they do. For example, the unemployment rate among women is 40 per cent higher than among men, and women's salaries average only 73 per cent of men's, despite the fact that women have as much education as men.[1] Only 17 per cent of representatives in the Czech Parliament are women, and in higher levels of government women are no more than 12 per cent. These statistics are much lower than most European countries. The gender distribution in political leadership is mirrored in sport organizations – only 8 per cent of all the executive committee members across the various Czech sport federations are women.[2]

Various laws protect against discrimination based on sex, but the country does not yet have a specific gender equity law.[3] In 2004, however, an amendment to the labour code took effect making sexual harassment in the workplace illegal. This change brings the labour code into line with that of other European Union nations.

Every year 30 to 40 children in the Czech Republic die because of physical violence. Violence against women is looked upon as a natural and common part of women's lives, and abused women are often accused of being responsible for the abuse themselves.[4] In 2006, for the first time ever, a coach was sentenced for having sexually abused two girls in sport.

Research Design

In 2001 the Women and Sport Committee of the Czech Olympic Committee, in cooperation with the Czech Sport Union, initiated a research project addressing women in sport. The goal was to assess the present role and situation of women in sport and in sport organizations. The project's stated aim was to develop knowledge about the influence and the meaning of gender relations in the lives of female athletes.

One of the research questions was designed to survey the amount of harassment experienced by female athletes, and it represents the only 'study' done in Czech sport on this subject to date. The participants, 595 female athletes and exercisers from 68 sport disciplines from all areas of the country, answered a structured questionnaire. The respondents ranged from 15 to 55 years old, with an average age of 23 years. A total of 226 participants were under 21 years old. A semi-structured interview was also conducted with nine elite-level athletes who had been sexually harassed by a coach.

For analytical purposes the participants were divided into three groups: elite-level athletes (229), non-elite-level athletes (224) and exercisers (142). To be considered elite, the athletes had to practise at least four times a week and have participated either at the international level during the past two years or in the Olympic Games, world championship or European championship. The non-elite group consisted of athletes who were competing but did not qualify for the elite group. The exercisers were those who practised sport but did not compete. The elite athletes were the youngest (average age of 22 years) and the exercisers the oldest (average age 24 years).

Key Findings

Physical harassment

Though this study primarily surveyed experiences of sexual harassment, the questionnaire contained one question about experiences of physical harassment: "Have you ever been slapped on the face, head or ears by a coach, teacher or a member of a sport management team?" A total of 53 athletes (9 per cent) answered yes. More of the elite athletes had been slapped compared with the two other groups. One of the interviewees described how physical punishment was used to create fear:

> "We got different kinds of slaps and I think that the main meaning with this was that they wanted us to be afraid. They wanted to endanger us ... the coaches do this as a form of punishment, and we never ... we never perceived it as a fair punishment. It was of course different with different coaches I have had through my life, but it's clear especially in my sport, which I participated up until my 19th year, that the coaches directed all my life. They decided everything – for example, we were forbidden to take a holiday with our family."[5]

The female athletes were also asked if they had ever experienced certain situations described as follows:

a) "Unwanted physical contact, body contact (for example pinching, hugging, fondling, being kissed against your will, etc.)"

b) "Repeated unwanted sexually suggestive glances, comments, teasing and jokes, about your body, your clothes, your private life, etc."

c) "Ridiculing of your sport performance and of you as an athlete because of your gender or your sexuality (for example, 'Soccer is not suitable for girls')."

For each question the participants were asked to indicate whether the behaviour had been perpetrated by a male or female coach, a male or female athlete, a male or female member of the management team, a male or female teacher, a male or female student, or a male or female family member, or from other males or females outside sport. In presenting the results, "experience of sexual harassment" means that a subject marked one or more forms of sexual harassment; it does not indicate the severity, frequency or total number of these experiences.

Almost half of the participants (45 per cent) had experienced sexual harassment by someone in sport. This means that the participants had marked one or more of the three harassing behaviours, either by a coach, an athlete or a member of the management team. The chance of being harassed by someone inside sport increased with performance level, from 33 per cent among the exercisers to 55 per cent among the elite athletes. The perpetrators of sexual harassment had been:

- Another athlete: 30 per cent of respondents;
- A coach: 27 per cent of respondents;
- One or more managers: 9 per cent.

Further analysis of the subgroups revealed that the highest percentage (38 per cent) was found among the elite-level athletes who had been harassed by a coach.

The most commonly experienced harassing behaviours were:

- "Repeated unwanted sexually suggestive glances, comments, teasing and jokes, about your body, your clothes, your private life etc." – 33 per cent;
- "Ridiculing of your sport performance and of you as an athlete because of your gender or your sexuality (for example, 'Soccer is not suitable for girls')" – 21 per cent;
- "Unwanted physical contact, body contact (for example pinching, hugging, fondling, being kissed against your will etc.)" – 14 per cent.

As an example of this last category one athlete told the following story:

> "It happens quite often that people try to hug people, but with this particular coach it is very clear that it was in a sexual context, so you have to be really insistent to keep him away from yourself. I experienced it as unpleasant … It mainly happens during the training where he uses opportunities like when someone is coming to practice and he comes to hug and says 'I'm really glad to see you'. But during the hug he can move his hands on the body, which is unpleasant."

Among the nine interviewees who had been harassed by their coaches the average age at interview was 24.6 years old. They spent a lot of time in their sport; in addition to competition, they practised an average of 29.5 hours per week.[6] But, consistent with other studies, many of their bad experiences had taken place when they were quite young, although no precise age data were collected. Though the interview focussed on their experiences of sexual harassment, the analyses revealed an abusive sport culture, illustrated by the following quotes from these young women:

> "When I was not getting as good achievements as we both would like, I would hear comments like I can't run, or that I'm clumsy. Also I heard from him that I should put off some weight and what I should eat or shouldn't eat. And then of course he tried to seduce me as he tried to seduce many other women."

> "And very often we go to tournaments, and there the coach and the male players provoke various games with sexual contact. For example, a game called 'spin the bottle', where you sit in a group and you spin a bottle, and where the bottle points the person is supposed to take off a piece of clothing…"

> "We had the same locker room as our [male] coaches. When you are 12 to 13 years I don't think it is OK. Many jokes were told when we were changing, and many with a sexual content. When you are 13 years of age that is not fun … It happened that we often had 'common showering days'. The coaches suggest then that we shower together and that they wash us girls on the back. This happens quite often. Or they ask if they can shower together with us."

According to Thoresen the transition from the pinching and hugging to a sexual relationship seemed to be quite short, particularly for younger athletes.[7] Many of them had either had, or knew about others who had had, a sexual relationship with their coaches that started when they were 14 to 17 years of age. One told us about a relationship that had lasted for eight or nine years but which had begun when the girl was 14 years of age.

Almost all the participants mentioned that a sexual relationship between a coach and an athlete was quite common. Many also mentioned that many of the coaches only had relationships with athletes they were coaching and that they often changed which of the girls (on the team or in the club) they were having sex with. It was not uncommon for the coaches to be having sex with several girls or young women at the same time. One respondent said, for example:

> "This man has only been together with those girls he has coached. I don't know about any other relationships that he had had. Before the one he lives with now, he lived with one of the other girls he coached."

Reflections

Based on this study, the authors[8] recommended development of a policy for educating and protecting people in sport from sexual harassment. It should help them to:

- Recognize (through education) what is meant by sexual harassment;
- Protect athletes and coaches against sexual harassment;
- Protect coaches against false allegations of sexual harassment;
- Refer concerns about sexual harassment to the authorities;
- Be confident that their concerns and reports will be taken seriously;
- Ensure that coaches or athletes who are proved guilty of harassment are sanctioned.

This has partly been fulfilled; in December 2006, about one year after the study was published, the Women's Committee of the Czech Olympic Committee developed an information brochure about sexual harassment. It was sent to all sport federations that were members of the Czech Olympic Committee.

Though the authors have not found any studies about abusive experiences among Czech children in sport, some of the participants in the study were under 18 years of age, a group that was particularly numerous at the elite level. Among the three groups, the elite-level athletes had experienced the most sexual harassment. There is therefore a strong need in the Czech Republic for research focusing on the experiences of children in sport.

Notes

1. Benninger-Budel, C. and J. Hudecova, 'Violence against women in the Czech Republic', report prepared by prepared by World Organisation Against Torture for the 28th Session of the United Nations Committee on Economic, Social and Cultural Rights, 2005.
2. Fasting, K. and N. Knorre, *Women in Sport in the Czech Republic: The experience of female athletes*, Norwegian School of Sport Sciences & Czech Olympic Committee, Oslo and Prague, 2005.
3. Marksova-Tominova, M., 'Gender equality and EU accession: The situation in the Czech Republic', information sheet from Women in Development Europe based on the Gender Assessment Report produced by KARAT (a regional coalition working on women's issues in Eastern and Central Europe) (https://nihsrvv20-3.nih.no/exchweb/bin/redir.asp?URL=https://nihsrvv20-3.nih.no/exchange/Kari.Fasting/Kladd/VS:%2520%257BDisarmed%257D%2520U NICEF%2520book%2520queries.EML/1_text.htm%23_msocom_3) as part of the UNIFEM-sponsored project 'Gender and Economic Justice in European Accession and Integration', 2003.
4. World Health Organization (WHO), 'Highlight on women's health in the Czech Republic', WHO Regional Office for Europe, Copenhagen, 2000.

5. Thoresen, T., 'Fra spøk til alvor' – Kommunikasjon mellom kvinnelige idrettsutøvere og deres trenere – en kvalitativ studie' ('From jokes to serious talk – communication between female athletes and their coaches'), unpublished master's thesis, Norwegian School of Sport Sciences, Oslo, 2007.
6. Thoresen, T., ibid.
7. Thoresen, T., op cit.
8. Fasting and Knorre, op. cit.

CHAPTER 21. PERCEPTIONS AND PREVALANCE OF SEXUAL HARASSMENT AMONG FEMALE STUDENT-ATHLETES IN FLANDERS, BELGIUM[1, 2]

Yves Vanden Auweele, Joke Opdenacker, Tine Vertommen, Filip Boen, Leon van Niekerk, Kristine De Martelaer and Bert De Cuyper

In all definitions of sexual harassment and abuse in sport, the athlete's 'perception' of a coach's sexual attention, rather than the coach's 'intention', has become the standard. The notion of perceived acceptability implies possible variation according to norms, influenced by such factors as gender and culture. It also implies a continuum of coach behaviour, from behaviour with no perceived sexual connotation[3] to behaviour that is clearly sexual harassment or sexual abuse.[4-7] The prevalence rates for harassment and abuse reported in the international research literature lie between 20 and 50 per cent. These figures have to be interpreted with caution as they result from research that varies in definitions, categorizations, samples and response rates.

No data about sexual harassment in sport were available from Belgium, so the main purpose of the study presented here was to quantify the reported prevalence of 'unwanted' sexual experiences among female student-athletes in the Flemish part of Belgium. Our study focused on student-athletes in universities with different philosophical orientations. (This followed reporting of a pilot study at the Catholic University of Leuven suggesting the possibility of low tolerance of sexual issues due to the stringent Catholic environment. It was thus hypothesized that a higher level of tolerance among student-athletes in a secular, more liberal environment might result in higher prevalence.)

Research Design

Survey Instrument

A survey was developed listing 35 coach behaviours, noted from previous research, that might or might not challenge the athletes' critical personal boundaries (see table 6).[8-11] The participants were asked to answer two questions with respect to each behaviour. First, they were asked to rate their perception of the acceptability of the coach's behaviour on a five-point rating scale. Specific labels were used for each score: 1, the behaviour is completely acceptable; 2, the behaviour is acceptable with reservations; 3, the behaviour is unacceptable but not so serious; 4, the behaviour is unacceptable and serious; and 5, the behaviour is unacceptable and very serious. Second, they were asked to indicate how frequently they had personally experienced the behaviour, also on a five-point scale: 0, never; 1, once; 2, two to three times; 3, often (five to ten times); 4, very often (at least once a week); and 5, always.

Participants

The questions were posted in 2005 and 2006 on an Internet page of the Catholic University Leuven (K.U.Leuven) and the Free University Brussel (VUB), known for its free-thinking, liberal, secular orientation. The K.U.Leuven sample consisted of 291 athletes aged 18-21 years. The VUB sample consisted of 144 respondents aged 18 to 19 years.

Statistical analysis

Different thresholds were defined for each item. All items were grouped with a cut-off mean score of minimum 4.50 and a standard deviation of less than 1 in a category 'very serious and unacceptable behaviour'. A second category, with a mean score of 3.50 and a variance around or above 1, was defined as 'serious and unacceptable'. The third category was named 'unacceptable but not serious' behaviour if the mean score was below 3.50 and above 2.50 with a variance higher than one. A fourth category was named 'acceptable behaviour', having a cut-off score being beneath 2.50 and a low variance.

Means and standard deviations, both at item and category level, describe the athletes' perceived acceptance of each of the 35 coach behaviours. The reported prevalence is described below in percentages: no experience versus at least one incident. Independent sample T-tests were used to compare the perceptions at item level. The Chi-square statistic was used to compare the reported prevalence of the experiences at both item and category level.

Findings

The reported prevalence figures of the coach behaviours revealed a considerable resemblance between the two universities; no statistically significant differences emerged between the two student samples (see table 6).

Table 6. Perceptions and experiences of coach behaviours, K.U.Leuven and VUB students

Coach behaviour	Perceptions		Experiences	
Your coach...	Leuven (N=291)	Brussels (N=144)	Leuven (N=291)	Brussels (N=144)
	Mean (SD)	Mean (SD)	Per cent	Per cent
16. Proposes a sexual encounter, promising a reward in return	4.97 (0.31)	4.69 (0.79)**	1.4%	1.4%
34. Touches your private parts or forces you to touch someone else's	4.95 (0.34)	4.62 (0.75)**	1.8%	2.8%
18. Shows you his/her private parts	4.95 (0.35)	4.71 (0.79)**	1.1%	2.8%
8. Proposes sexual encounter and issues threats for rejection	4.95 (0.41)	4.76 (0.79)*	1.8%	1.4%
5. Stares at you during showering	4.71 (0.70)	4.30 (1.01)**	3.9%	6.9%

142

Coach behaviour	Perceptions		Experiences	
Your coach...	Leuven (N=291)	Brussels (N=144)	Leuven (N=291)	Brussels (N=144)
	Mean (SD)	Mean (SD)	Per cent	Per cent
20. Kisses you or embraces you with a sexual undertone	4.66 (0.63)	3.75 (0.87)**	3.5	7.1
37. Kisses you on your mouth	4.65 (0.67)	4.24 (0.91)**	3.6	2.8
10. Showers with you and the other members of the team	4.46 (1.03)	3.79 (1.29)**	5.3	9.1
17. Makes a sexual remark about you	4.20 (0.81)	3.47 (0.90)**	11.4	21.8*
25. Gives you a massage on the front side of your body	4.05 (1.08)	3.34 (1.08)**	5.0	7.7
31. Stares at your breasts/buttocks/pubic area	4.02 (0.90)	3.31 (0.85)**	15.0	20.6
30. Asks you about your personal sex life, private sexual matters	4.01 (0.93)	3.42 (0.88)**	9.2	12.7
38. Touches you unnecessarily, deliberately (not instruction related)	3.99 (0.99)	3.47 (0.87)**	13.6	12.7
40. Has an intimate relationship with an athlete below 18 years of age	3.97 (1.23)	3.93 (1.04)	7.9	3.5
6. Gives you a (romantic) present	3.93 (1.00)	3.51 (1.00)**	4.9	9.8
14. Flirts with you and/or others in your team	3.91 (1.01)	3.35 (0.98)**	19.5	28.5*
33. Comes into your locker room before the time agreed	3.72 (1.07)	3.31 (0.89)**	13.9	21.3%
26. Sleeps in your room during tournaments	3.39 (1.24)	2.95 (1.10)**	7.1	8.6
36. Asks you about your menstruation	3.30 (1.26)	2.66 (0.96)**	16.4	23.2
27. Tells dirty jokes or stories	3.33 (1.03)	3.05 (0.81)*	13.9	14.1
39. Calls you at home about matters unrelated to sport	3.26 (1.23)	2.79 (0.90)**	14.6	19.9
28. Invites you to the movies, dinner, etc.	3.18 (1.13)	2.79 (0.96)**	13.1	18.3
24. Gives you a massage on the back side of your body	3.18 (1.27)	2.61 (1.02)**	17.7	27.5*
9. Becomes a second family (surrogate parent).	3.08 (1.11)	2.71 (0.93)**	17.8	21.7

Coach behaviour	Perceptions		Experiences	
Your coach...	Leuven (N=291)	Brussels (N=144)	Leuven (N=291)	Brussels (N=144)
	Mean (SD)	Mean (SD)	Per cent	Per cent
21. Compliments or makes comments about your figure.	2.99 (1.07)	2.43 (0.75)**	42.0	54.9*
13. Invites you home under pretext of sport matters	2.90 (1.29)	2.94 (0.99)	16.7	15.3
4. Comments on your physical appearance	2.73 (0.98)	2.54 (0.86)*	46.8	57.6*
22. Makes sexist jokes	2.56 (1.07)	2.31 (0.69)*	46.8	47.2
15. Shows more attention to an individual athlete (instruction related)	2.46 (1.10)	2.33 (0.71)	65.0	70.4
32. Compliments your clothing	2.35 (0.99)	2.11 (0.70)*	37.9	52.1*
41. Has an intimate relationship with an athlete above 18 years of age	2.35 (1.26)	2.39 (0.95)	19.8	19.1
3. Makes stereotypical/derogatory remarks on men and women	2.28 (0.84)	2.29 (0.76)	58.7	65.3
2. Stands/sits close to you while giving instruction	1.37 (0.60)	1.67 (0.59)**	87.8	81.3
1. Gives you a lift in his car	1.10 (0.39)	1.21 (0.44)*	79.8	76.4

Statistical significance figures: *p < .05; **p < .05/35 = .0014 (after correction) –> Significant differences between the two groups as result from *t*-test (perception) or χ^2 (experience). N = number of respondents.

Note: Items are ranked according to the K.U.Leuven students' mean perceptions on the acceptability of the coaches' behaviour.

However, K.U.Leuven students' perception scores differed significantly from those of VUB students on all but four items. VUB students systematically perceived the same coach behaviours as less unacceptable when compared with K.U.Leuven students.

In an effort to go beyond item level and get a more comprehensive view of the reported prevalence of unwanted sexual behaviour, we took into account the grouping of the items according to the differences in perceptions between the universities (see table 7).

Table 7. Experiences per coach abuse category according to the perceptions of students from K.U.Leuven and VUB

Category	Experience (Per cent who experienced at least one behaviour in the category)		
	Leuven (N=291) (per cent)	Brussels (N=144) (per cent)	p*
Categories according to the perceptions of KULeuven students			
Very serious and unacceptable: Items 16, 34, 18, 8, 20, 5, 37	7.9	13.7	0.080
Serious and unacceptable: Items 10, 17, 31, 38, 25, 40, 30, 14, 6, 33	44.2	50.4	0.252
Unacceptable but not serious: Items 35, 26, 27, 24, 36, 39, 28, 9, 21, 13, 4, 22	74.8	83.2	0.061
Acceptable behaviour: Items 15, 32, 3, 41, 2, 1	98.9	98.6	1.000
Very serious and unacceptable: Items 8, 18, 16, 34	2.1	4.9	0.139
Serious and unacceptable: Items 5, 37, 40, 10, 20	17.2	19.6	0.589
Unacceptable but not serious: Items 25, 17, 31, 30, 38, 6, 14, 33, 35, 26, 36, 27, 28, 24, 9, 13, 4	72.7	81.1	0.084
Acceptable behaviour: Items 21, 22, 15, 32, 41, 3, 2, 1	98.9	98.6	1.000

* Result (2-sided) from χ^2 between the two groups
Note: The cut-off mean scores to differentiate between the categories were 4.5, 3.5 and 2.5. N = number of respondents.

Table 7 reveals that K.U. Leuven students perceived more behaviours as serious and unacceptable than did VUB students. The latter perceived more coach behaviours to be in the unacceptable but not serious zone. We then assessed whether the grouping of the items according to the same cut-off scores in both universities revealed other frequencies of experiences. Using the more tolerant VUB norms, very serious and unacceptable behaviour was reported only by 2.1 per cent of the K.U.Leuven students and 4.9 per cent of the VUB students. Serious and unacceptable behaviour was reported by 17.2 per cent of the K.U.Leuven students and 19.6 per cent of the VUB students (table 7).

Reflections

Despite important differences in perceptions of what is unacceptable, there were no significant differences at item level in the reported prevalence of coach behaviours between the two samples. Major differences in reported prevalence only appeared after the behaviours were grouped according to the respective perceptions of K.U.Leuven or VUB students.

The explanation for the differences in perceptions may lie in the different philosophical orientations of the two universities, exemplified in the different type of student who chooses each university and the different curricula. None of the reported differences, however, reached the normal threshold for statistical significance in the social sciences ($p < 0.05$). The most important finding to emerge from this study, therefore, is that differences in perception made no difference when it came to reported prevalence. This has important political implications since it suggests that perceived abuse cannot be attributed merely to the sensitivity of certain kinds of female athletes.

The figures based on the most tolerant perception revealed an alarming 20 per cent prevalence of reported serious and unacceptable behaviour from the coach. Moreover, if the athlete's perspective is considered an indicator of inflicted harm, it is important not to take the most tolerant perception as a reference. Prevalence figures of unacceptable and serious coach behaviour in Flanders/Belgium vary between 20 per cent and 50 per cent. Although we are aware of difficulties related to international comparisons, we conclude that the Flanders/Belgium figures are comparable to those found in the United States, United Kingdom, Australia and the Scandinavian countries. They undoubtedly suggest an evidential trend that sport governing bodies cannot deny.

Notes

1. Flanders is the Dutch-speaking part of Belgium and includes 60 per cent of the population.
2. For their collaboration we would like to thank Jos Feys, Karlien Van Kelst and Christophe Indigne.
3. Although apparently innocent coach behaviour may not be so innocent at all: the grooming process can be used to entrap unsuspecting athletes into sexual cooperation.
4. Brackenridge, C.H., '"He owned me basically..." Women's experience of sexual abuse in sport', *International Review for the Sociology of Sport*, 1997:32, pp. 115-130.

5. Fasting, K., 'Research on sexual harassment and abuse in sport', 2005, available at www.idrottsforum.org/researchers/faskar.html.

6. Fejgin, N. and R. Hanegby, 'Gender and cultural bias in perceptions of sexual harassment in sport', *International Review for the Sociology of Sport*, 2001:36, pp. 459-478.

7. Leahy, T., G. Pretty and G. Tenenbaum, 'Perpetrator methodology as a predictor of traumatic symptomatology in adult survivors of childhood sexual abuse', *Journal of Interpersonal Violence*, 2004:19, pp. 521-540.

8. Volkwein, K. A. E., F.I. Schnell, D. Sherwood and A. Livezy, 'Sexual harassment in sport', *International Review for the Sociology of Sport*, 1997:32, pp. 283-295.

9. Brackenridge, C.H. op. cit.

10. Toftegaard Nielsen, J., 'The forbidden zone: Experience, sexual relations and misconduct in the relationship between coaches and athletes', *International Review for the Sociology of Sport*, 2001:36, pp. 165-183.

11. Fejgen, N. and Hanegby, R., op.cit.

CHAPTER 22. ROLE CONFLICT AND ROLE AMBIGUITY AMONG SWIMMING COACHES IN RESPONSE TO CHILD PROTECTION MEASURES IN ENGLAND[1]

Joy D. Bringer and Lynne H. Johnston

In 1995, a former British Olympic swimming coach was sentenced to 17 years in prison for sexually abusing swimmers he had coached. Since his conviction and several other high-profile cases of sex abuse by coaches, development of child protection policy in sport has increased exponentially in the United Kingdom.[2, 3] Governing bodies now require many coaches to receive child protection training. In 2005, the Football Association reported that nearly 100,000 coaches had attended child protection workshops, and another coach education organization reported that nearly 30,000 coaches attended their child protection workshops between 2006 and 2007.[4, 5]

When our research started in 1999, previous research on abuse in sport had focused or was focusing on athletes' experiences of abuse,[6, 7] prevalence rates[8, 9] and athlete responses to abuse.[10, 11] Aside from a couple of studies examining coaches' perceptions of harassment and abuse,[12, 13] the experience of coaches with child protection measures had generally been ignored. If policy makers are to reduce opportunities for coach harassment and abuse, it is important first to understand the reasons coaches give for making decisions about appropriate and inappropriate behaviour. Therefore, this study took a qualitative approach to identify what might influence the perceptions of male swimming coaches in England about the appropriateness of coach-athlete sexual relationships.[14]

Based on coaches' comments during the first phase of data collection, the focus of the study shifted to examining the impact of child protection measures on the swimming coaches. This chapter provides a brief review of both areas of this research study, which is published in more depth elsewhere.[15, 16]

Research Design

Nineteen male swimming coaches participated in one of four focus groups, and three additional coaches were interviewed individually. Males were selected rather than females not only because they are over-represented in coaching at the high school,[17] university[18] and elite levels[19, 20] but also because males perpetrate the majority of reported sexual abuse.[21, 22] Brackenridge and Kirby have hypothesized that athletes within the 'stage of imminent achievement' (high-level athletes who have the potential to earn elite honours but have not yet done so) may be most vulnerable to coaches who groom them for sexual abuse.[23] Therefore, this study addressed males coaching swimmers within this 'imminent' age range of about 13 to 17 years old at international, national and developmental levels. The coaches ranged in age from 27 to 67 years old, had been coaching for an average of 17 years and spent on average 22 hours a week coaching swimming.

In line with grounded theory techniques (whereby themes are extracted from data with no prior assumptions being made about what might be found),[24] our initial analysis of the focus groups guided the selection of three swimming coaches (who had not participated in the focus groups) for individual interviews. These coaches were selected to further our emerging understanding of coaches' perceptions of the appropriateness of child protection measures and their effect on coaching. One of the three coaches had been convicted of sexually assaulting a female swimmer in his care, the second was in a committed relationship with a swimmer whom he was coaching and the third had been suspended (and then cleared) by the Amateur Swimming Association during an investigation into allegations of sexual misconduct. Ethical considerations such as confidentiality, researcher safety and procedures for dealing with new allegations of abuse were all addressed prior to commencing data collection.[25] The procedures used for the data collection and analysis are detailed elsewhere and therefore are not repeated here.[26, 27, 28, 29]

Key Findings

Perceptions of appropriateness

The results from this study indicate that coaches in the focus groups first and foremost used the legal age of consent as the basis for deciding about the appropriateness of sexual relationships with swimmers. All the coaches in this study agreed that sex with an athlete under the age of consent in England (16 years old) would be unacceptable. With regard to sexual relationships with athletes above the age of consent, opinions ranged from "it would be totally inappropriate" to "it's a question of civil liberties." In general, the coaches expressed that they held themselves to a higher standard of behaviour compared with how they would judge their fellow coaches.

Specifically, some coaches seemed willing to reduce opportunities to develop close relationships with athletes in response to the pressures generated by greater awareness of child sexual abuse and the emergence of child protection policies in sport. Coaches also reported that the potential for false accusations, power imbalances and negative performance consequences influenced their own beliefs about whether or not a relationship would be appropriate. However, awareness of career-damaging false accusations and attempts at maintaining civil liberties contributed to the coaches' stated reluctance to intervene with other coaches when suspicions of inappropriate coach-athlete relationships arise.

Role conflict and role ambiguity

In analysing the data from the focus groups, we became aware that the problem most relevant to the research participants was not how they distinguished appropriate from inappropriate sexual relationships but how child protection initiatives were affecting their roles as swimming coaches. Using the approach of drawing out themes from the data,[30, 31, 32] we started with a broad focus allowing the area of concern most important to the coaches to emerge from the data. This core category was labeled *role conflict and role ambiguity* to reflect how the coaches were questioning their role as coaches after the development of child protection guidelines and increased public scrutiny. Definitions of these concepts provided by Kahn and his colleagues[33] were used for role conflict, referring to conflicting role expectations, and role ambiguity, referring to insufficient information about role expectations. For example, in one of the focus groups, a coach stated,

> "There are going to be some athletes that could be very great athletes but they will fail as athletes, because we will fail them as coaches. Because we will not be coaching them as to how they need to be coached with some of these rules and regulations."

Role conflict and role ambiguity thus became the centre of our model,[34] which provided the structure for reporting the findings from this study.[35] It is important to note that the elements of the model interact over time to influence the core category. For example, the consequences of a coach's response to role ambiguity will influence how he experiences role ambiguity and may influence the conditions for experiencing role ambiguity in the future.

The starting point for the model is the factors that raise awareness of child protection issues among the coaches. These included personal experience or knowledge of child protection allegations, increased cultural awareness of child abuse, media coverage of child abuse and increased legislation on child protection issues. These prerequisite conditions influenced the conditions leading to role conflict and ambiguity and included awareness/acceptance of child protection issues, coaching behaviours and compatibility/incompatibility of coaching behaviours and child protection guidelines. Once the coaches experienced role conflict or ambiguity they had three main strategies for attempting to resolve it: defining (or redefining) what it means to be an effective coach, assessing one's own morals standards and intentions, and assessing the risks involved in not adhering to child protection guidelines.

Reflections

A common limitation of conducting research with people is the difficulty in ascertaining whether participants are responding honestly or are responding in a socially desirable manner.[36, 37] The use of focus groups potentially increases the likelihood of such responses, as participants may be concerned about the other participants unfavourably judging them. While this may have happened to some degree in the focus groups, there was sufficient variability in responses to indicate that it was not a serious problem. In two of the individual interviews, however, the lead researcher felt that the participants were withholding information; for example, the convicted coach denied that the abuse happened. The coach who was cleared of allegations was reluctant to talk about the situation, and the researcher did not pressure him into discussing the details of the case.

As this was an exploratory study, a further limitation is that the emerging themes reported in the study cannot be generalized to the wider population of swimming coaches. The role conflict/role ambiguity model presented is empirically grounded but requires further testing before claims about causality can be made.

There is scant research examining sexual harassment and abuse in sport and the impact of child protection policies on sport coaches, so there are many possibilities for future research. Theory development in this area will benefit from research examining cross-sport differences, female coaches and recreational-level sport. As child protection policies become embedded in all government-funded youth sport programmes in the United Kingdom, it will be important to examine whether different groups of coaches experience role conflict and role ambiguity in the same way as the coaches in this study. For example, male coaches, who may feel more scrutinized, may experience more role conflict and ambiguity from child protection measures than female coaches. (A study of carers of foster children found that male carers were more concerned about false allegations of abuse than were female carers.[38])

It would also be useful to interview coaches from a sport that does not yet have a well-developed child protection policy or from countries with different cultural norms. This would allow examination of the impact of cultural awareness on perceptions of appropriateness, role conflict and role ambiguity. In addition, a longitudinal study following a group of coaches within a sport that is developing and implementing a child protection policy would provide insight into the development of role conflict and ambiguity. It also might highlight strategies for decreasing the experience of conflict and ambiguity.

The child protection in sport movement could also benefit from pedagogical research examining the best methods for raising awareness and improving coaching practice without contributing to role conflict and ambiguity. This research should be conducted soon to avoid the detrimental effects of role conflict and ambiguity. As theory develops in this area, it will be possible to develop evidenced-based practices that will encourage positive sporting experiences for both athletes and coaches. The objectives of both protecting and developing children may be achieved by assisting coaches to develop professional standards and teaching them how to care and be professionally friendly without overstepping the boundary into intimate friendship, while also teaching parents and athletes how to recognize inappropriate coaching behaviour.

Finally, it is important to note that, while role ambiguity and role conflict may be uncomfortable experiences, the consequences need not be negative.[39] These experiences challenge the conceived role and encourage flexibility and change, which can facilitate improvement in a coach's role. Thus, by constantly re-evaluating ideal coach-athlete interactions and discussing difficult, often unanswerable questions, it is possible to create and maintain professionalism.[40]

Notes

1. The data for this paper originated from the first author's doctoral thesis at the University of Gloucestershire. We thank the Amateur Swimming Association and the Institute of Swimming Teachers and Coaches who funded the research and the British Association for Swimming Teachers and Coaches, who provided logistical support. Celia Brackenridge and Lynne Johnston supervised the research.

2. Boocock, S., 'The Child Protection in Sport Unit', *Journal of Sexual Aggression*, 2002:8, 2, pp. 99-106.

3. Sport England, 'Safeguarding the Welfare of Children in Sport: Towards a standard for sport in England', Sport England, London, 2001.

4. Football Association, *The FA Annual Review 2004-2005*, London, 2005.

5. Sports coach UK, *sports coach UK Annual Report 2006/2007*, Coachwise Business Solutions, Leeds, 2007.

6. Bowker, L.H. 'The coaching abuse of teenage girls: A betrayal of innocence and trust', in: L. H. Bowker (ed.), *Masculinities and Violence*, Sage, London, 1998.

7. Brackenridge, C.H., "'He owned me basically...': Women's experience of sexual abuse in sport', *International review for the Sociology of Sport*, 1997:32, 2, pp. 115-130.

8. Kirby, S., L. Greaves and O. Hankivsky, *The Dome of Silence: Sexual harassment and abuse in sport*, Zed Books, London, 2000.

9. Leahy, T., G. Pretty and G. Tenenbaum, 'Prevalence of sexual abuse in organised competitive sport in Australia', *Journal of Sexual Aggression*, 2002:8, 2, pp. 16-36.

10. Fasting, K., C.H. Brackenridge and K. Walseth, 'Coping with sexual harassment in sport: Experiences of elite female athletes', *Journal of Sexual Aggression*, 2002:8, 2, pp. 37-48.

11. Hassall, C.E., L.H. Johnston, J.D. Bringer and C.H. Brackenridge, 'Coach and athlete perceptions of ambiguous behaviours and sexual harassment: Implications for coach education', *Journal of Sport Pedagogy*, 2002:8, 2, pp. 1-21.

12. Toftegaard Nielson, J., 'The forbidden zone: Intimacy, sexual relations and misconduct in the relationship between coaches and athletes', *International Review for the Sociology of Sport*, 2001:36, pp. 165-182.

13. Bringer, J.D., C.H. Brackenridge and L.H. Johnston, 'Defining appropriateness in coach-athlete sexual relationships: The voice of coaches', *Journal of Sexual Aggression*, 2002:8, 2, pp. 83-98.

14. Bringer et al. ibid.

15. Bringer et al. op cit.

16. Bringer, J.D., C.H. Brackenridge and L.H. Johnston, 'Swimming coaches' perceptions of sexual exploitation in sport: A preliminary model of role conflict and role ambiguity', *The Sport Psychologist*, 2006:20, pp. 465-479.

17. Lackey, D., 'Sexual harassment in sports', *The Physical Educator*, 1990:47, 2, pp. 22-26.

18. Acosta, R.V. and L.J. Carpenter, *Women in Intercollegiate Sport: A longitudinal study - Twenty-five year update, 1977-2002*, Brooklyn College, Brooklyn, NY..

19. Kirby, Greaves and Hankivsky, op. cit.

20. West, A. and C.H. Brackenridge, *Wot! No Women Coaches: A report on issues relating to women's lives as sports coaches*, PAVIC Publications, Sheffield, 1990.

21. Fergusson, D.M. and P.E. Mullen, 'Childhood sexual abuse: An evidence based perspective', in: A.E. Kazdin (Ed.), *Developmental Clinical Psychology and Psychiatry Series*, Sage, London, 1999.

22. Grubin, D., *Sex Offending Against Children: Understanding the risk*, Policing and Reducing Crime Unit, London, 1998.

23. Brackenridge, C.H. and S. Kirby, 'Playing safe: Assessing the risk of sexual abuse to elite child athletes', *International Review for the Sociology of Sport*, 1997:32, pp. 407-418.

24. Strauss, A.L. and J. Corbin, *Basics of Qualitative Research: Techniques and procedures for developing grounded theory*, Sage, London, 1998.

25. Bringer, J.D., *Sexual Exploitation: Swimming coaches' perceptions and the development of role conflict and role ambiguity*, unpublished doctoral thesis, University of Gloucestershire, United Kingdom, 2002.

26. Bringer et al. 2002 op cit.

27. Bringer et al. 2002 op cit.

28. Bringer, J.D., L.H. Johnston and C.H. Brackenridge, 'Using computer assisted qualitative data analysis software (CAQDAS) to develop a grounded theory project', *Field Methods*, 2006:18, 3, pp. 245-266.

29. Bringer, J.D., L.H. Johnston and C.H. Brackenridge, 'Maximizing transparency in a doctoral thesis: The complexities of writing about the use of QSR*NVIVO within a grounded theory study', in: A. Bryman (ed.), *Qualitative Research 2: Qualitative data analysis*, Sage, London, 2007, pp. 63-82.

30. Strauss, A.L. and J. Corbin, op.cit.

31. Glaser, B.G. and A.L. Strauss, *The Discovery of Grounded Theory: Strategies for qualitative research*, Aldine de Gruyter, New York, 1967.

32. Strauss, A.L. and J. Corbin, *Basics of Qualitative Research: Grounded theory procedures and techniques*, Sage, London, 1990.

33. Kahn, R.L., D.M. Wolfe, R.M. Quinn, J.D. Snowek and R.A. Rosenthal, *Organizational Stress: Studies in role conflict and ambiguity*, Wiley and Sons, London, 1964.

34. Strauss and Corbin, op cit.

35. Bringer, J.D., C.H. Brackenridge and L.H. Johnston, 'Swimming coaches' perceptions of sexual exploitation in sport: A preliminary model of role conflict and role ambiguity', *The Sport Psychologist*, 2006:20, pp. 465-479.

36. Reynolds, W.M, 'Development of reliable and valid short forms of the Marlowe-Crowne Social Desirability Scale', *Journal of Clinical Psychology*, 1982:38, 1, pp. 119-125.

37. Ballard, R. and M.D. Crino, 'Social desirability response bias and the Marlowe-Crowne Social Desirability Scale', *Psychological Reports*, 1988:63, pp. 227-237.

38. Swan, T.A., 'Problems in caring for sexually abused girls: Care providers speak out', *Community alternatives: International Journal of Family Care*, 1997:9, 1, pp. 71-87.

39. Kahn, et al. op.cit.

40. Sockett, H., *The Moral Base for Teacher Professionalism*, Teachers College Press, New York, 1993.

CHAPTER 23. CHILD ATHLETES' NEGATIVE EMOTIONAL RESPONSES TO THEIR COACHES IN THE UNITED KINGDOM

Misia Gervis

In the pursuit of excellence, sport is demanding more and more from its young elite performers. Young athletes are training longer and harder and are spending significantly more time with their coaches. Sport completely dominates their lives, and their relationships with their coaches can become more important to them than those with their parents. The prevailing culture in elite sport requires child athletes to comply with the coach's demands in order to succeed. The emotional and psychological response of such child athletes to these conditions and the potential for mental injury in these circumstances has largely been ignored. The outside world does not perceive the children to be 'at risk'; indeed, the perception is generally the opposite. Performance achievements mask the process through which they are realized, and there is an acceptance that the ends justify the means.

Until now the understanding of emotional abuse of children has developed from outside of sport and has essentially focused on child-parent relationships. This research has examined the pairing of parental behaviour with the child's emotional well-being. This dual focus on parental fault and state of the child is evident in the literature, with questions being raised about establishing a causal relationship between parental behaviour and child psychopathology.[1]

It has been recently acknowledged that all forms of child maltreatment have an emotional or psychological consequence for the child. However, because it is often internalized and therefore 'invisible', emotional abuse has received less attention from clinicians and researchers than other forms of child maltreatment. It may, however, have consequences that greatly outweigh and outlast the physical injuries or the physical results of neglect or sexual abuse (see figure 6).

Research into child maltreatment has demonstrated that emotional abuse occurs within dysfunctional relationships between adult and child, and understanding these relationships and the arising emotional and psychological consequences have been at its heart. However, no such spotlight has been aimed at understanding the psychological impact and emotional response to the relationships between elite child athletes and their coaches. Consequently, this chapter takes a child-centred approach to examining the emotional responses of elite child athletes to their coach's behaviour.

The research that supported and underpinned this work originated primarily from the child maltreatment field. The majority of literature on emotional abuse has come from the disciplines of child psychiatry, psychology, paediatrics, social work and law. The work most influential in beginning the dialogue on emotional abuse was undertaken by Garbarino in the late 1970s and 1980s. The seminal work, in which he termed emotional abuse the 'elusive crime', opened up an area that had previously been ignored.[2] Garbarino highlighted adult behaviours towards children that were emotionally abusive, including humiliating, belittling, shouting, threatening and rejecting. Thus, he presented a framework from which the majority of work on emotional abuse has developed.

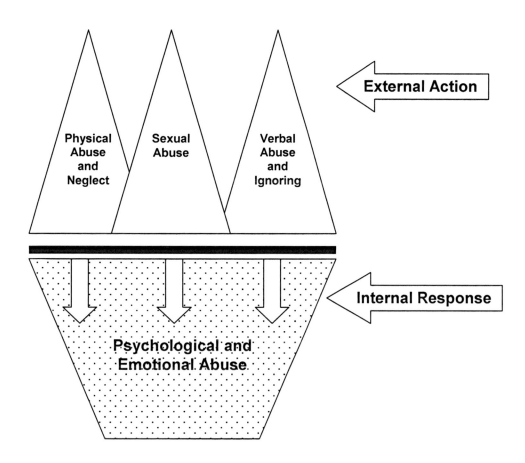

Figure 6. Schematic illustration of the 'iceberg' model of child maltreatment

Emotional abuse is not always observable, and the damage it causes may only manifest itself much later in life, perhaps long after athletes have retired from competing. Apparently mild acts repeated over a long period of time can have a severe damaging outcome. Thus, it is the 'drip, drip' effect of children constantly experiencing the abusive behaviour or action that can result in psychological and emotional damage.[3] Emotional abuse constitutes the series of interactions or patterns of behaviour within a relationship, as can be the case between coach and child athlete. This contrasts with the isolated event, as is often the case with sexual or physical abuse. Furthermore, research has shown that children who suffer emotional abuse can exhibit a range of symptoms, including depression, diminished feelings of self worth, anxiety, emotional instability and eating disorders.[4]

The recognition of emotional abuse is further complicated by the culture or context within which it occurs. When it is so common, and therefore accepted by those within the culture, there is no acknowledgement that the outcome could be emotionally damaging.[5] Thus, the prevailing culture can mask emotionally abusive behaviour because it becomes normalized. This describes the situation within elite sport, where intensive coaching methods are an integral part of the culture and are rarely challenged because they produce winning results. Furthermore, because the damaging effects of the emotional abuse may not be realized until athletes have stopped competing, the explanation for the retired athletes' condition is generally not attributed to their experiences in sport.

Research Design

This chapter summarizes a series of studies employing mixed methodologies. The primary purpose was to explore and test the 'theoretical process model of negative emotional response in child athletes' through both qualitative and quantitative methods. Key components of this model (see figure 7) posit that (1) elite child athletes will experience negative behaviour from their coach similar to the adult behaviour previously described by Garbarino as emotionally abusive;[6] (2) they will experience this behaviour frequently and repetitively; (3) athletes will have a negative emotional response to the behaviour that will lead them to exhibit emotional problem symptoms; and (4) this will only occur within a 'power-over' culture of coaching in which coaches assume a hierarchically superior position over athletes.

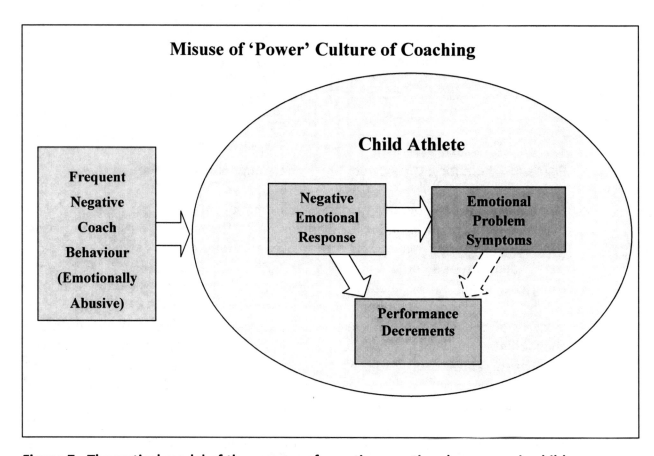

Figure 7. Theoretical model of the process of negative emotional response in child athletes

In the first study, 12 former elite child athletes (four males and eight females) were interviewed about their experiences of being coached as elite child athletes. The interviews were framed to test the theoretical model. These athletes had all been on world class performance programmes or equivalent and had been identified as elite when they were children, with a mean age of identification of 13.1 years. Participants were asked to reflect on their past experiences as elite child athletes, so their responses represented the residual impact of their experiences.

The second series of studies focused on testing the model with larger and more diverse athlete populations. This was achieved through development of a new instrument, the 'sport emotional response questionnaire' (SER-Q), a retrospective self-report measure of athletes' remembered perceptions of behaviour by their coaches. The instrument is a 20-item questionnaire that measures the frequency, emotional response and performance effect of each item of negative coach behaviour. Each item was generated from the interview source data from the first study.

A total of 502 volunteer participants completed the questionnaire (326 males and 175 females). Regarding competitive level, 64 were at club level, 207 at regional level, 133 at national level and 97 at international level. All participants were student athletes studying sport science at university. Participants came from 32 different sports, both team and individual.

Key Findings

The results from all the studies confirmed the theoretical model as having currency within sport. In the first qualitative study, all of the athletes reported that they had experienced some or all of the negative behaviours from their coach while training as elite child athletes. The most frequently experienced behaviours were belittling, humiliating, threatening and shouting. These negative behaviours were considered to be part of their coaches' day-to-day coaching methods.

Athletes reported the occurrence of these behaviours independent of the gender of their coach, the sport participated in and whether it was a team or individual sport. The athletes reported a range of residual emotional problem symptoms, many of which stayed with them long after they stopped competing. This was typified in the following responses:

> "I was meant to be one of the best but I never felt like this, I always felt like I was rubbish and worthless generally."

> "All it did was to destroy me as a person, to make me feel worthless."

> "I gave up because I had no confidence, because she constantly told me that I was crap and worthless all the time. I believed this and it carried on into general life and I am now scared of rejection, failure because of the things she did."

Interestingly, all the athletes reported that their coach's behaviour worsened once they had been identified as elite. A typical example of this was reported by a footballer who commented:

> "He became a power maniac … because I was good he thought it was all his doing."

These athletes reported having to cope with the pressures of training and competing at the highest level in a climate of sustained attacks on their self-esteem when they were still vulnerable children. But the behaviour of their coaches went unchallenged, as they were all successful athletes. The outside world viewed them as victorious achievers and, as such, they went unnoticed as potentially being at risk.

The results from this study may lead to the hypothesis that these athletes' experiences are not likely to be isolated cases but are indicative of accepted coaching practice. Consequently, the subsequent quantitative studies were designed to address this issue and access larger populations through the SER-Q. Preliminary results indicated that the proposed 'theoretical process model of negative emotional response in child athletes' seemed also to hold true for larger populations of athletes. Significantly, as athletes reported an increase in the frequency of negative coach behaviour, the reported response was an increase in negative emotion. This would support the notion that it is the 'drip, drip' effect of coach behaviour that caused the athletes to report a negative emotional response. Thus, it poses a risk to the child athlete when a coach adopts a methodology that includes frequent negative behaviour such as humiliating, belittling, threatening and shouting.

Further findings from this study revealed that the athlete's level of competition played a significant role in the frequency of reported emotionally abusive behaviour and the emotional response to it. Elite athletes – those at international and national level – reported greater frequency of negative coach behaviour and a significant increase in their negative emotional response to it. The club-level athletes reported the least experience of this type of coach behaviour and consequently reported neutral emotional responses.

These findings would suggest that elite child athletes experience a different coaching climate from that of their recreational counterparts. A number of factors may contribute to this. One is that elite child athletes spend more time with their coaches, providing more opportunities to experience the negative behaviour. Some elite child athletes spend more time with their coaches than with their parents. Long periods of closeness between adult and child are the classic ingredients that, outside sport, have been found to lead to various forms of child abuse and maltreatment. Also, coaches are dependent on these athletes for their own career aspirations. A coach's reputation is built on the athletes that he or she produced.

Reflections

It must be clearly stated that this work is truly in its infancy; researchers are still at the early stages of conceptualizing, measuring and testing. However, a re-examination of the data appears to provide strong evidence supporting the proposed theoretical model. Clearly, however, a more detailed investigation is needed to explore all aspects of the model. Nevertheless, it is apparent even from these early studies that elite child athletes appear to be 'at risk' and, as such, every effort should be made to protect them. Until now, children participating at elite levels in sport would not normally be considered 'at risk', so researchers and child protection workers have not previously identified them as vulnerable. This position clearly needs to be reconsidered.

It is not yet known what are the long-term consequences to children who have experienced this emotional abuse, but if they follow the pattern of children who are emotionally abused in other contexts the outlook is not good. We have a responsibility towards child athletes to ensure that they do not endure the emotionally and psychologically debilitative effects of emotional abuse at the hands of their coaches.

Notes

1. Kavanagh, C., 'Emotional abuse and mental injury: A critique of the concept and recommendation for practice', *Journal of American Academy of Child and Adolescent Psychiatry*, 1982:21, pp.171-177.
2. Garbarino, J., 'The elusive 'crime' of emotional abuse', *Child Abuse and Neglect*, 1978:2, pp. 89-99.
3. O'Hagan, K., 'Emotional and psychological abuse: Problems of definition', *Child Abuse and Neglect*, 1995:19, pp. 449-461.
4. Bingeli, N., S. Hart and M. Brassard, *Psychological Maltreatment of Children*, Sage, California, 2001.
5. Navarre, E.L., 'Psychological maltreatment: The core component of child abuse', in: M.R. Brassard, R. Germain and S.N. Hart (eds.), *Psychological Maltreatment of Children and Youth*, Pergamon Press, New York, 1987.
6. Garbarino, J., E. Guttman and J.W. Seeley, *The Psychologically Battered Child*, Jossey-Bass Publishers, California, 1986.

Part 4
GLOBAL ISSUES: POLICIES AND CHARTERS

CHAPTER 24. ENSURING THE HUMAN RIGHTS OF YOUNG ATHLETES

Paulo David

Historically, human rights and sport have an extremely modest record of interaction. Little and sporadic research exists on the relationship between the two; isolated policy and law development has taken place at country and international level. Though many rights-related concerns have emerged in the public domain since the democratization and huge expansion of the sport system in the 1970s, the human rights of athletes remain an often hidden issue. The issues include doping; racism and discrimination; labour disputes; various forms of violence, including physical, psychological and sexual abuse; excessive training; and economic exploitation.

Youth sport has traditionally been identified as an exclusively positive activity for children's development. Today a more balanced view is emerging. The many positive aspects that sport can bring to a child's holistic development are clear. Nevertheless, competitive sports can also increase children's vulnerability to various forms of violence, abuse, neglect and exploitation.

International human rights law is framed by nine core, legally binding international treaties, including the Convention on the Rights of the Child, which was adopted in 1989 after a long decade of negotiations among States. No provision of the Convention explicitly refers to sports, but in fact 37 of the 42 substantive provisions directly apply to sports. They include:

- The right to non-discrimination (art. 2);
- The principle of the best interests of the child (art. 3);
- The right to be provided appropriate direction and guidance (art. 5);
- The right to development (art. 6);
- The right to an identity and nationality (art. 7);
- The right not to be separated from their parents (art. 9);
- The right to have their views taken into account (art. 12);
- Freedom of expression and association (arts. 13 and 15);
- Protection of privacy (art. 16);
- The right to access appropriate information (art. 17);
- Protection from abuse and neglect and other forms of violence (art. 19);
- The right to health (art. 24);
- The right to education (arts. 28 and 29);
- The right to rest, leisure, recreation and cultural activities (art. 31);
- The right to be protected from economic exploitation (art. 32), illegal drugs (art. 33), sexual exploitation (art. 34), abduction, trafficking and sale (art. 35) and other forms of exploitation (art. 36);
- The right to benefit from rehabilitative care (art. 39);
- The right to due and fair process (art. 40).

The Convention has been ratified by all but two states (the United States and Somalia). It defines a child as 'every human being below the age of eighteen years unless under the law applicable to the child, majority is attained earlier' (art. 1).

Rights recognized in the other eight international human rights treaties also implicitly apply to persons below 18 years of age.

The Convention on the Rights of the Child is a powerful tool to guarantee the protection of children's rights. Among its provisions are a legal and policy framework; the obligation of the State, parents "or any other person who has the care of the child" to guarantee respect of the child's rights (art. 19); recognition of "the evolving capacity of the child" to exercise progressively his or her own rights (art. 5); and the right of the child to remedy (art. 4). The Convention recognizes the child as an active subject of rights, rather than solely a passive object of protection.

Despite persistent resistance, it is today nevertheless increasingly accepted that the rule of law also applies to the sport field. International human rights law, which is meant to be reflected in domestic legislation, therefore also applies to athletes. In the context of sport, public authorities have a direct obligation to ensure protection of the rights of young athletes; private sport federations, parents and other adults involved also have an indirect responsibility. In the view of the United Nations Committee on Economic, Social and Cultural Rights,[8] the obligation to respect rights requires States to *refrain* from interfering directly or indirectly with people's enjoyment of their human rights; the obligation to protect requires States to *take measures that prevent third parties* (such as parents, coaches or sports organizations or authorities) from interfering with human rights; and the obligation to *fulfil* requires States to adopt appropriate legislative, administrative, budgetary, judicial, promotional and other measures towards the full realization of human rights.

Respect for children's rights and competitive sports are perfectly compatible when the rights of athletes, as recognized in international human rights law, are guaranteed. Contrary to popular belief, the search for excellence can be achieved without infringing on the rights of young athletes if the sport environment is truly rights oriented. Sport legislation, policies, regulations, jurisprudential decisions, by-laws, programmes and practices need to ensure systematic integration of the requirements of the Convention on the Rights of the Child. Few sport authorities, including the International Olympic Committee, have done this so far. For example, an athlete under age 18 accused of illegal doping should not be tried or judged under the criteria used for adults. In 2001, in a remarkable initiative, the Irish Sports Council and the Sports Council for Northern Ireland (the highest domestic sport authorities) united to adopt a Code of Ethics and Good Practice for Children's Sport in Ireland,[9] which affirms that:

> "As citizens, adults have a responsibility to protect children from harm and to abide by government guidelines in responding to and reporting child protection concerns. This responsibility exists wherever such concerns might arise, whether inside or outside sport. Guidelines contained in the Code of Ethics and Good Practice for Children's Sport in Ireland *took account of the UN Convention on the Rights of the Child* and are in accordance with government guidelines. (*Emphasis added*) Recognising the human rights of

young athletes will empower them and potentially increase their capacity to protect themselves from all forms of sport related violence, abuse, neglect and exploitation and, at the same time, enable them to perform with dignity and in safety."

Conclusion

At least two major arguments can be made to promote respect for child rights in the context of competitive sport:

- Respect for the rule of law: The sporting world, like any other, is bound by human rights laws and policies and can no longer remain an entirely closed and hermetically sealed system.

- Elimination of harmful side effects: The potentially harmful side effects of sport must be addressed to ensure that competitive sport remains a largely positive experience for young people and to minimize the number of athletes whose holistic development is irreversibly affected. Applying the rule of law to the sport sphere can potentially increase the quality of sport services delivered.

Notes

1. UN Committee on Economic, Social and Cultural Rights, 'The right to the highest attainable standard of health', article 12 of the International Covenant on Economic, Social and Cultural Rights, General Comment No. 14, E/C.12/2000/4, Geneva, United Nations, 2000.
2. Irish Sports Council and Sports Council for Northern Ireland, 'Code of Ethics and Good Practice for Children's Sport in Ireland', Dublin, Irish Sports Council, 2001.

CHAPTER 25. STANDARDS FOR PROTECTING CHILDREN IN SPORT IN THE UNITED KINGDOM

Steve Boocock

The United Kingdom's 'Child Protection in Sport Action Plan' (2000) identified the need to establish standards for sport organizations introducing child protection policies. The purposes of the standards were to:

- Help create a safe sporting environment for children and young people and protect them from harm;
- Provide a benchmark to assist those involved in sport to make informed decisions;
- Promote good practice and challenge practice that is harmful to children.

When the standards were first developed, under the aegis of the Child Protection in Sport Unit (CPSU), they were intended to be relevant to all sports at all levels, although initially they applied only to national sport governing bodies. The standards were developed so that umbrella funding and controlling bodies could use them, for example, to raise the quality of athlete welfare, assist in decision making about abuse referrals or for enforcement of rules about recruitment. Participating organizations receiving government funding are required to meet the standards as a condition of funding.

Alongside child protection organizations, several sport organizations participated actively throughout the development of the standards. There was also wide consultation with other relevant organizations. In developing the standards, the CPSU was aware of the diverse size, resources and capacities of national governing bodies and other sport organizations. It was therefore accepted that the standards would only be fully implemented after a five-year period. After endorsing the standards, sport organizations were expected to work towards implementation, which became an expectation of funding arrangements.

The standards cover 10 areas, each having been identified as a key component of effective child protection practice:

1. Policy

A child protection policy makes clear to all what is required in relation to the protection of children and young people. It helps to create a safe and positive environment for children and to show that the organisation is taking its duty of care seriously.

2. Procedures and systems

Procedures provide clear step-by-step guidance on what to do in different circumstances. They clarify roles and responsibilities and lines of communication. Systems for recording information and for dealing with complaints are also needed in order to ensure implementation and compliance. Procedures help to ensure a prompt response to concerns about a child's safety or welfare. They also help an organisation to comply with and implement legislation and guidance.

3. Prevention

Some people who work or seek to work in sport, in either a paid or voluntary capacity, pose a risk to children and young people. It is possible to minimise the risks and to prevent abuse by putting safeguards in place.

4. Codes of practice and behaviour

Codes of practice describe acceptable standards of behaviour and promote good practice. Children's sport should be carried out in a safe, positive and encouraging atmosphere. Standards of behaviour for all set a clear benchmark of what is acceptable. They can help to minimise opportunities for abuse and help to prevent unfounded allegations.

5. Equity

Abuse happens to male and female children of all ages, ethnicities, social backgrounds, abilities, sexual orientations, religious beliefs and political persuasions. Some children, such as disabled children, are particularly vulnerable. Prejudice and discrimination can prevent some children getting the help they need. Organisations should take steps to combat discrimination and actively include all children and young people in their safeguarding measures.

6. Communication

Policies and procedures are only effective if people are aware of them, have some ownership of them and have the opportunity to express their views on how they are working.

7. Education and training

Everyone in contact with children has a role to play in their protection. They can only do so confidently and effectively if they are aware and have the necessary understanding and skills. Organisations providing sporting activities for children have a responsibility to provide training and development opportunities for both staff and volunteers.

8. Access to advice and support

Child abuse is distressing and can be difficult to deal with. Organisations have a duty to ensure that advice and support are in place to help people to play their part in protecting children. Children need someone to turn to when they are being abused. Often they do not know where to turn for help.

9. Implementation and monitoring

Policies, procedures and plans have to be implemented across and in all parts of the organisation. Checks are needed to ensure this is happening consistently. The views of those involved inside and outside the organisation can help to improve the effectiveness of any actions taken.

10. Influencing

A number of sports organisations have both a strategic and a service/activity delivery role in relation to children and young people. Where partnership, funding or commissioning relationships exist with other organisations they can exert influence to promote the implementation of safeguarding measures. Partnership, funding and commissioning criteria can include a requirement for child protection policies and procedures.

The CPSU recognizes three levels of achievement of the standards:

- Preliminary level: Achieved by producing a written child protection policy (Standard 1) and implementation plan (Standard 9).

- Intermediate level: Achieved by implementing elements of the standards governing procedures and systems (Standard 2), prevention (Standard 3), education and training (Standard 7) and access to advice and support (Standard 8).

- Advanced level: Achieved by implementing elements of the standards governing codes of practice and behaviour (Standard 4), equity (Standard 5) and communication (Standard 6).

To demonstrate achievement of each of the standards, sport organizations are required to provide evidence of action in specified criteria. The portfolios of evidence are evaluated by independent assessors who present their report and recommendations to a review panel that considers whether the requirements have been met. The panel comprises representatives from Sport England and the CPSU, together with the relevant portfolio assessor. An organization that does not accept the panel's decision can appeal the outcome through a second evaluation process.

It was recognized that sport bodies would need specialist support to help them achieve the standards. The CPSU has been the main source of this support through consultancy and training services. It has also facilitated the establishment of learning sets (groups of mutually supporting learners) and regional group meetings for child protection/welfare officers in national governing bodies.

Guidance has also been developed for sport organizations working to achieve the safeguarding standards. This guidance describes the assessment process as a whole, explains the rationale behind success criteria and suggests some of the types of evidence needed to demonstrate achievement of the criteria.

The process of adopting and achieving the standards has been positive but challenging for all involved. The standards have given a clear framework for sport bodies and an objective process for evaluating progress made. They have provided a basis for collaboration and sharing of best practice across sports and provided a means of measuring progress in the development of child protection practices.

CHAPTER 26. BILL OF RIGHTS FOR YOUNG ATHLETES IN THE UNITED STATES

The Bill of Rights for Young Athletes was developed in the 1980s by Dr. Vern Seefeldt, professor emeritus at the Institute for the Study of Youth Sports (Michigan) and Dr. Rainer Martens in response to growing concerns regarding the abuse of young athletes. A number of national organizations have used the bill of rights as a guideline for coaches and parents, and it can be used freely so long as the authors and the Institute for the Study of Youth Sports are recognized. It is reprinted from R. Martens and V. Seefeldt (Eds.), Guidelines for Children's Sports, Washington, D.C., American Alliance for Health, Physical Education, Recreation and Dance, 1979.

The 10 rights are:

1. Right to participate in sports.
2. Right to participate at a level commensurate with each child's maturity and ability.
3. Right to have qualified adult leadership.
4. Right to play as a child and not as an adult.
5. Right of children to share in the leadership and decision-making of their sport participation.
6. Right to participate in safe and healthy environments.
7. Right to proper preparation for participation in sports.
8. Right to an equal opportunity to strive for success.
9. Right to be treated with dignity.
10. Right to have fun in sports.

CHAPTER 27. PANATHLON DECLARATION ON ETHICS IN YOUTH SPORT

Panathlon International is a worldwide network of sport organizations. It encourages sport, with an emphasis on fair play, as a means of promoting friendship and cultural values. Its Panathlon Declaration, formally endorsed on 24 September 2004, aims to encourage the development of positive values in youth sport. Details are available at http://eng.panathlon.net/news/?id=573.

This declaration represents our commitment to go beyond discussion and to establish clear rules of conduct in the pursuit of the positive values in youth sport.

We declare that:

1. **We will promote the positive values in youth sport more actively with sustained effort and good planning.**

   - In training and competition we will aim for four major objectives in a balanced way: the development of motor (technical, tactical) competence, a healthy and safe competitive style, a positive self-concept, and good social skills. In this we will be guided by the needs of children.
   - We believe that striving to excel and to win and to experience both success and pleasure, and failure and frustration, are all part and parcel of competitive sport. We will give children the opportunity to cultivate and to integrate (within the structure, the rules and the limits of the game) this in their performance and will help them to manage their emotions.
   - We will give special attention to the guidance and education of children according to those models which value ethical and humanistic principles in general and fair-play in sport in particular.
   - We will ensure that children are included in the decision making about their sport.

2. **We will continue our effort to eliminate all forms of discrimination in youth sport.**

   This coheres with the fundamental ethical principle of equality, which requires social justice, and equal distribution of resources. Late developers, the disabled and less talented children will be offered similar chances to practise sport and be given the same professional attention available to early developers, able-bodied, and more talented children without discrimination by gender, race or culture.

3. **We recognise and adopt the fact that sports also can produce negative effects and that preventive and curative measures are needed to protect children.**

   - We will maximise the child's psychological and physical health through our efforts to prevent cheating, doping, abuse and exploitation, and to help children to overcome the possible negative effects of these.
   - We accept that the importance of children's social environment and of the

motivational climate is still underestimated. We will therefore develop, adopt and implement a code of conduct with clearly defined responsibilities for all stakeholders in the network around youth sport: sport governing bodies, sport leaders, parents, educators, trainers, sport managers, administrators, medical doctors, physical therapists, dieticians, psychologists, top athletes, children themselves, etc.

- We strongly recommend that the establishment of bodies on appropriate levels to govern this code should be seriously considered.
- We encourage registration and accreditation systems for trainers and coaches.

4. **We welcome the support of sponsors and media but believe that this support should be in accordance with the major objectives of youth sport.**

- We welcome sponsorship from organizations and companies only when this does not conflict with the pedagogical process, the ethical basis of sport and the major objectives of youth sport.
- We believe that the function of the media is not only to be reactive, i.e. holding the mirror up to the problems of our society, but also to be proactive, i.e. stimulating, educational and innovative.

5. **We therefore formally endorse 'The Panathlon Charter on the Rights of the Child in Sport'.** All children have the right:
- to practise sports;
- to enjoy themselves and to play;
- to live in a healthy environment;
- to be treated with dignity;
- to be trained and coached by competent people;
- to take part in training that is adapted to their age, individual rhythm and competence;
- to match themselves against children of the same level in a suitable competition;
- to practise sport in safe conditions;
- to rest;
- to have the opportunity to become a champion, or not to be a champion.

All this can only be achieved when governments, sports federations, sports agencies, sports goods industries, media, business, sport scientists, sport managers, trainers, parents and children endorse this declaration.

CHAPTER 28. INTERNATIONAL OLYMPIC COMMITTEE CONSENSUS STATEMENT ON TRAINING THE CHILD ATHLETE[1]

The Consensus Statement was drafted by an IOC Medical Commission Expert Panel whose members were: Arne Ljungqvist, Chairman (IOC Medical Commission); Patrick Schamasch (Medical Director, IOC Medical & Scientific Department); Susan Greinig (Medical Programmes Manager, IOC Medical & Scientific Department) and a team of experts led by Lyle Micheli (Harvard Medical School).

Protecting the health of the athlete is the primary goal of the International Olympic Committee's Medical Commission. One of its main objectives is the promotion of safe practices in the training of the elite child athlete. The elite child athlete is one who has superior athletic talent, undergoes specialised training, receives expert coaching and is exposed to early competition. Sport provides a positive environment that may enhance the physical growth and psychological development of children. This unique athlete population has distinct social, emotional and physical needs which vary depending on the athlete's particular stage of maturation. The elite child athlete requires appropriate training, coaching and competition that ensure a safe and healthy athletic career and promote future well-being. This document reviews the scientific basis of sports training in the child, the special challenges and unique features of training elite children and provides recommendations to parents, coaches, health care providers, sports governing bodies and significant other parties.

Scientific Basis of Training the Elite Child Athlete

Aerobic and anaerobic fitness and muscle strength increases with age, growth and maturation. Improvements in these variables is asynchronous. Children experience more marked improvements in anaerobic and strength performance than in aerobic performance during pubescence. Boys' aerobic and anaerobic fitness and muscle strength are higher than those of girls in late pre-pubescence, and the gender difference becomes more pronounced with advancing maturity. Evidence shows that muscle strength and aerobic and anaerobic fitness can be further enhanced with appropriately prescribed training. Regardless of the level of maturity, the relative responses of boys and girls are similar after adjusting for initial fitness.

An effective and safe training programme incorporates exercises for the major muscle groups with a balance between agonists and antagonists. The prescription includes a minimum of two to three sessions per week with three sets, at an intensity of 50 to 85 per cent of the one maximal repetition (1RM).

An optimal aerobic training programme incorporates continuous and interval exercises involving large muscle groups. The prescription recommends three to four, 40 to 60-minute sessions per week at an intensity of 85-90 per cent maximum heart rate (HRM).

An appropriate anaerobic training programme incorporates high intensity interval training of short duration. The prescription includes exercise at an intensity of about

90 per cent HRM and of less than 30 seconds duration to take into account children's relatively faster recovery following high intensity exercise.

A comprehensive psychological programme includes the training of psychological skills such as motivation, self-confidence, emotional control and concentration. The prescription applies strategies in goal-setting, emotional, cognitive and behavioural control fostering a positive self-concept in a healthy motivational climate.

Nutrition provided by a balanced, varied and sustainable diet makes a positive difference in an elite young athlete's ability to train and compete, and will contribute to optimal lifetime health. Adequate hydration is essential. Nutrition requirements vary as a function of age, gender, pubertal status, event, training regime, and the time of the competitive season. The nutrition prescription includes adequate hydration and individualises total energy, macro- and micro-nutrient needs and balance.

With advancing levels of maturity and competitiveness, physiological and psychological training and nutrition should be sport-specific with reference to competitive cycles. Confidential, periodic and sensitive evaluation of training and nutritional status should include anthropometric measures, sport-specific and clinical assessment.

Special Issues in the Elite Child Athlete

Physical activity, of which sport is an important component, is essential for healthy growth and development.

The disparity in the rate of growth between bone and soft tissue places the child athlete at an enhanced risk of overuse injuries particularly at the epiphyses, the articular cartilage and the physes (growth plates). Prolonged, focal pain may signal damage and must always be evaluated in a child.

Overtraining or "burnout" is the result of excessive training loads, psychological stress, poor periodisation or inadequate recovery. It may occur in the elite child athlete when the limits of optimal adaptation and performance are exceeded. Clearly, excessive pain should not be a component of the training regimen.

In girls, the pressure to meet unrealistic weight goals often leads to the spectrum of disordered eating, including anorexia and/or bulimia nervosa. These disorders may affect the growth process, influence hormonal function, cause amenorrhoea, low bone mineral density and other serious illnesses which can be life-threatening.

There are differences in maturation in pubertal children of the same chronological age that may have unhealthy consequences in sport due to mismatching.

Elite child athletes deserve to train and compete in a pleasurable environment, free from drug misuse and negative adult influences, including harassment and inappropriate pressure from parents, peers, health care providers, coaches, media, agents and significant other parties.

Recommendations for Training the Elite Child Athlete

The recommendations are that:

- More scientific research be done to better identify the parameters of training the elite child athlete, which must be communicated effectively to the coach, athlete, parents, sport governing bodies and the scientific community;

- The International federations and national sports governing bodies should:
  - Develop illness and injury surveillance programmes;
  - Monitor the volume and intensity of training and competition regimes;
  - Ensure the quality of coaching and adult leadership;
  - Comply with the World Anti-Doping Code.

- Parents/guardians develop a strong support system to ensure a balanced lifestyle including proper nutrition, adequate sleep, academic development, psychological well-being and opportunities for socialisation;

- Coaches, parents, sports administrators, the media and other significant parties should limit the amount of training and competitive stress on the elite child athlete.

The entire sports process for the elite child athlete should be pleasurable and fulfilling.

Note

1. Adopted 14 November 2005, www.olympic.org/uk/organisation/commissions/medical/full_story_uk.asp?id=1551.

CHAPTER 29. INTERNATIONAL OLYMPIC COMMITTEE CONSENSUS STATEMENT ON SEXUAL HARASSMENT AND ABUSE IN SPORT [1]

In its role of promoting and protecting the health of the athlete, the IOC Medical Commission recognises all the rights of athletes, including the right to enjoy a safe and supportive sport environment. It is in such conditions that athletes are most likely to flourish and optimise their sporting performance. Sexual harassment and abuse are violations of human rights, regardless of cultural setting, that damage both individual and organisational health. While it is well known that sport offers significant potential for personal and social benefits, this potential is undermined where such problems occur.

Sexual harassment and abuse occur worldwide. In sport, they give rise to suffering for athletes and others, and to legal, financial and moral liabilities for sport organisations. No sport is immune to these problems which occur at every performance level. Everyone in sport shares the responsibility to identify and prevent sexual harassment and abuse and to develop a culture of dignity, respect and safety in sport. Sport organisations, in particular, are gatekeepers to safety and should demonstrate strong leadership in identifying and eradicating these practices. A healthy sport system that empowers athletes can contribute to the prevention of sexual harassment and abuse inside and outside sport.

This document summarises current scientific knowledge about the different forms of sexual harassment and abuse, the risk factors that might alert the sport community to early intervention and the myths that deflect attention from these problems. It also proposes a set of recommendations for awareness raising, policy development and implementation, education and prevention, and enhancement of good practice.

Defining the Problem

Sexual harassment and abuse in sport stem from power relations and abuses of power. *Sexual harassment* refers to behaviour towards an individual or group that involves sexualised verbal, non-verbal or physical behaviour, whether intended or unintended, legal or illegal, that is based upon an abuse of power and trust and that is considered by the victim or a bystander to be unwanted or coerced. *Sexual abuse* involves any sexual activity where consent is not or cannot be given. In sport, it often involves manipulation and entrapment of the athlete. Sexual harassment and abuse occur within an organisational culture that facilitates such opportunities. Indeed, they are symptoms of failed leadership in sport.

Gender harassment, hazing and homophobia are all aspects of the sexual harassment and abuse continuum in sport (see figure 8). *Gender harassment* consists of derogatory treatment of one gender or another which is systematic and repeated but not necessarily sexual. *Hazing* involves abusive initiation rituals that often have sexual components and in which newcomers are targeted. *Homophobia* is a form of prejudice and discrimination ranging from passive resentment to active victimisation of lesbian, gay, bisexual and transgendered people.

SEX DISCRIMINATION

⟶

SEXUAL & GENDER HARASSMENT

⟶

HAZING &   SEXUAL ABUSE

⟶

I N S T I T U T I O N A L ....P E R S O N A L

'The chilly climate'	'Unwanted attention'	'Groomed or coerced'
Vertical and horizontal job segregation	Written or verbal abuse or threats	Exchange of reward or privilege for sexual favours
Lack of harassment policy and/or officer or reporting channels	Sexually oriented comments, jokes, lewd comments or sexual innuendoes, taunts about body, dress, marital situation or sexuality	Groping
Lack of counselling or mentoring systems		Indecent exposure
	Ridiculing of performance	Forced sexual activity
Differential pay or rewards or promotion prospects on the basis of sex	Sexual or homophobic graffiti	Sexual assault
	Practical jokes based on sex	Physical/sexual violence
Poorly/unsafely designed or lit venues	Intimidating sexual remarks, propositions, invitations or familiarity	Rape
Absence of basic security	Domination of meetings, play space or equipment	Incest
	Condescending or patronising behaviour	
	Undermining self-respect or work performance	
	Physical contact, fondling, pinching or kissing	
	Vandalism on the basis of sex	
	Offensive phone calls or photos	
	Stalking	
	Bullying based on sex	

Figure 8. The sexual exploitation continuum

Source: Adapted from C.H. Brackenridge, 'Sexual harassment and sexual abuse in sport', in: G. Clarke and B. Humberstone (eds.), Researching Women in Sport, London, Macmillan, 1997.

Scientific Evidence: Prevalence, Risks and Consequences

Research indicates that sexual harassment and abuse happen in all sports and at all levels. Prevalence appears to be higher in elite sport. Members of the athlete's entourage who are in positions of power and authority appear to be the primary perpetrators. Peer athletes have also been identified as perpetrators. Males are more often reported as perpetrators than females.

Athletes are silenced by the sexual harassment and abuse process. The risk of sexual harassment and abuse is greater when there is a lack of protection, high perpetrator motivation and high athlete vulnerability (especially in relation to age and maturation). There is no evidence that the amount of clothing cover or the type of sport are risk factors: these are myths. Research identifies risk situations as the locker-room, the playing field, trips away, the coach's home or car, and social events, especially where alcohol is involved. Team initiations or end-of-season celebrations can also involve sexually abusive behaviour against individuals or groups.

Research demonstrates that sexual harassment and abuse in sport seriously and negatively impact on athletes' physical and psychological health. It can result in impaired performance and lead to athlete drop-out. Clinical data indicate that psychosomatic illnesses, anxiety, depression, substance abuse, self harm and suicide are some of the serious health consequences. Passive attitudes/non-intervention, denial and/or silence by people in positions of power in sport (particularly bystanders) increases the psychological harm of sexual harassment and abuse. Lack of bystander action also creates the impression for victims that sexually harassing and abusive behaviours are legally and socially acceptable and/or that those in sport are powerless to speak out against it.

Relationships in Sport

Sexual harassment and abuse in sport do not discriminate on the basis of age, gender, race, sexual orientation or disability. Athletes come from many different cultural and family backgrounds and are the centre of a system of relationships focused on helping them to achieve their sport potential. There is always a power difference in an athlete's relationships with members of their entourage (coaches, scientific and medical staff, administrators etc.). This power difference, if misused, can lead to sexual harassment and abuse and, in particular, to exploitative sexual relationships with athletes.

These relationships require that a significant amount of time be spent together in the emotionally intense environment of competitive sport. This situation has the potential to put the athlete at risk of isolation within a controlling relationship where his/her power and right to make decisions is undermined.

All adults in an athlete's environment must adopt clear guidelines about their roles, responsibilities and appropriate relationship boundaries. It is essential that each member of the entourage, and any other authority figure, stays within the boundaries of a professional relationship with the athlete.

Prevention Strategies

Accepted prevention strategies include policies with associated codes of practice, education and training, complaint and support mechanisms and monitoring and evaluation systems. Regardless of cultural differences, every sport organisation should have these provisions in place.

The policy is a statement of intent that demonstrates a commitment to create a safe and mutually respectful environment. The policy should state what is required in relation to the promotion of rights, well-being and protection. It allows the organisation to generate prompt, impartial and fair action when a complaint or allegation is made. It further allows it to take disciplinary, penal and other measures, as appropriate.

Codes of practice describe acceptable standards of behaviour that, when followed, serve to implement the policy. Standards of behaviour set a clear benchmark for what is acceptable and unacceptable (see box). They can help to minimise opportunities for sexual harassment and abuse and unfounded allegations.

Recommendations

All sport organisations should:
1. Develop policies and procedures for the prevention of sexual harassment and abuse;
2. Monitor the implementation of these policies and procedures;
3. Evaluate the impact of these policies in identifying and reducing sexual harassment and abuse;
4. Develop an education and training programme on sexual harassment and abuse in their sport(s);
5. Promote and exemplify equitable, respectful and ethical leadership;
6. Foster strong partnerships with parents/carers in the prevention of sexual harassment and abuse; and
7. Promote and support scientific research on these issues.

Through sexual harassment and abuse prevention in sport, sport will become a safer, healthier and more positive environment for all.

Criteria for Sexual Harassment and Abuse Policies and Codes of Practice in a Sport Organisation

The policy on sexual harassment and abuse should:
- Identify and address these issues;
- Be clear and easily understood;
- Involve consultation with athletes;
- Be widely communicated through publication and education;
- Be approved by the relevant management body (e.g. Management Board or Executive Committee) and incorporated into its constitution and/or regulations
- apply to all involved in the organisation;
- Be supported by a comprehensive education and training strategy;
- Be reviewed and updated on a regular basis, particularly when there is a major change in the constitutional regulations of the organisation or in the law.

The policy should:
- State that all members have a right to respect, safety and protection;
- State that the welfare of members is paramount;
- Identify who has responsibility for implementing and upholding it;
- Specify what constitutes a violation;
- Specify the range of consequences for such violations;
- Specify procedures for reporting and handling complaints;
- Provide details of where to seek advice and support for all parties involved in a complaint;
- Specify procedures for maintaining records;
- Provide guidance for third party reporting ('whistleblowing').

There should be codes of practice on sexual abuse and harassment for specific member roles in a sport organisation. The code of practice on sexual harassment and abuse should:
- Provide guidance on appropriate/expected standards of behaviour from all members;
- Set out clear processes for dealing with unacceptable behaviours, including guidance on disciplinary measures and sanctions.

Note

1. The Consensus Statement, adopted 8 February 2007, was drafted by an IOC Medical Commission Expert Panel. Panel members were Arne Ljungqvist, Chairman (IOC Medical Commission); Patrick Schamasch (Medical Director, IOC Medical & Scientific Department); Susan Greinig (Medical Programmes Manager, IOC Medical & Scientific Department); Agnès Gaillard (Projects Assistant, IOC Medical & Scientific Department); Margo Mountjoy (Coordinator, IOC Medical Commission); Celia Brackenridge, Programme Consultant (United Kingdom); Kari Fasting, Programme Consultant (Norway). Participants were Steven Boocock (United Kingdom), Charlotte

Bradley-Reus (Mexico), Joy Bringer (United Kingdom), Paulo David (Switzerland), Margery Holman (Canada), Sheldon Kennedy (Canada), Kimie Kumayasu (Japan), Sandra Kirby (Canada), Trisha Leahy (Hong Kong, province of China), Petra Moget (the Netherlands), Debbie Simms (Australia), Jan Toftegaard-Stoeckel (Denmark), Ian Tofler (United States) and Maarten Weber (the Netherlands). Details at www.olympic.org/uk/organisation/commissions/medical/full_story_uk.asp?id=2064.

CHAPTER 30. EUROPEAN FEDERATION OF SPORT PSYCHOLOGY POSITION STATEMENT ON SEXUAL EXPLOITATION IN SPORT

The European Federation of Sport Psychology is the leading sport psychology organization in Europe. It has published a number of position statements including this one (No. 6) on sexual exploitation in sport, originally authored by Celia Brackenridge in 2002.

Exploitation and abuse in sport has been recognised as an issue only within the past two decades. Awareness of both sexual harassment and sexual abuse grew as a consequence of initiatives for gender equity in sport in the 1970s and 1980s; emotional and physical abuses are under-researched but have also been highlighted in studies of the elite level of athlete performance. There is an emerging body of knowledge that now underpins both harassment-free sport and child protection policy initiatives. These initiatives should have practical benefits for all athletes.

Sport frequently involves close personal relationships, both among groups of athletes and between individual athletes and their coaches or leaders. There is evidence of high levels of bullying between athletes, sometimes serious enough to cause an athlete to leave his or her sport. The trust that develops between the athlete and leader is often regarded as an essential part of training for success. Sometimes, however, more powerful individuals take advantage of those with less power, using demeaning sexually harassing behaviour – such as sexist jokes or unwanted touching – or in the most extreme cases abusing them sexually, emotionally or physically. In the most serious cases it is thought that the abuser is motivated by a desire to control the athlete: they may thus use sex to achieve and maintain power, rather than power to achieve sexual gratification.

Sexual Exploitation and Gender

Sexual exploitation affects both males and females athletes and may be perpetrated by both adult authority figures and by athletes themselves. Given the gender distribution in sport, and the over-representation of males in coaching and other authority positions, it is much more likely that perpetrators of sexual exploitation will be males. This is reinforced by research findings.

The sexually abusive coach is frequently a kind of 'father or mother figure' for the young athlete, especially where the child's natural parents are either absent or show no interest in their sporting progress. Homophobia is linked to sexually exploitative behaviour, often where the perpetrator is him/herself uncertain about their sexual identity and seeking to reinforce their own perceived boundaries between the acceptable and unacceptable. Sexual exploitation can also occur in group settings where senior athletes engage rookies or newcomers in bullying, physically challenging or sexually explicit rituals as part of hazing or initiation rites. Such rituals have been observed in some women's sports but are much more commonly associated with male sports, especially traditional team sports.

Sport as a Protection from Sexual Exploitation

In addition to its health and fitness benefits, sport has long been promoted as a medium for the development of self-confidence and assertiveness. Physical fitness helps to develop self-confidence and this, in turn, can assist with building an individual's capacity to resist sexually harassing behaviours. Self-confident athletes with strong family support are less likely to exhibit the vulnerability that marks out a potential victim of a sexual abuser.

Each sport has developed its own culture and norms. In some sports, training in deference to authority and respect for the rules helps to instil norms that protect athletes from sexual exploitation. Athletes whose lives involve a mix of activities and who enjoy a balance between academic studies, sporting practice and social pursuits, are also less likely to become dependent upon a single individual who might draw them into a sexually abusive relationship.

Sport as a Site of Risk of Sexual Exploitation

There may be a proportion of young athletes in any club who have suffered sexual abuses in their family, and these individuals require particular support and care in order to avoid them being targetted a second time. Sports which involve early peaking – i.e. where elite level performance is reached in the lower teenage years, at or around puberty – are thought to present more risk of sexual exploitation to athletes than those sports with higher peaking ages, since this time coincides with the transition from child to adult during which sexual identity and maturity are achieved.

At the club level, young athletes may fall prey to their 'sporting idols' in whom they may place unqualified trust. At the elite level, young athletes are often expected to accept responsibilities that are more usual for adults, such as travel arrangements and money management. Their athletic development or 'sport age' is thus well in advance of their social and physical development, which can create tensions and sexual uncertainty.

Sport psychologists have a special role to play here as they are in a privileged position to spot early signs of distress and abuse as part of their professional practice. Indicators of possible abuses suffered by athletes include: sudden mood swings, changes in behaviour or performance standard, loss of enthusiasm for sport, misleading or telling lies about their whereabouts, development of addictions and/or disordered eating patterns, social withdrawal, uncharacteristic exhibitionism or unusual sexual knowledge for their age. The sport psychologist can also work with coaches to ameliorate the effects of autocratic coaching styles and, in this way, minimise the chances of abuse by coaches and other authority figures in sport.

Four Dimensions of Protection from Sexual Exploitation in Sport

Sports psychologists should attend to four dimensions of protection in relation to sexual, physical and emotional abuse:

1. **Protecting the athlete from others:** Recognising and referring to legal and/or medical authorities anyone who has been subjected to sexual misconduct or abuse by someone else, whether inside sport (by another staff member or athlete) or outside sport (by someone in the family or peer group);

2. **Protecting the athlete from oneself:** Observing and encouraging good practice when working with athletes in order to avoid perpetrating neglect or abuse of any kind;

3. **Protecting oneself from the athlete or others:** Taking precautions to avoid false allegations against oneself by athletes or their peers or families;

4. **Protecting one's profession:** Safeguarding the good name and integrity of sport, coaching and sport science.

Recommendations for Minimising the Risk of Sexual Exploitation

1. Adopt harassment-free policies and procedures that are in line with international ethical and human rights statutes;
2. Encourage open debate about sexual harassment, homophobia and exploitation of women and men in sport;
3. Embed both an equitable balance of males and females in all roles and also democratic leadership styles to mitigate against abuses of power;
4. Act as advocates of harassment-free sport through education and training programmes for every member of the sport;
5. Actively monitor the effectiveness of all anti-harassment initiatives;
6. Initiate research into men's, women's and children's experiences of abuse and bullying within their sport;
7. Give active representation to athletes in decision-making at every level of the sport.

Part 5
LOCAL PROGRAMMES

CHAPTER 31. JUSTPLAY: MONITORING THE CONDUCT OF YOUTH SPORT PARTICIPANTS (CANADA)

Elaine Raakman

Volunteers are crucial to the success of grass-roots sports, but they can also pose limitations. Volunteers often lack the educational qualifications and administrative skills needed to operate a youth sport organization. But they have one important qualification – the enthusiasm and willingness to do the job. 'Justplay', a Canadian NGO that promotes sportsmanship and works to prevent violence in youth sports, set out to provide a tool that would improve the effectiveness of these administrators and promote good behaviour by all participants in youth sport.

Justplay's behaviour management programme, launched in 2000, is a system that allows sports officials to collect and analyse information about the conduct of coaches, players and spectators. By identifying and quantifying the variables that contribute to problem behaviour in team sports, it aims to help administrators make the evidence-based staffing and policy decisions needed to anticipate, respond to and prevent problematic behaviour. For example, a sport league administrator might use data from Justplay to evaluate the effectiveness of programmes designed to improve the conduct of participant groups.

It was decided that officials (referees) would be the most appropriate people to acquire data objectively, and that the variables most likely to affect conduct would be venue, age, skill, gender and game type. This led to creation of the Justplay 'conduct report card', independently filled out by each official following every game. The officials rate the conduct of the coaches, players and spectators of each team on a scale of 1 (very good) to 5 (very poor). Importantly, they use the same scale to rate their own personal satisfaction about the game. This satisfaction rating is not an evaluation of how they feel about their officiating, but rather represents their enjoyment in carrying out their duties during the game.

Officials receive pads of blank conduct report cards for logging their ratings at each game. A couple of times a week they enter the data onto the Justplay website, which takes only a few moments. All data entered by officials is cross-tabulated against their age, years of experience, role within the game and level of certification. The information entered into the database is then organized and displayed in a library of dynamic graphs available on a password-protected basis.

Officials' ratings for 'poor' and 'very poor' behaviour are pooled, and the graphs then depict the overall percentage of problematic behaviour by coaches, players and spectators. This allows identification of the most problematic games, leagues, age groups and so on. Critical incidents are tracked separately to determine more precisely where, when and under what circumstances problem behaviour occurs. All graphs can be viewed with the team name identified or hidden, allowing administrators to print or show graphs while protecting the anonymity of the participant groups. Administrators also have the capability to give access to people in their association.

Currently Justplay is working with hockey, soccer, baseball, football and basketball teams throughout Canada. The feedback from both administrators and officials is extremely positive. Administrators use the information to set and enforce behaviour standards, evaluate policy and implement interventions to address identified concerns, as well as to help in selecting coaches and resolving disputes. They also use it to identify trends in officiating, review the impact of poor conduct on official satisfaction, identify officials with low satisfaction ratings and help assign officials to games that are optimal for them and the participant groups.

The Justplay system is a valuable research tool, given the volume of data it generates, the diversity of sports and geographical areas covered (or potentially covered), ease of data collection and analysis, and ability to correlate/contrast the data with official data and socio-economic indicators. Justplay has collaborated on a number of research projects. Recently the programme was adapted to collect data from child hockey players in an effort to examine bullying behaviour. Players aged 8 to 18 years were asked to fill out an online card, similar to the conduct report card, following every game. The information indicated whether the child felt they had been bullied before, during or after the game from teammates or other players, coaches, officials or spectators from either team. Children could provide this information in the privacy of their own home, under the supervision of their parents if necessary. In November 2007 another project was initiated to study the factors that contribute to officials' satisfaction.

Justplay has the potential to revolutionize how youth sports are administrated. Given the importance of ensuring protection of children's rights in the sport environment, a tool that monitors the conduct of the participant groups consistently and continuously is essential.

For more information see www.wejustplay.com.

CHAPTER 32. PLAY BY THE RULES: TEACHING SPORT CLUBS TO PREVENT CHILD ABUSE (AUSTRALIA)

Mary Duncan

Play by the Rules is an Internet-based programme designed to help individuals and clubs identify, prevent and manage (if not resolve) discrimination, harassment and child abuse in sport. Launched in 2001, it was one of the first Australian websites to provide free, online training to those involved in community/club sports – which are characterized by a reliance on volunteers, a shortage of people, high turnover of personnel and a lack of skill and expertise in legal and administrative matters.

But the programme doesn't exist in a vacuum. Over the years federal, state and territory sport and recreation agencies have developed many resources to support club sports. Play by the Rules complements and builds on those materials by providing a variety of interactive, informative and easy-to-read documents, activities and case studies on subjects relevant to coaches, players and administrators. It focuses on helping people understand issues, rights and responsibilities and giving them the skills and confidence to act appropriately. Scenarios and case studies provide examples of relevant situations, while templates of concise and simply written model policies and procedures, consistent with state and national organization guidelines, provide tools for response.

To supplement the scenarios and templates, Play by the Rules provides downloadable posters, publications and DVDs to promote fair and safe behaviour. This material comes with practical suggestions for spreading the message. The DVDs, like all the programme materials, focus on everyday issues faced by those involved in sport. In child protection, for instance, one scenario explores the inappropriate demonstration of skills and another shows the verbally abusive coach – both problems that frequently affect children's enjoyment and safety in sport. The DVD on reporting child abuse encourages people to act if they have concerns (which are defined) rather than simply offering technical explanations of abuse or overwhelming people with detailed descriptions of legal obligations.

The programme is a unique collaboration and funding partnership among the Australian Sports Commission, Australian Human Rights Commission, all state and territory sport/recreation and anti-discrimination agencies, and the Queensland and New South Wales Commissioners for Children and Young People.

Strategic direction and budget are set by a management committee, comprising representatives from the executive directors of both commissions, four state and territory sport and recreation agencies, four anti-discrimination commissioners and two children's commissioners (or their delegates). A national reference group of 19 managers from federal, state and territory agencies informs the direction of programme activities. Involving so many agencies in a project presents a number of communication challenges, but generally the structure has worked well, enabling Play by the Rules to help clubs develop safe and harassment-free sport.

Since its inception, Play by the Rules has steadily increased the range and scope of its materials, often in response to perceived needs. In 2007, the national reference group found that sport clubs did not know where and how to get assistance in dealing with problems. Play by the Rules and partner agencies responded by developing an agency referral guide for each state and territory, identifying the resources available to assist in achieving a safe, harassment-free sports environment.

During development of these guides it became apparent that clubs needed more support in resolving problems, particularly those involving behaviour that was inappropriate or unfair rather than clearly unlawful. As a consequence, the online courses were reviewed, and the whole programme is undergoing a significant upgrade and restructure. It will continue to be a portal to the best resources available for preventing and managing discrimination, harassment and child abuse in sport. But it will also provide materials to help clubs handle challenging situations and to assist them in learning from those experiences.

Play by the Rules now includes:

- Upgraded online learning courses on discrimination, harassment and child protection;

- A problem-solving section that provides practical information on dealing with a comprehensive range of issues. Users simply click on their role (e.g. administrator, coach, umpire) to access information tailored to their needs;

- Short, interactive problem-based learning scenarios on a wide array of issues (e.g. girls playing in boys' teams, sexual harassment, team selection) to provide further depth to the existing online learning;

- The pilot version of an interactive tool to assist club administrators handle complaints.

Busy club volunteers, whether coaches, umpires or administrators, usually involve themselves in sport with the best of intentions. Many of them want to be supportive, inclusive and proactive and are often committed to establishing positive systems and processes. The reality, however, is that they don't often have the time, knowledge or skills to do so. Play by the Rules provides them with the information and resources they need. In addition to its templates and advice, it helps people understand challenging issues through simple, engaging and interactive problem solving. Using its resources, clubs and communities can create environments where children can *play by the rules* – safely, fairly without harassment or abuse.

For more information see www.playbytherules.net.

CHAPTER 33. TEN SIGNS OF A GOOD YOUTH SPORT PROGRAMME (UNITED STATES)

Brooke de Lench

Moms Team, a website offering advice and resources for parents of children in sports, offers these suggestions for recognizing a well-run youth sport programme:

1. **It has implemented comprehensive risk-management and child protection programmes.** A good youth sports programme recognizes that it owes a duty of care to every child who participates. It has identified best practices and implemented a child protection programme, including background checks of all adults working with children, to reduce the number of out-of-control parents, abusive coaches and bullying teammates, spectators and volunteers, as well as to prevent catastrophic injuries and deaths.

2. **It is child-centred.** The emphasis on winning in youth sports is a result of adults wanting to win. Studies that ask boys and girls what they would like to see changed about youth sports repeatedly find that the vast majority would like to reduce the emphasis on winning. A good youth sports programme listens to what children say they want; it emphasizes having fun, building skills and ensuring fair play; and it keeps winning, losing and competition in proper perspective.

3. **It does not exclude children before the age of 13-14 years.** Childhood is a time to prepare children for adulthood by giving them a chance to develop coping skills and the self-confidence to succeed in the adult world, while in a safe and nurturing environment. Many researchers say that cutting children from athletic programmes fosters an environment that hurts, rather than fosters, self-esteem.

4. **Before eighth grade its teams are comprised of children of the same age, from the same neighbourhoods and of mixed abilities.** There is no proof that forcing 'better' players to play with those who appear less skilled when young keeps them from developing their 'talent' or that they deserve to play with similarly 'gifted' players. Every child deserves a chance to play, receive the best coaching and play on the best fields.

5. **It uses independent evaluators, not parent coaches, to select its teams.** Tryouts run by parent coaches are unacceptable because of concerns about the fairness, politics and behaviour associated with such a selection process.

6. **It has implemented and enforces rules requiring equal playing time (before sixth grade) and significant playing time (sixth grade and above).** Requiring all participants to have equal/significant playing time creates a win-win situation for the players (who play together more as a team, are less selfish and feel less pressure to excel in order to earn more playing time), parents (who, knowing that their child will get the same or significant playing time as every other player, are less likely to pressure their child to perform), and the coach (the rule

eliminates two of a coach's major headaches: complaints from players and complaints from parents about playing time).

7. **It is accountable to parents and solicits their input.** A good youth sports programme asks for input from parents; publicizes its mission statement, bylaws, and the names, telephone numbers and e-mail addresses of board members and other administrators; limits the terms of directors; holds open board meetings; and measures its progress against other, similar programmes.

8. **It requires that coaches receive accredited training and be evaluated after every season.** Coaches need training not only in the sport they are coaching but in first aid and child development. Evaluations are needed to identify those who should no longer be coaching because they are abusive, violate equal playing time rules or overemphasize winning at the expense of fun and skill development.

9. **It requires parent training.** Parents who have been trained are better able to handle the stress of watching their child compete.

10. **It sets sensible limits on the number of practices and games per week.** Understanding that nearly half of the sports injuries children suffer each year are overuse injuries, the programme sets age-appropriate participation limits.

For more information see <www.momsteam.com>.

CHAPTER 34. RECREATION AS A COMPONENT OF COMMUNITY DEVELOPMENT: CITY OF KITCHENER (CANADA)[1]

John R. Cooper

The City of Kitchener supports public recreation based on the belief that it enhances community development. Children's right to participate in a safe sport environment and to enjoy recreation and sport is supported through municipal government policies and agreements with local agencies and other service providers.

Located 100 kilometres southwest of Toronto, Kitchener is a cosmopolitan community of 200,000 with the fourth largest immigrant population in Canada. Twenty-two percent of the population is foreign born, and over 60 languages are spoken. In 2004 there were 50,000 children and youth under age 20 (26,000 males and 24,000 females). About 35 to 40 per cent of children and youth ages 3 to 19 participate in organized sport. Many youth under 14 participate in more than one sport during the same season. Some athletes play on both community and school teams.

Grants and other forms of support and services are provided to not-for-profit, volunteer-controlled groups in diverse sectors, including sport, arts/culture and senior citizens. This focus on community development enhances the city in many ways, making it strong, viable and democratic. It also creates a large base of trained volunteers who work on numerous small and large community events including provincial, national and international sport tournaments.

The City Council has passed legislation and adopted policies aimed at ensuring a safe environment for children participating in sport. These include the Minor Sport Affiliation Policy, the Unacceptable Behaviour Policy and the Child Abuse Reporting Policy.

Affiliated with the city are 40 sport groups for children and youth. To be affiliated, the groups must be not-for-profit, inclusive and democratic and must provide instructional, recreational or competitive programmes primarily to residents 18 years and younger. The Minor Sport Affiliation Policy aims to ensure that sport takes place in an organized, responsible, safe and sustainable way. The policy provides the municipality with some degree of influence over sport clubs, for example by helping to standardize approaches to child welfare. Two athletic coordinators are employed to assist the development of sport and sport clubs, ensure the viability and sustainability of clubs, and enforce the policies.

Clubs must have a volunteer management system, including a structured process for recruiting, screening, evaluating, recognizing, disciplining and removing volunteers. All volunteers are expected to complete an application form, be interviewed by a small committee, sign a job description and code of conduct, and, if they are to have close access to children, go through a police record check. Clubs must have a policy stating that volunteer coaches will not be alone with an athlete. This requirement is included in the job description and code of conduct signed by coaches.

The Unacceptable Behaviour Policy aims to encourage safety and a positive atmosphere. It forbids such activities as fighting and harassing, using obscene language and disrupting activities. It also forbids use of cell phones and other devices in change rooms and toilets at public recreation facilities to prevent inappropriate photography.

The Child Abuse Reporting Policy is a legal agreement with Family and Children's Services of Waterloo Region requiring municipal employees and sport volunteers to report any suspected or actual abuse of children. Sport volunteers can report suspected cases of abuse by parents or coaches without repercussion to themselves.

To resolve sport-related disputes in a confidential, safe and positive setting, the Sport Mediation and Resolution Team, or SMART, was formed through collaboration between Kitchener and the nearby city of Waterloo in cooperation with Community Justice Initiatives of Waterloo Region. SMART provides volunteer mediators trained in sport-related conflict to help deal with disputes involving players, coaches, referees or parents, as well as training to prevent conflicts from escalating. After a case is reviewed, two mediators invite all the parties to work at resolving the conflict. The process is usually completed within 30 days. Discussions are held in a confidential, safe and positive setting. The mediators listen to all sides of the dispute. They do not decide who is right or wrong, but help those involved to reach their own solutions.

Note

1. Adapted from 'The Safety and Empowerment of Children in Sport, Kitchener Canada', a presentation by John R. Cooper to the International Symposium on Child Welfare in Sport, 'Promoting Children's Rights, Welfare and Life Chances', International Children's Games, Coventry, England, 2005.

CHAPTER 35. PREVENTING SEXUAL HARASSMENT IN RUGBY LEAGUE (AUSTRALIA)

John Brady

In 2004, allegations of sexual assault were made against six members of an Australian rugby club. While criminal charges did not result, changes most certainly did. The so-called Coffs Harbour incident led to profound changes and helped to revolutionize attitudes both inside and outside of sport.

In response to the allegations, the chief executive of the National Rugby League (NRL), David Gallop, initiated a project to delve into player attitudes towards women. Through its Welfare and Education Committee, NRL organized a research committee and enlisted the services of several professionals: Associate Professor Catharine Lumby, at the time a researcher at Sydney University; Wendy McCarthy, who had worked on organizational gender reform with state and federal governments as well as the private sector; Karen Willis, Director of the New South Wales Rape Crisis Centre; and Dr Michael Flood, at the time lecturing at the Australian National University in Canberra.

As a first step, Professor Lumby and her assistant, Dr Kath Albury, conducted face-to-face interviews with several players from every professional rugby club in the country. Most players also completed surveys that explored a range of attitudes and included a tool for determining men's beliefs on such issues as myths around consensual sex. Players were questioned on the best ways to deliver messages about changing attitudes and behaviours.[1] McCarthy organized discussion forums involving administrators, players' wives, women who worked in the game professionally as administrators or support staff, journalists who covered the game and board members from rugby clubs.

The research committee spent almost a year studying the attitudes of current and past players as well as the perceptions common in a male-dominated sporting culture. The committee also looked at how the issue of sexual harassment was affecting sports in other countries. The committee met with American researcher Jackson Katz, who had pioneered sexual harassment prevention programmes in the American military and the National Football League. Katz said the scope of what was taking place in the NRL was beyond anything he had seen in any other sport in the world.

In December 2004 the research committee released its report summary and recommendations, 'Playing by the Rules'. It included recommendations for handling complaints about sexual harassment; establishment of interactive forums to promote awareness of the need for harassment prevention in every club; development of player mentors to encourage responsible behaviour; establishment of charters of social responsibility; promotion of women in management roles; and promotion of family involvement at matches.

At the start of the 2005 season, the NRL Rookie Camp unveiled the first 'Playing by the Rules' seminars aimed at changing attitudes and behaviours towards women. The seminars, delivered by recently retired players, were based on findings that had emerged during the previous year's research.[2] Though the sessions at first seemed confrontational, the frankness and understanding of the Rookie Camp participants persuaded the league to hold similar seminars with each of the first grade teams. What started as a defensive response in sport turned into a series of open forums that dealt with the challenges faced by many thousands of young Australians at party and dance venues every night, while also examining the extra challenges of celebrity. So successful was the approach that the league also delivered the session to junior representative teams.

The league administration and the players association, along with individual clubs, also become prominent supporters of UNIFEM's White Ribbon Day campaign, which decries any violence against women. The game's involvement in this campaign provided players with a chance to show leadership on an issue that extends well beyond the sporting community.

'Playing by the Rules' has evolved every year, along with an increasing focus on player education. In 2008 every player in the league's new under-20 competition attended the seminar and also participated in programmes focussing on cultural awareness, abuse of alcohol and illicit substances, and off-field career education. The league also mandated non-training days in which players under 20 are to focus on study, traineeships or employment.

Inevitably rugby players, especially the young ones, will continue to get into trouble and make bad choices. The NRL is committed to ensuring that players are aware of these risks in advance and understand how to avoid them.

An important component of any education process is ensuring that support structures are in place. The league now provides a counselling service in all clubs, which is equipped to provide confidential support on any issue. It also ensures that welfare officers are in place at every club to help guide players.

In 2006 the New South Wales government recognized the league, the Rugby League Professionals Association and the clubs in its Violence Against Women awards. Ultimately, commitment to a cause cannot be measured in numbers alone, but the fact that the 'Playing by The Rules' workshop has been delivered to more than 2,000 players, both at the league level and the game's junior elite competitions, is an indication of how far the programme has reached.

Notes

1. This research included questions drawn from the Rape Myth Acceptance Scale first devised by M.R. Burt, 'Cultural myths and supports for rape', *Journal of Personality and Social Psychology*, 1980:38, pp. 217-230.
2. Michael Buettner, Ben Ikin, Scott Sattler, Jason Stevens.

CHAPTER 36. SAFE SPORT EVENTS: WELFARE PLANNING FOR YOUTH SPORT EVENTS (UNITED KINGDOM)

Anne Tiivas

Most young people have an enjoyable sporting experience when training or participating away from home. However, research and experience have shown that young athletes are particularly vulnerable to abuse and harm when they are in unfamiliar surroundings, with unfamiliar people and when they are homesick, under pressure to perform and/or highly dependent on the adults looking after them.

The National Society for the Prevention of Cruelty to Children (NSPCC) Child Protection in Sport Unit (CPSU), jointly funded with Sport England, works with sport to ensure that all children are protected from harm (see chapter 9). The CPSU has prepared best practice guidelines to help sport clubs develop welfare plans for sports events to ensure that young people can participate in a safe and enjoyable environment.

The concept of welfare planning for young people in sport was first formalized in 1999 by the work of Celia Brackenridge in developing a plan for the United Kingdom's Millennium Youth Games. The CPSU worked with Sport England to develop a welfare plan template for the 2002 Sport England Active Sport Talent Camps, which served 10,000 young people at nine multi-sport camps across England. The template provided a framework for the event organizers, sport national governing bodies, participants and parents to ensure the highest standards of welfare through customized plans for each event. Each plan was scrutinized by the CPSU, and implementation of all the plans was subject to monitoring and review as a condition of being accepted. Training was developed and delivered to event organizers and welfare staff.

In 2003, the CPSU and Sport England produced the 'Safe Sports Events' guide to assist event organizers and stakeholders with welfare planning for young people's sporting events at all levels. The guide also includes a one-day training package prepared by the CPSU.

This approach has been further developed in subsequent youth games events and was adopted by the 2005 International Children's Games in the United Kingdom and the UK School Games in 2006. Welfare planning is now seen as integral to the success of such games, and providing the highest standards of welfare is included in their objectives.

Key Elements of Welfare Planning

Providing the highest possible standards of welfare should be a stated objective of all sport events for children and young people. The written welfare plan should form an integral part of the event plans. There should be an agreed policy statement that clearly outlines the event's underlying values and principles, which should be underpinned by the Convention on the Rights of the Child. Principles for participation may include fair play, equity, inclusiveness, tolerance and responsibility. The key elements of welfare planning are described below.

Event personnel: Roles and responsibilities

- A clear policy and procedures should be developed for the recruitment, selection and supervision of staff and volunteers – including safeguarding checks, validation of identity and qualifications.

- All personnel, whether paid or unpaid, should have clear role descriptions, and these should be specific about the welfare responsibilities of the role. For each role, specifications should outline the required knowledge, skills, experience and qualifications.

- All staff and volunteers must be appropriately trained to fulfil their roles and responsibilities. The welfare plan must specify minimum training required prior to the event. This should include the relevant level of safeguarding/child protection training and orientation to their role in respect of the welfare plan at the event.

- The event coordinator should have overall responsibility for athlete welfare and implementation of the welfare plan. There should be an event welfare coordinator, and each team should have a welfare officer.

- Team managers have a duty of care for their participants' welfare and play a key role in ensuring the well-being of young people when they are away from home.

- To ensure the event is enjoyable for all, codes of conduct need to be established for staff, volunteers and athletes. These set the tone for expected standards of behaviour. These should be formally agreed, and procedures must be in place to deal with breaches.

Policies and procedures for child welfare and protection

- Written procedures for responding to all welfare issues that may affect children and young people should be developed, and all participants should know the chain of reporting for any concerns. Procedures need to clarify the process for reporting child protection concerns to statutory agencies and for dealing with missing participants. Athletes must be told whom they can talk to if they have any concerns.

- Evaluation of events has revealed that many welfare issues arise from poor planning. While some issues are minor, all have an impact on children's experience of the event. Examples include lack of planning for athletes' dietary requirements; lack of water at outdoor facilities in summer, leading to injuries caused by dehydration; lack of security at accommodations; and accommodations shared with unknown adults.

- Event complaints and disciplinary procedures must be in place in advance. Event procedures need to be consistent with the procedures of individual sports and with those of the statutory agencies at the event location.

- Regular welfare briefing sessions should be held throughout events. These enable emerging issues to be addressed and provide the opportunity to inform people about incidents.

Practicalities

- Venues need to be visited and risk-assessed by key personnel in advance of events. There must be clear lines of responsibility for facilities and equipment including provision for shade/shelter; access to food, drinking water and toilets; lifeguard and other safety staff; site maps; and security staff. All personnel need to be given time to become familiar with the venue.

- For residential events, accommodation must be appropriate to the athletes' needs and must be safe and secure. Accommodations must be checked on arrival. Personnel and athletes must be made familiar with fire alarm procedures. There must be access to on-call staff at all times. Athletes must not share rooms with adults unless the event allows accompanying parents/carers to stay with their children. Particular care must be taken when there is no alternative to sharing accommodation with adults not involved in the event. Athletes and personnel need to understand house rules governing drinking and smoking, lights-out times and access to rooms.

- Use of host families is not recommended unless the organizers can complete satisfactory background/safeguarding checks in advance.

- The welfare plan must link with each facility's operating and emergency procedures.

- The registration process must be agreed in advance. Contact details for personnel and participants (including emergency contacts and medical details/consents) must be obtained ahead and easily accessible throughout the event. Welfare staff, event managers and security staff need to be able to communicate easily, ideally through two-way radios and mobile telephones so information can be shared confidentially.

- Arrangements for athletes to contact their parents/carers must be in place, and parents need event/team contact information for emergencies.

- Responsibility for fulfilling the event's 'duty of care' to athletes must be clear at all times. Agreed supervision ratios must be implemented, both when athletes are participating in their sport and during recreational time. Risks to participants are heightened when they are moving between venues and where there is a handover of duty of care.

- Transport must be arranged through a reputable, fully insured organization that uses appropriately vetted staff. Vehicles must meet safety requirements including provision of seat belts. Athletes must be supervised on all journeys. Staff, parents and athletes must be given written information about collection and drop-off details and procedures for dealing with a failure to collect.

- All personnel and athletes should be provided with photo identification cards. Zones are recommended for multi-sport sites, so access can be limited to suitably identified personnel.

- Ideally, the roles of all personnel should be identifiable through colour-coded clothing.

- Health and safety procedures should include facility and event normal and emergency operating procedures, event risk assessment, insurance coverage, accident and safety procedures, first aid and procedures for dealing with sports injuries.

- Personnel from local statutory agencies and emergency services should participate in planning. Personnel must be familiar with relevant procedures through training/briefing and provision of written information.

- Guidelines for photography and media access need to be included in the event welfare plan. Most major events have a media plan that identifies the purposes of media participation in terms of promoting the event and the sport/s involved. These need to be clear to all. Parents and athletes need to provide written consent for taking/using athletes' photographs.

- Expectations of reporters and photographers need to be clear. Professional photographers should be accredited and given identification. They should receive a written brief that clarifies acceptable behaviour and content of images.

- Unsupervised access or access outside the event or lodging should not be permitted.

- A policy should be developed on the use of mobile phones with cameras and the use of photography by visitors and parents who wish to photograph or videotape their child.

Monitoring and evaluation

The welfare plan should clarify how it will be monitored and evaluated, including a structure to obtain feedback from all stakeholders, including athletes and their parents. This feedback has been integral to major events planning in the UK.

Conclusion

In the early years of the CPSU, many organizers and sport administrators were concerned about the potential bureaucracy involved in developing specific welfare plans for children's sporting events. However, welfare planning for children's and young people's sport events has since been fully vindicated.

CHAPTER 37. LEISUREWATCH: PREVENTING SEXUAL ABUSE IN LEISURE FACILITIES (UNITED KINGDOM)

Celia Brackenridge

The idea that our living environment can be a boon to criminals is not a new one. Since the 1980s, it has been recognized that poor street lighting, footpaths with high-sided fences and concrete stairwells on housing estates all provide opportunities for the ill-intentioned.[2]

As a response to improve public safety from sex offenders, the multi-agency Derwent Initiative (TDI) was established with funding from the Home Office following the child abuse scandals in Cleveland in the 1980s, in which paediatricians were accused of exaggerating evidence of intra-family sexual abuse, resulting in many children being taken away from their families.[3] One component of that initiative, Leisurewatch, first piloted in 2002, is now working to prevent sexual abuse of children. It was prompted by forensic psychiatrist Don Grubin, whose work in preparing pre-sentence reports drew his attention to the potential for surveillance of grooming behaviour in public leisure facilities such as swimming pools, parks and entertainment and amusement arcades. Grubin subsequently contacted the head of the TDI and together they developed the concept for Leisurewatch.

The aims of **Leisurewatch** are to:

- Increase awareness of the potential risks to children by sexual offending in public leisure spaces;
- Reduce the risks by educating responsible groups in the community;
- Empower responsible groups to take action.

The core of the scheme is training for staff in leisure-focused faculties. It teaches them to recognize typical grooming behaviour and the signs and symptoms of sex offending. It also equips them with knowledge of the agencies that manage sex offenders and their powers, as well as procedures for responding to suspicious situations.

Staff in the leisure facilities are put in touch with named police officers responsible for community safety in their area. They then work together to implement a system for responding appropriately to concerns about any individual in the facility. The assumption is that, by intervening early, potential offences may be stopped and potential offenders detected.

The scheme has led to some small but important design changes in facilities, such as moving first aid rooms to the poolside, adding porthole windows and installing secure turnstiles at changing room entries. Today everyone is acutely aware of the presence of surveillance systems in our lives.[4] But proponents of Leisurewatch see these actions as 'positive surveillance' and an antidote to what Hughes describes as the 'destructive vigilantism' that has characterized some earlier community responses to paedophilia.[5]

Since its inception in the northeast of England, Leisurewatch has expanded into a number of other communities and commercial venues. TDI is establishing regional offices throughout the United Kingdom with a view to setting up Leisurewatch systematically to meet demand from both police authorities and leisure agencies. TDI's own evaluations show that the scheme has reduced all crime in and around leisure centres and swimming pools. According to its coordinator, Leisurewatch continues to be refined, building on the successes demonstrated in an audit of the pilot period during 2002. However, it is unclear how results were measured and precisely what were the data. Some sceptics argue that crimes have simply been deflected to other venues. But for the leisure facility staff involved, there is some reassurance in enhancing safety on their own patch.

At a presentation on the scheme by Hughes to an NSPCC-sponsored conference in Leeds in 2003, police officers in the audience folded their arms and began to scowl. Their view was that they, the experts, knew best how to manage sex offenders in the community. Contrary to this rather hierarchical approach, Leisurewatch encourages community involvement and partnerships. It starts from the philosophy that offender management is a shared responsibility rather than something to be handled only by specialists such as the police or probation service. Indeed, TDI reports that police services became increasingly enthusiastic about the scheme during the pilot period, recognizing its contribution to their own intelligence network and to community safety. To that extent, Leisurewatch is contributing to much-needed public education about sex offending in a way that should be welcomed.

Notes

1. This chapter is adapted from an article prepared in 2006 for the newsletter of the National Organisation for the Treatment of Abusers (United Kingdom).
2. Silverman, J., 'Making life harder for paedophiles', 2004, retrieved from http://news.bbc.co.uk/go/pr/fr/-/1/hi/magazine/3431173.stm
3. The Derwent Initiative, <www.thederwentinitiative.org.uk>.
4. Foucault, M., *Discipline and Punish: The birth of the prison* (translated by Alan Sheridan), 1979, London, Penguin.
5. Hughes cited in J. Silverman, op. cit.

CHAPTER 38. SPEAK OUT: PREVENTING SEXUAL ABUSE IN SPORT (CANADA)

Michelle Zubrack and Sandra Kirby

Following the scandal provoked by revelations of the sexual abuse of professional ice hockey player Sheldon Kennedy in Canada (from 1997 onwards), the Canadian sports authorities introduced a number of programmes and practices to prevent such abuses occurring again. One such scheme is Speak Out, which encourages whistle blowing in sport. This chapter describes the programme and assesses its impact.

The Speak Out campaign took root in February 1997 as a proactive response of the Canadian Hockey Association and the Red Cross to the ordeal of Sheldon Kennedy, who played ice hockey with the National Hockey League in North America. The legal case and media reporting about it abruptly revealed the realities of sexual abuse of young male athletes to the ice hockey community and the wider world of sport. The Speak Out campaign has since grown into a successful national programme that educates and empowers athletes, parents and coaches to recognize and report abuse in ice hockey. It is one of the many ways in which the Canadian Hockey Association has established itself as an exemplary organization for proactive approaches to sport-related abuse and harassment.

The development of the Speak Out campaign is illustrative of how local initiatives can develop. In the initial year of the Speak Out campaign, the Canadian Hockey Association (CHA) established a committee aiming to develop policies and educational programmes to prevent harassment and abuse. CHA took the bold step of inviting help from others inside as well as outside the ice hockey realm. The association opened itself to public scrutiny at a time when it was vulnerable to severe criticism. Doing so earned it the respect of those whose help it sought, including parent groups, child protection leaders in related fields, and researchers and writers. This frank and honest approach became fundamental to the success of the Speak Out campaign.

The CHA recognized the different strengths that diverse individuals and resources could bring to the issue of sexual harassment and abuse. Along the way, key 'non-hockey' people took on leadership roles within the association. These included, for example, the national coordinator of abuse prevention services for the Canadian Red Cross (Judi Fairholm) and the advisor on rights and responsibilities at Concordia University (Sally Spilhaus) in addition to current and former ice hockey leaders.

The Prevention of Harassment and Abuse Committee was subsequently formed, with members from an array of backgrounds. They included Justice David Watt, who came from a prominent background in law and had been a CHA director from 1991 to 1997; Jamie McDonald, manager of coaching and director of development for the CHA; and Mike McGraw, a member of the CHA's administrative staff. In 1999, with CHA committing staff resources, Todd Jackson became the first full-time paid manager of the committee. Jackson, now senior manager of safety and insurance for the CHA, is on the 2008 committee along with Fairholm and Spilhaus, both of whom volunteer their professional advice about harassment and abuse prevention.

The core of the Speak Out programme is initiatives developed and implemented by the Prevention of Harassment and Abuse Committee. One critical initiative is the production of educational materials and training programmes for coaches, and easy-to-read materials on preventing abuse for all players. In addition, volunteer coordinators were trained to assist at the community level, such as by working with local sport associations to develop prevention policies and to convey local, provincial, territorial and national resources to local/community audiences.

Many educational and prevention materials are available at the Speak Out website, including age-specific posters and brochures, a parents' guide and various materials for safe recruiting of coaches and volunteers.

Another project is the Kids Help Phone, a national toll-free service providing callers with access to trained counsellors. The number is prominently displayed on all Speak Out educational materials, as well as on bag-tags distributed free for player equipment bags. The telephone project provides a safe, confidential and respectful place for callers to speak, be heard and remain anonymous. It receives 800 to 1,000 calls daily from children across Canada, on issues ranging from harassment and abuse to family relationships and suicide.[1] Callers are referred to community resources drawn from a large database of listings for children's services.

Thanks to Sheldon Kennedy (an athlete who dared to speak out), the Canadian Hockey Association (a sport organization that dared to open its doors at its most vulnerable moment) and to the Red Cross (which offered its immediate assistance), the Speak Out campaign now provides comprehensive training and education on bullying, harassment and abuse for players, parents, coaches, team managers, sport administrators and safety personnel. The 'Speak Out! Act Now' guide assists local sports clubs and associations,[2] and a similarly named manual was prepared for national distribution with the assistance of the Harassment and Abuse in Sport Collective, Sport Canada, the Canadian Association for the Advancement of Women and Sport and Physical Activity, the Canadian Centre for Ethics, and the Canadian Red Cross.[3]

Through actions such as these, the CHA has become the recognized leader of abuse/harassment prevention in sport, spending over CDN$300,000 annually on developing and disseminating policies and educational materials.[4] The programme incorporates the diverse backgrounds and experiences of ice hockey volunteers in its efforts to promote respectful leadership, team-building and positive communication. This approach creates a domino effect: If participants feel safe, they can enjoy hockey for a number of years, develop leadership skills and decide to volunteer in the positive hockey environment.

The Speak Out material is presented in simple, clear points, using language that is accessible to all. The campaign has come a long way in its short life, thanks to the commitment of the CHA to expose the problem of abuse and aggressively seek solutions. By embracing the expertise and support of individuals from a variety of backgrounds, and by emphasizing positive change through education, the CHA has built a strong foundation for the prevention of abuse and harassment – not only in ice hockey, but in all sports.

However, the campaign's effectiveness has yet to be formally evaluated. The degree to which it prevents abuse is not known. Formal evaluation is an important next step.

Speak Out materials and information are available on the CHA website (www.hockeycanada.ca).Further information on the Speak Out course, offered through the National Coaching Certification Program (NCCP), can be obtained from the NCCP section on the CHA website.

Notes

1. www.hockeycanada.ca/index.cfm/ci_id/7835/la_id/1/document/1/re_id/0/file/so_nl_01_e.pdf, p. 2, retrieved 2 September 2008.
2. www.hockeycanada.ca, retrieved 2 September 2008.
3. CAAWS, www.canada2002.org/e/progress/worldwide/chapter3_america.htm, retrieved 2 September 2008.
4. Speak Out newsletters: www.hockeycanada.ca/7/8/7/3/index1.shtml, retrieved 13 August 2008.

CPSIA information can be obtained at www.ICGtesting.com
Printed in the USA
LVOW09s1817030516

486489LV00017B/479/P

9 781508 549123